Hugh Anderson was born in Paris relatively soon after the end of WW2. He was educated privately for the most part. When it became clear he wasn't learning anything, he was let loose on an unsuspecting society. He tried his hand at many different jobs before finding his utopia in the transport industry. He has had more jobs than birthdays to date. Finally, he married and took up writing which he had dabbled with for several years. His other interests include, but are not confined to motorbikes, reading, big birds, sunny days, wine and the origin of vines.

For everyone who can unfailingly find the funny side in any of their dire circumstances during their everyday lives. Laughing always brings solutions.

Denise Rogers.

Chunky Chicken, here's your special copy that'll help you make it fly!!
Thank you so much for all your help and promotions. I really appreciate it.
Keep Smiling,
LJ Dickson.   (Chunky)

Hugh Anderson

MILESTONE

AUSTIN MACAULEY PUBLISHERS™
LONDON • CAMBRIDGE • NEW YORK • SHARJAH

Copyright © Hugh Anderson 2024

The right of Hugh Anderson to be identified as author of this work has been asserted by the author in accordance with sections 77 and 78 of the Copyright, Designs and Patents Act 1988.

All rights reserved. No part of this publication may be reproduced, stored in a retrieval system, or transmitted in any form or by any means, electronic, mechanical, photocopying, recording, or otherwise, without the prior permission of the publishers.

Any person who commits any unauthorised act in relation to this publication may be liable to criminal prosecution and civil claims for damages.

All of the events in this memoir are true to the best of the author's memory. The views expressed in this memoir are solely those of the author.

A CIP catalogue record for this title is available from the British Library.

ISBN 9781035834037 (Paperback)
ISBN 9781035834044 (ePub e-book)

www.austinmacauley.com

First Published 2024
Austin Macauley Publishers Ltd®
1 Canada Square
Canary Wharf
London
E14 5AA

My son, Josh, and his partner, Angela, for encouraging me to write down the stories they so enjoyed listening to. My wife, Belén, gave me her unwavering support in writing this book and also her help with the Spanish translation (work in progress). Peter Sylvester-Smith, whose enduring friendship and loyalty gave me such confidence. Probably the most important was his expert assistance in editing my work. Mar Encinas, for being my mentor, giving me excellent professional feedback and helping me edit out what I had believed to be great swathes of literary genius. Ronny Walsh, whose friendship and especially humour helped me so much during my early driving years and in the pub. I also remember all my workmates of the era. I liked them all, including those who didn't like me, but I can't believe there were many of those!

Prologue

There was a song years ago and it went something along the lines of... what old men dream about is what they did in their youth.

I can't remember the name of the song, or any more than that, or even who sang it or wrote it, but I can still remember the tune. It was a song I loved and as I enter the twilight of my years I realise how true those words are. Anyone who has plenty of time on their hands to sit and stare into space will understand. I have a plethora of memories so I'm never bored, despite what my wife would tell you.

I met a man once who became a relatively good friend despite us having practically nothing in common apart from Gordons Gin. He told me he'd spent 40 years of his life working in a government office. He went to the same building, sat at the same desk, on the same chair, (I think that bit was memory failure), and did the same work from 9am to 5pm every single working day. He said he bicycled to work every day and the only thing which varied his life was where he was living at the time and how far it was from the office. How many memories has he got to keep himself amused in times of boredom?

I worked for thirty-five years in an industry which I adored from the outset. I met hundreds of people, and my recollections are all about them. We all had so many things to say and tell each other during the infrequent times we met up. My stories are mostly recounted through dialogue. I can still remember those conversations practically verbatim. The majority of them were amusing, and I still howl with laughter over others.

All the surnames and company names I've mentioned are fictitious. Many Christian names have been replaced with nick names in order to protect the innocent! If you think you recognise yourself, you're probably mistaken.

I never made any notes during my working years, so all the tales come directly from my head. My doctor says I have amazing recall. Personally I believe I have a good sense of humour which makes some things worth remembering. For example if I were to lose my keys or bank card, I would think it's just a punch line to a poor joke which I can't remember.

Over my working life I have driven many types of both two, four and multi-wheeled vehicles. I've never been a petrol or diesel geek so I wasn't very interested in who made them or what the model number was. In what little spare or free time I had, I very much enjoyed riding motorbikes. I still do. Even so, I have always found it difficult to keep track of model numbers for motorcycles, to which many people now refer when speaking about which one they ride. For instance, I have no idea which company makes a ZZR or a GSXR8GT. It's a maze. Why don't they just say, I ride a BSA or a Velocette!

All the stories come from a different age. It's history, as kids will often tell you nowadays. There are some parts of the story about which you may have strong views, but my advice is to avoid comparison with modern life. Things have changed remarkably in such a short time. We begin in approximately 1970. It's over fifty years ago when even a mobile phone was space age material.

It's easy getting a job!

Not everyone in life is lucky enough to fall into a job they adore at a relatively early age. Nor even to secure a specific job through trying relentlessly to get it. Most people get one just to pay your way because 'you should get a job lad, you know you have to try'. Others get pushed into doing something they don't want and end up loathing it, but can't get out of it. Some just get told what to do by their fathers, but fortunately those days were mostly over when my turn came. It wasn't as if I'd hankered after a job on the road. My main concern after school was simply earning enough money to pay for beer and motorbikes. It didn't sound like a long term ambition, but my future never saw me looking any further forward than tomorrow's breakfast. Not very ambitious I grant you, but nonetheless exceptionally important in my early working life. Well, all of it actually.

From 1971 until 1975 I'd worked whenever and wherever there were jobs to be had. In those days there were plenty. What I aimed for was a job which paid as much as possible for the least amount of effort. In modern terms I believe it's called efficiency. As a plan it resulted in me having achieved thirty nine jobs in only four years. It couldn't have been far short of an entry in The Guinness Book of Records. After my promising start in England my parents retired to southern France before moving to Spain. It deprived me of a sensible and remarkably inexpensive place to live. I decided I'd go too and work my way round the great big continent.

I managed to convince a friend to join me and we bought a car. His father told us we had to have some sort of a plan. We signed on for the grape harvest, allowing plenty of time to get disgustingly legless in Paris. It could have been the title of a film – Legless in Paris. Grape picking wasn't all it was cracked up to be and we were soon on our way to Italy via St. Tropez. After a flying visit to peer into the crater of Vesuvius, it was on to Sardinia and then Corsica. My mate got bored and went home. I spent a year in Nice working the boats in dry dock, making caravans and fibreglass yachts. It was the only job for which I trained and I even got a 'stificate'. It was probably granted more for attending than accomplishing a trade. I enjoyed working there and every time we finished a boat, the boss had it hauled to the port. It was put in the water to make sure it wouldn't sink. On one occasion the boat was very big and expensive with all sorts of flash fittings. We put it in the water and it floated perfectly. Boss decided to celebrate and took us all to lunch. When the coffee was served we peered out of the window to gaze upon our super-yacht. To our huge consternation it wasn't where we'd left it. Looking further out to sea it was perfectly visible, floating merrily away towards Africa. What a laugh! Boss commandeered a speed boat, and quick as a flash, went to the rescue. Very soon afterward I returned to the comfort zone which we used to call Great Britain.

I settled down in a dull job as a trainee manager in a garage and renewed my old friendships in the town. My wage was £21.87p per week. The only reason I remember it clearly is because I always brought it to mind when future jobs got me down. To be fair it was reasonable pay in those days, but there were better rates to be had. It was job No 46, and I hadn't quite reached the ripe old age of twenty-one.

In my spare time I amused myself by drinking beer, riding my motorbike, (a Triton), and playing in a card school. We mostly played 7-card-brag. I think it was a bit like poker, but for simpletons. Anyway it involved an increasing 'pot' which was only won by putting more and more money in each round. It continued until someone paid enough or was 'seen' by the remaining player. Most often the pot didn't get won for at least half an hour.

'Well, shit! It happens to me every time! The one round where I've got a really winning hand and I bloody run out of money! Anyone lend me?'

'No lad. You knows the rules. Own money in or give it up.'

'You want to get a better job with more money, Yooee.' My name's Hugh but many people find pronunciation challenging, even in their mother tongue.

'We'm all drivers mate. Well, nearly all. Us earns over a ton a week. Get yourself a license and get on the winning side, Yooee.'

Fundamentally that's what happened. After borrowing an absolute fortune to train to pass the test, I became a Class 1 HGV driver.

The mid-1970s lorry driving test

Ho ho ho! If you compare this to 21st century procedures you'll laugh your socks off. I arrived on my first day at a disused airfield on top of a windy hill in the middle of absolutely nowhere. The old runway was littered with road cones. The instructor greeted us. There were three of us and there were the same quantity of what looked like vaguely serviceable lorries. They were attached to empty forty foot flat trailers.

'Good morning to you all. We'll get started right away. Driving a lorry is not very much different to driving anything else. The most noticeable thing is it is very much larger than a car. It's wider, longer and heavier and, in this case it is articulated. Which means the lorry can be separated from the semi-trailer. Therefore, when the whole lot is joined together it bends.'

'The requirements to pass the test are all practical. You will be required by the examiner to demonstrate you can drive it in a forward motion, and also in reverse. The route you follow may vary, but as you know, it is a very small town, so the options are limited. Various junctions and corners are used and we know exactly which ones they are, as will you when the time comes. If you've never reversed anything with a trailer do not worry, because the reversing test is precisely the same each time. We have worked out a method to do it which is mathematical. If you do precisely what we teach you, even your dog could manage it.'

There was nervous laughter from the assembled group of trainees. Rodney, who had already declared ownership of a dog, was shaking his head.

'You will be asked a few very basic questions about drivers' hours' regulations, and you will be asked questions with regard to road signage specifically pertinent to lorries.'

'When you have achieved this momentous task and received your Class 1 driving licence you will be in a position to apply for any lorry driving job. Our advice in that endeavour is to at least look like a driver, even if you have zero experience. So,' he looked pointedly at one of my companions. 'Don't use binder twine to hold your trousers up. Not as a belt nor as braces. Oh, and brush the straw out of your hair Rodney.' We were going to be trained to pass a test, not taught how to drive a lorry.

So it was. After ten days of driving around, we all took the test and passed. Whoopeee! That day was a milestone in my life. Despite the tests' simplicity, I can swear to you I was never involved in any RTA whilst in a lorry in 35 years apart from two mishaps with illegally parked cars.

Let's take a test in the 21st century

For all vehicles modern tests are considerably more complex. They take much longer to pass and are very expensive. There are two theory tests, and then the practical test. In addition, there is a course for lorry drivers to attend entitled the CPC, or Certificate of Professional Competence. Potential LGV drivers must also take a medical examination. Personally I'm in favour of the modernisations, but I'm not in favour of all the duplications. I consider them to be nothing more than an exercise in raising revenue and increasing bureaucracy. For example, you don't need to have a medical examination to take a motorcycle test or a car test. But if you do both of those, you do a near duplication of the theory tests.

For the lorry test the theory is marginally different, but frankly, not much. I would imagine once you've done the motorcycle A1 test, followed by the A test, the car test and later the lorry test, you would be able to recite the theory tests by rote. It is probably reasonable to point out at this juncture what is stated in the Government website. If you take the motorcycle test first you don't have to repeat the theory test when you do the car test. However, if you do those tests in the reverse order, you do! Who thinks up these rules? Why on earth are the theory tests not required just the once? Every vehicle on the road is a potential hazard, irrespective of which type you drive. It would do away with a lot of duplication, expense and time. In addition, when you've achieved a car or motorcycle test you have it for life. The lorry licence requires you to repeat the CPC every five years, despite there not being many significant changes in law. Suffice it to say I disagree with the need for increased paperwork and to raise revenue from those people who do not have regular employment as drivers.

That's my view and I'm sticking to it.

The hunt was on for job No 47.

I could smell the real money

I had never had any trouble finding a job. I suppose it was because I was an unskilled labourer and willing to try my hand at absolutely anything in my quest for untold riches with completely no effort. Of course I had been fired from several jobs for lack of interest and I'd voluntarily retired from many for the same reason. In 1975 I discovered I was in a different boat. There was no point at all in accepting a job stacking shelves in a supermarket after I'd invested such a large quantity of funds, (some £1500), getting myself a qualification. This put me in a very disappointing situation and drove me into penury.

I couldn't afford my lodgings and had to spend a while living in a friend's car. I laugh now, but it was quite serious. I would have lived in my car, but I only had a motorbike which would be chilly in winter. Job No 47 was becoming quite elusive. I had no qualms about knocking on doors and begging for employment, so I just kept at it. I was rewarded for my perseverance about four months after my momentous achievement of being the recipient of my HGV licence. In those days it was a little red booklet. Some bloke in the sticks offered me a driving job. It was mostly farm work, hauling straw or cattle feed and the occasional load of timber. In any event, it was the job I'd been hunting for. Driving lorries.

Job No47

Most haulage bosses just take it for granted if you hold an HGV licence you automatically know how to do the job. It is simply not the case. In my case it was completely the reverse as I found out to my horror. Within minutes of starting work I got myself into some very tricky and dangerous situations. The up side was my wage, which compared to the garage had increased by 100%. Getting started in your chosen career is difficult because no one knows who the hell you are and you have no track record. Once off the starting grid friends and contacts grow rapidly. So for me the apparent ease of gaining a spot in the Guinness Book of Records was still on the cards. I wasn't very happy working at the country haulage firm. The feeling was clearly mutual. The boss once passionately told me,

'You'll never make a fucking driver Yooee!'

I was determined to prove him wrong. My short time there was interesting nevertheless and I did go through an extremely steep learning curve and survived. I learned how to tie the drivers' knot which was called the dolly. I sort of learned how to cover a load. I learned the hard way why you can't carry tree trunks without using chains to secure them. I learned rudimentary diesel engine repairs, many of which I had to do myself. My only tools were a hammer and an electrical screwdriver!

I carried a load of Christmas trees. They were not the big ones they put in village squares. There were literally hundreds of little household ones, just for me. I had to offload them by hand on Christmas Eve in Bristol. There were about 40 delivery points. It was raining all day. The lorry stopped itself at every set of lights and I had to tip the cab, (to access the engine), short the solenoid and start again. I got back at midnight having made a late start in the morning at 6am. The boss paid me my wage and would you believe gave me a £2 bonus!

We parted company after about 6 months. I felt it was a mutual decision, but his parting words to me were along the lines of,

'Fuck off Yooee! And never darken my door again.'

I had been given a tip by my new landlady where I'd secured lodgings in a village much closer to civilisation. Landladies are an endless font of local information because they know and talk to so many people. Immediately after receiving her snippet, I nipped down to the transport yard mentioned and secured myself a position in job No 48. He wasn't overly taken by the extent of my experience, but luckily he was desperate for a driver and hired me.

Job No48

He didn't have any articulated lorries so all his vehicles were what are known as 'rigids'. They don't bend in the middle, or anywhere else for that matter, unless the driver rams one into a wall. It would be another skill learned for me. Even so, I did want to find a bigger company to work for which had the right kit. So the hunt for job No 49 was on immediately. I didn't spend long with the 'rigids', but I did learn a lot more and the other drivers were friendly and helpful. I think it was because they were paid by the hour rather than a percentage of earnings or bonus. They had plenty of time to waste if no one was watching. I saw a lot more of the UK and discovered the existence of places like Blackpool, which I can tell you, is a bloody long way away from sleepy Somerset. It also took forever to get there at an average speed of 27mph. There were only about a quarter of the amount of motorways which are available today.

For the most part, lorries carried an outgoing load away from base and then someone, mostly the driver, searched for a return load to make the money up. The rigids nearly always returned empty as outgoing work was very busy. I imagined the company got paid both ways or at least for a part of the return. Otherwise it wouldn't have been profitable. But what did I, a lowly driver, know about the complex business of management?

I hadn't been there long when I heard a whisper Rodes Transport was possibly hiring. I rang them up and was told to come and see Michael on Saturday morning.

Result.

Rodes

I arrived at Michael's office, which was also his home, at 9.30am on the dot.

'Good morning Sir, I've come to see Michael.'

'I am he. You must be Hugh. Come and sit down. Let's have a chat.' I sat.

'Now then, you sound a trifle over qualified to be driving lorries.'

'Oh no, Sir. I'm not at all.' I said as eagerly as possible,

'Right, well, let's start at the beginning. Do you have any qualifications?'

'Yes. I've got an HGV Class 1 license.'

'Mmmm, it's a good start lad, but what I meant was do you have many qualifications from school and university.'

'Not many and I definitely never went to university.'

'Which ones do you have?'

'Yes, well, I've got a few O levels.'

'I thought as much. How many and in what subjects?'

'I've got one in English language and…'

'Yes, yes, OK. But just out of curiosity, how many do you have?'

'Four.'

'Which are they?'

'I have English Language as I said, English Literature, French and Mathematics.'

'Mmmm, and why have you got so many?'

'My father told me I had to have a minimum of four O levels before I left school to go to work, which was what I wanted above all. They had to be my own language, a foreign language, mathematics and one other which wasn't carpentry or welding or suchlike.'

'Very sensible Dad you've got.'

'Yes I suppose, but it took me six attempts to get maths.'

'OK, so anyway you'll find English language useful for deciphering the array of accents I have driving my lorries. Literature should keep you from boring yourself to death while waiting to load, unload, or waiting in a phone box for someone to call you back. French will very probably be useless, although you never know. Mathematics, on the other hand, will be very useful for keeping your records straight. I take it then, you can add up and take away?'

'Oh yes, and I can do fractions, equations, long division and multiplication, but I've always had problems with logarithms.'

'Yes, well you'll definitely find adding up and taking away useful for filling in your Ministry of Transport hours sheets. So you'll be able to add up the amounts of hours you've driven and take away the ones which add up to too many by law.'

I wasn't at all sure whether it was meant as a joke or not, but I later learned he was in earnest.

'Do you know the drivers' hours regulations?'

'Yes.'

'They change on an almost hourly basis, so keep on top of it.'

It was all sounding remarkably positive, I thought.

'Out of interest, what did you do before you got your lorry licence?' I wasn't going to tell him about all those jobs just as he might be on the point of offering me job No 49, so I said,

'Well I tried my hand at a number of things after school, and then I went to France and Italy and worked for a couple of years making yachts.'

'Did you go on your own? How did you get there?'

'No, I bought a cheap car and drove with a friend, but he got bored after 6 months and went home. I stayed for another 18.'

'How did you get on with the language?'

'Hit and miss really, but I survived.'

'So, you've demonstrated perseverance and resilience and obviously you can read a map?'

'Oh yes, I like geography.'

'Right, I'm going to give you a job, but I've learned from your existing boss your experience is practically zero. Though he says you're a quick learner and keen. So, as I have no vehicle readily available for you, I'm going to put you with another slightly more experienced driver for three months or so. It will be his dubious pleasure to teach you all he knows until a lorry becomes free for you to drive on your own.'

'I somewhat doubt Jack will require a whole three months to divulge the quantity of his knowledge, but you should learn the rudiments well enough to do them in your sleep. I'm absolutely certain he'll find you a help in reading and understanding maps. You will work with him and share the same lorry to sleep in. You'll probably find it a bit cramped. He'll teach you the rules of the road and the rules of the company.'

'When you get your own lorry I'll have another chat with you. I'll pay you £60 per week flat rate plus overnight expenses. Give your boss one week's notice as is customary and come and see me again next Saturday at the same time. Good. Welcome aboard Hugh, as they are prone to saying on the dock. You will be the most educated driver I've ever employed, but don't worry I'm not going to post it on the notice board.'

'Oh, that's wonderful! Thank you Sir. Oh thank you, thank you, thank you.'

'Enough! It's a deal done and my name is Michael. Don't call me Sir. I expect your father drilled it into you but it's not required here. Go on, off you go and get pissed, or whatever you lads do to celebrate. Oh, just one other thing I'm obliged to ask you. Have you ever been in trouble with the police?'

'Never! Apart from bike riding warnings, but I was never nicked.'

'They don't count. Right, on your way!'

I was so deliriously happy I ran out of the yard whooping and singing and punching the air while dancing along the street until I noticed people staring at me. After a couple of hundred yards I remembered I'd come on my motorbike, so I had to go back and get it. It was only half past ten so I decided to race back to my boss, Jeff, and tell him the news. I was sure he desperately wanted to hear it as much as I wanted to tell him. I had secured job No 49!

Do you feel safe?

Drivers' hours regulations were introduced in 1970. I believe they were started partially for reasons of workers' rights, to increase revenue, and to create what I consider to be unnecessary bureaucracy. The implementation of the 40 hour week was a wonderful advancement and I can well remember when Saturday working was considered both acceptable and a commercial prerequisite. I believe wholeheartedly in these changes, but they were never applied in full to transport drivers. Drivers' hours regulations appear to be a concession to industry while partially appeasing workers' demands.

The introduction of drivers' hours' rules was sold to the general public on the basis of road safety for all. This is how safe it was and is.

Drivers' hours rules

An HGV driver may be required to work no more than 15 hours in the entire daily duty period. Every four and a half hours maximum, (although continental European police forces prefer it to be four hours), the driver must take a rest of 45mins, whether it's from driving or other work. Therefore you can calculate, in the whole 15 hour duty period which is allowed, the driver may actually work no more than thirteen and a half hours in one day.

The maximum actual driving period allowed each day was 9 hours which could be increased to 10 hours twice a week. How many workers in any other heavy industry would agree to such a scheme?

At the end of each shift the driver was required to take an 11 hour rest. It could be reduced to nine hours twice a week.

At the end of the working week drivers had to take a minimum of 24 hours rest. On the second week it was 45 hours.

If the vehicle was being operated by two drivers in the same cab, the vehicle could be driven for a maximum of eighteen hours daily and twenty hours twice a week. The only difference for the team system was both drivers had to take a 56 hour break each week. I grant you the figures may not be completely correct for 2021 rules because they change frequently, but they are very similar. In the team system, I can tell you it is almost impossible to get complete rest in a moving vehicle.

However it's calculated, those rules allowed an HGV driver to be required to do almost two days' work, every single working day. Some drivers were, and possibly still are, paid on a bonus arrangement or a percentage of the vehicles' earnings. This does away with the necessity for the employer to pay overtime.

Please don't misunderstand me. Many drivers enjoy that there are a lot of working hours available to them each day. For example, it could allow them to get home at the end of a shift. However, in terms of workers' rights the laws are not equal to all.

If you believe regulating drivers hours to allow nearly two days' work in every one has anything to do with road safety, you are most definitely living on another planet.

Now, how safe do you think you are with regard to your own road safety by regulation?

I am not suggesting drivers hours rules should be further restricted. I'm simply pointing out they have nothing whatever to do with road safety. One thing has never failed to fascinate me. Who is the mathematical genius who thought up those numbers? How could a 45 hour break at the end of a working week be arrived at? It doesn't appear to have any connection with the other numbers. Then there's the 15 hour duty period. Where does it come from? Is there something I've been missing, or am I right and it's nonsense?

Just before I leave this topic I'd like to point out these rules do not apply to any other group of workers as far as I know, except perhaps air crews and train drivers. Let's imagine someone works in an office and has a demanding job. During busy times he or she may spend as much as eighteen to twenty hours working at a computer screen, making phone calls and taking difficult decisions. During the day, he or she might grab a quick cup of coffee and possibly eat a working lunch without leaving their desk. Finally at the end of the day, they finish, go to the pub for a relaxing drink and then drive home for an hour. There is no law to prevent them doing so and they are not considered to be a danger to other road users, despite being very probably dog tired.

We all get tired. It's how the human body works. Why would lorry drivers need their rest periods regulated when no one else has it imposed on them? Well, the answer is it's easy to control, creates employment for those who police the rules and raises revenue.

On the move

Jeff was firmly clutching his tenth cup of coffee of the morning when I went into the office.

'Morning, Yooee. It so happens, I've just come off the 'phone to Michael. I understand he's offered you a job. I can't say I didn't expect it. I don't think you been completely happy here and wanted to get on to 'artics', (articulated lorries which separate the power end from the load carrying trailers). It's been sort of mutual and I'm not too sorry to see you go. Anyway, I've given you a good reference, don't you worry 'bout that. Michael has more time to train someone.

So I wish you well, but I suppose you're here to give me a week's notice. It would be very useful as I've got a lot on, as you know.'

'Yes Jeff, it is why I'm here and I thank you for being so understanding. I'll work till next Friday night.'

'All right boy, until Friday'

I couldn't understand why everyone was being so pleasant. I was sure there was something I hadn't figured out yet. The last week at Jeff's passed without incident and before I knew it Saturday morning had arrived, so I rode up to see Michael once again.

Job No.49 Getting started for real

'Good morning Hugh.'

'Morning Michael.'

'Hugh, Jack's not in this morning, which is to say he's already left. So I won't be able to do the introductions. I've instructed him to pick you up in front of The Egremont hotel at 6.30am on Monday morning. He'll have a lorry similar to that one over there,' he indicated, 'and he'll be pulling a low loader. Do you know what one of those is?'

'Er, no.'

'It's like one of those trailers over there,' he indicated again, 'but the significant differences are it's shorter, the rear axle seems like it's following the lorry at a distance, and the loading bed is practically on the floor. Rodes is the only company within a 20 mile radius which operates one. Obviously, the lorry is brightly sign-written with my name. I'm pretty sure you won't confuse it with the hundreds of other lorries hanging around outside The Saloon Bar at 6.30 on a Monday morning.'

'No, of course not Michael,' I said trying not to laugh as I wasn't sure of his humour yet.

'Don't be late, as you're both due on site at 7am to move an excavator to another site.'

'I'll be there.' I rode away looking forward immensely to my new job.

One of the problems of life is the more you want something to happen, the less likely it is to occur. Murphy's Law will intervene with a vengeance and fuck up your dreams. Whether it's your own fault or not, you'll mostly find if something is going to go wrong it will always go wrong just at the moment you don't want it to. I wanted the job with Rodes more than anything in my life.

I was late. I missed the boat. I missed the bus. I missed the low-loader. Oh shit! I remembered I'd been fired from several jobs in the past for tardiness. It was grouped into the general heading of lack of interest. So I was worried indeed. Shaking with fear might have been more accurate. I grabbed my lunch box which my landlady so immaculately prepared each day, my flask and bike gear. I flew through the lanes like I was on a practice for the Isle of Man TT. I arrived sweaty but alive at Street's yard at about 8.15am. There didn't seem to be anyone about, but there was a furious hammering noise going on in the workshop. I wandered down hoping I looked a bit like a professional Class 1 HGV driver.

The foreman emerged for some air, followed by a cloud of smoke and peered at me.

'Ah, you must be the new boy what's gone with Jack and the low-loader,'

I nodded shamefacedly.

'Late on your first day is not a good omen. Never mind, Michael's not in yet and we just brewed a cup of tea. Want one?'

'Oh yes please.'

'We take it with milk and 3 sugars. That OK with you?'

It wasn't, but I didn't want to be difficult. 'Fine,' I said.

'We'll take it out here. Steve'll bring yours out cos it's a bit smokey inside. Steve! Make another and bring it out,' he shouted into the fog.

We waited.

'You're Yoo, ain't you?'

'Close enough.'

'Michael'll be in 'bout 9. He'll come out here after he's settled in. Arrrter tea I should grab a broom if I were you and look busy. Cheer up, don't look so miserable, 'snot the end of the world, like what it is inside that fuckin' workshop.'

Michael arrived just before 9 and went into the office. Two minutes later he was out in the yard and coming my way.

'Good morning Hugh. You've overslept I see. Don't look so miserable.'

'Morning, Michael. I'm really sorry. I truly promise it won't happen again.'

'I should hope not. Look, we all oversleep from time to time. It's not a crime but it's very inconvenient for everybody else. We work as a team here. If anyone is late it just screws up the day for everyone else. Got it? Right, that's done. Now, Jack should be back about 12.30 and I'll see you both together then. In the meantime, get yourself down to the dock and present yourself to Harold. Don't see Arnold as he's a miserable bastard and he'll call me up to moan. I can't deal with him before I've had my coffee. I'll speak to Harold. He can use you to help him to load and sheet, (cover with large tarpaulins), a few trailers before Jack gets back. I'll call him when I'm ready to see you. Off you go.'

So I did, feeling very stupid, ashamed, relieved and happy all at the same time. I rode down to the dock. Harold was quite an old boy by my standards, but he probably wasn't much past 60 years old, if that. He was sort of mid height with not much hair, which was cropped short. He looked strong but not fat, with a weather-beaten face. He wore an enormous welcoming grin and flapped a cloth cap in his hand.

'Hello lad. Your bike looks like a nice bit of kit, (650 BSA A10 Café racer in cream). You better park it at the side of the weighbridge out the way, in case any of these nutcases convert it into a wrecking ball. Come in here and have a nice cup of tea with me and Arnie-the-ass before we get started again. What did Michael say your name was?'

'Hugh.'

'Righto. Will Yooee do? It's easier for me.'

'Course,' I said obligingly.

We went into the weighbridge office.

'Arnie, this is Yooee,' Harold began.

'I know who the fuck he is and we need him like a hole in the head!'

'You better wait outside Yooee, I'll bring your tea out in a minute.' I left and Harold closed the door. I heard raised voices and some shouting from Arnie. There was a pause and Harold emerged.

'Don't let Arnie-the-ass get you down Yooee. He's still stuck in the class wars of the 50s. He fancies himself as a bit of a revolutionary trade unionist, although he never got anything for us.'

'Not even a wage rise. Unlike 'im on the docks who be pretty good at it. Anyway you'll probably find quite a lot of that. You always do in big companies.

There's some who'll dislike you from the off, for where they think you come from, not who you are. Just stay out of his way till you finds your feet.'

He gave me my tea.

'That's OK Harold, it's sound advice. I've come across it plenty of times. I've only done manual work since I left school five years ago. My first driving job gave me a lot of it, but to be fair, it was probably deserved as I knew absolutely nothing. I don't know much now, but I really want to learn.'

'Look lad, I don't care where you come from, and I'll help you learn as much as you like so long as you're prepared to muck in.'

'Yeah, I'll do that. Shall we get started?'

'Hold on there, Yooee I haven't started my tea yet.'

Before Michael called for me I worked with Harold for a couple of hours. He was good fun with a quick sense of humour. He told me a few stories from the old days when he was long distance driving himself, and I looked forward to chatting with him again. Before I left I told Harold I'd been given notice at my lodgings. I asked him if he knew anyone in Watchet who would rent me a room.

'Well lad, there is a lady on the outskirts of town. Mrs Baker. I knows her pretty well. I don't know if she's still doing it, but she got a small self-contained flat which might suit you well. I'll ring her up today and ask for you. How's that? Come and see me at the end of the week and I'll have an answer.'

'Bloody hell, Harold, it sounds brilliant. Thanks a lot. I'll see you Friday.'

Michael introduced us.

'Hugh, this is Jack. Jack this is Hugh Late, but he won't be in future.' Jack grinned.

'Right, you both know what's required. Make sure you like each other. Take a load to Chard this afternoon, then pick up one for Caerphilly for tomorrow, and there'll be steel coming back. I'll put the collection notes in the box. Afterwards you can do a long trip. Hugh, get your overnight kit together and into the lorry one evening. Discuss the permissible quantity with Jack. I expect you've got a mate who can run it over for you in a car. If not, gather it together at home and load it when you're passing. All clear both of you? Good. Oh, and Hugh here's the keys to that garage over there. It's marked 593 for some reason. You can leave your bike in there. It'll save it getting wet, dirty or run over.'

'Wow, thanks Michael.' But he was gone. 'I shouldn't get too excited 'bout the garage mate, he'll probably charge you for it. Come on, we better get earning. Hop in and we'll go and pick up a Chard.'

Most of the trailers were kept loaded just outside the dock in a trailer park. If it filled up in busy times the excess was 'shunted' up to the company yard.

Getting hitched

Marrying a tractive unit, prime mover or lorry to a trailer is actually less complicated and safer than attaching a caravan or works trailer to your car. Technically an articulated lorry trailer is called a semi-trailer because it has no drawbar. In America the whole outfit, (lorry and semi-trailer), is referred to as a semi which they pronounce sem-eye! You've probably heard the term in American films.

The lorry carries a greased plate which is situated over the rear axle and has a circular hole in it. It is accessed via a V-shaped wedge cut out of the rear of the plate. The semi-trailer has a pin which is fixed to a similar greased plate and points down vertically.

The semi-trailer is attached to the lorry by sliding its pin into the hole in the plate on the lorry.

Many engineering processes do sound sexual don't they? Anyway, the two parts are joined together by reversing one into the other. The bars in the lorry plate automatically snap shut, thereby locking one to the other. I've always found it fascinating and slightly horrifying that the pin is the only part which keeps the semi-trailer coupled to the lorry.

In those heady days of the 1970s UK, we had progressed to having an air operated brake system on most lorries. The system was also used on semi-trailers, which in future, I'll just refer to as trailers. Obviously, to make the trailers' brakes work, there had to be a connection between it and the lorry. This was provided by flexible airlines which had to be connected up when you married one to the other. You've probably noticed different coloured lines behind articulated lorries when you've been travelling.

There were three differently coloured air lines which serve different purposes within the system. The red one was the emergency line. When a trailer was disconnected from the lorry, the brakes were automatically applied as the red line was removed. So obviously, they would be released when the red line was attached during the coupling process.

It's extremely important to apply the lorry hand brake before joining all the airlines from the lorry to the trailer.

In the early days of my employment at Rodes Michael employed his nephew as a driver. The very first trailer he coupled up was parked in the yard. Rodes yard was on a slight incline. He failed to put the handbrake on before going through the routine of joining the airlines. He connected the emergency line first. The trailer brakes released and the whole vehicle started forward down the hill. Drivers are as prone to panic in an emergency as anyone else, except hopefully surgeons. He panicked and tried to get off the lorry which fortunately he succeeded in doing. But he didn't reach the handbrake in time.

The same day Michael had hired a brand new forklift which had been parked in a safe place. His nephews' vehicle wrote it off. Experienced drivers would have known you only need to disconnect the red line in the instant the lorry starts rolling forward.

We live and learn.

Learning the ropes with Jack

Chard wasn't exactly the big wide world, especially if you lived only 40 miles away as I did. Although they say Chard is the birth place of powered flight, history books quote something quite different in citing the Wright brothers. Apparently someone called Stringfellow attached wings to a steamroller and 'rushed' it off some cliffs near Axminster. It did actually fly for some 5 yards and then plummeted onto the beach like an eagle after a rabbit.

Chard was also mentioned in the annals of history as being the English town with the highest rate of crime per capita. But it must be with the caveat it was the prison town for Taunton, the county town of Somerset. Other than that what more can be said? On the way back we stopped off at my gaff. I hurriedly gathered my sleeping bag, pillow, wash kit, various maps and a pair of overalls, so I wouldn't have to do it the next evening. We swapped trailers, secured the Caerphilly load and dragged it back to the yard. We fetched the loading notes for the steel from the cupboard where messages for drivers were left when the office closed.

Rodes Transport's business was built on the import and export of goods to and from Portugal. Lisbon I imagine, as it was a transit dock. The inbound cargo was predominantly timber for making pallets, but also included cork of varying dimensions and for different purposes. There was also steel and bags of stuff for mopping up spillages. Very occasionally there were one-offs of crockery and part loads of wine. Later the diversity increased to toilet rolls the size of a car!

Export cargo was generally steel, including stainless steel. There were tractors and sometimes wood pulp and even waste paper. The returning ships were not always loaded from Watchet. The only times we had to rush were when they were, or if an inbound shipload was all due for one destination. The latter caused immense queues and long waits at the delivery point where as Michael pointed out at my interview, my O level in English Literature became so rewarding.

One of those delivery points was Golbourne, a small town just north of Manchester. It was one of the many hubs of industry which I was to come to know well in the following years. The shipping company also used another small dock at Mostyn, in North Wales. Sometimes lorries arrived in Golbourne from both docks on the same day. The resulting queues of lorries stretched beyond the little town's limits. A shipload could weigh as much as 2000 tonnes which would equal 100 lorry loads per ship, multiplied by the two docks.

We set off for Caerphilly at 6am the next morning. I managed to get to the yard on time and Jack said he'd drive first. I think he wanted to gain some confidence in my abilities before he felt safe enough to doze off while I was driving. He wasn't going to risk it before breakfast. There was only one Severn Crossing back then and as we started the descent to the bridge my instruction began.

'Lorries take a long time to slow down from 60mph, Hugh.' Jack said, 'and need loads of power to pull away again. So I'll show the best way to pay the toll.'

We were doing close to terminal velocity when we reached the bottom of the hill. Jack powered off as the toll booths came into sight. He slowed down gently until we were almost at the end of the short queue. He found a low gear and eased forward without stopping. Our turn to pay arrived and we passed through without stopping. Jack sort of half threw and half put the money in the booth where a man sat. He seemed pretty used to it. He gave us a smile and waved us on.

'There you are,' Jack grinned at me, 'got to get it right or you spend the whole day stopping and starting. Sometimes, if there's no queue, I go through at 30 miles an hour but they get a bit pissed off about it. Rush, rush, rush, time is money. We're on bonus.'

'I'm not.' I said.

'No, but I am. What's he pay you, then?'

'£60 a week plus expenses.'

'Fuck me! Is that all?'

'Yep, but a year ago I only earned £20 a week.'

'You might have got more but he pays me £10 for learning you.'

'It's better than just being told.'

'When you get your own wagon, you'll be on the same as the rest of us.'

'How much is that?'

'It's a bonus system. We get a flat rate of £90 and then the wagon has to earn £260. After the £260 we get 20% of the lorry earnings. On a normal week you should make £180 including expenses and tax paid, unless of course the wagon breaks down on Wednesday.'

'Roll on the end of three months then.'

'Hey, don't you like me?' He joked, 'I wasn't looking forward to this schooling job to be honest, but so long as we get on it could be a good laugh.'

'I can get on with almost anyone, Jack.'

Caerphilly was a bustling, smallish town and just north of Cardiff. Not many places had ring roads then, Caerphilly included, but it had a castle and a river. We had to drive through the centre of town to get to our delivery. The streets were narrow and the river bridge was even narrower, and there was a sharp right just after it. There was never much traffic about first thing in the morning. So we got there, tipped, (unloaded), and we were soon on our way out. We waited at the lights to do a hard left to go over the bridge. I was still 'shotgun,' (riding as the passenger).

'There's a car pulling up on the near side, Jack. You seen it?'

'Yeah, yeah I have him.'

We were waiting as far to the right as possible in order to negotiate the tight left turn over the bridge. The car stopped about half way along the trailer on the inside. I supposed he realised how the lorry was going to make the turn. But no, the lights changed and Jack drove to the centre of the main road before making the turn, as is the procedure. As the lorry turned the car would have disappeared from his view in the mirror. The car driver was clearly perplexed, because instead of waiting he kept pace with us. I shouted at Jack to stop but at the same time I watched from my grandstand view as the disaster unfurled. As we made the turn the trailer cut the corner, as it is bound to. The two trailer axles mounted the car boot, sort of took off like an aircraft, bounced on top of the roof and then rolled elegantly off the bonnet. We stopped.

'Stay here Hugh, I'll sort this out.'

Jack grabbed a printed piece of paper and a pen and leaped out of the cab. I watched him talking to the car driver, writing some stuff down and copying the driver's details. He returned to the cab.

'You got to remember to pick up a handful of these papers from Michael, mate. They're disclaimers. You just got to convince the other bloke to sign it and we'll not hear another word, right?'

'OK.' I nodded, though not completely convinced.

'Turns out it was a brand new Moskovitch. He'd only done 5 miles in it. Time to replace with new, I reckon. Never mind, all done. I think he was suffering from shock. I told him to call in at the hospital. The car's still working, sort of. It just don't look very pretty. OK, let's get on and get some steel.'

'I could eat some breakfast.'

'Good idea. We'll stop somewhere.'

We stopped just outside the town. You can't beat a full Welsh breakfast.

I'd never been to a steel works before. The one in Cardiff was close to the docks. It was vast with loads of different sheds. All appeared clearly numbered. We arrived at the entry barrier where a bloke sat in glass box which was raised to the level of a lorry window.

'Morning, driver. Loading papers please.'

Jack greeted him and passed the loading notes.

'20 foot round bar. Know where to go?'

'Yes mate, No 4 shed?'

'That's the one lad, half way down on the left. Show your tickets to the loader before backing in.'

Jack stopped outside and we both went in to present ourselves. Outside it was relatively quiet but inside the shed the noise was deafening. The steel was made, stored and loaded it in the same shed. The loading foreman had a blackened face and wore the company overalls, heavy duty gloves and a yellow hard hat with big ear muffs secured over it. He didn't attempt to say anything and instead held out his hand for the notes but he was smiling. He looked at the notes and nodded. He leaned in close to the both of us and shouted.

'Get into position to back into that bay there. When I signal you to back in, reverse in until I indicate STOP. Make sure the dunnage is laid out sort of where it should be. My boys'll move it if they have to. Stay in the cab while we're loading. Yeah?'

We gave him a thumbs-up.

'Right Hugh, you set it up and back in when he calls us. Give me a hand with the dunnage[1]. Lucky I filched some from the pallet yard.'

Inside the shed it was exceptionally hot, noisy and dusty, but for me it was really exciting to watch the big gantry cranes running back and forth above the workshop floor. It only took five trips for the crane to put 20 tonnes on the trailer. Each bundle of steel weighed a tonne and was 20 feet long. There were four bundles in each crane journey. The loading crew was very efficient and they knew exactly what was required to spread the weight and load us safely. Within 15 minutes the foreman came over and shouted into our cab.

'Right lads, take it out and secure it. Then come back in and get your delivery tickets from the transport office up there.'

He pointed up to an office on a higher level.

'Way de go Yooee. Turn right out the shed and park up alongside.'

'Have we got to cover it?' I asked.

'Yeah, but only for appearances. We'll leave it down the dock so it doesn't have to be a special job. Four straps and rough cover it with the fly. Have you done any sheeting?'

'Yes of course, but I'm not very good at it.'

'Practice makes perfect. Come on, get the kit out. With a bit of rush we'll be back by 4.30 and still have time for lunch on the way. We'll stop at Gordano services.'

Jack showed me how the ratchet straps worked and how to tuck the sheet in under itself so it didn't flap in the wind. We made the sheet tight with a few ropes over the front, back and top and then collected the notes.

'Normally you just get two notes. One for the customer and one for him to sign, but this is an export order, so there are all sorts of customs papers with it. Don't lose any.'

---

[1] Dunnage has various meanings but in lorry driver terms it normally refers to lengths of timber on which to load the cargo. Drivers were expected to provide their own.

Within twenty minutes we were going through the gate and on our way home with me at the wheel.

'How do we know it's within the weight limits?'

'The steel is all pre-weighed before loading. They never put on more than 20 tonnes and we know we weigh 10.8 tonnes tare or empty. Don't worry mate, put your foot down, I'm getting peckish.'

After a light lunch we got back to base at around five and dropped the trailer. We put the mountain of notes in the dock office and drove up to the yard for diesel. Jack came out of the office with tomorrow's notes and a big smile.

'We're off to see the Queen mate.'

'What? Scotland?'

'No you idiot. The Big Smoke. London!'

'London? The last time I was there was when my dad took me to see the sights. I was only four.'

'You'll know your way around then.' He laughed.

I was terrified. London? In a lorry?

'We got to be there before 8am. 7.30 be best or else we'll catch the traffic. Which means, Hugh, we've got to leave the yard latest, 3.30am. We'll leave at 3am, right?'

I nodded despondently.

'It's a load of cork board. We'll pick it up now. Get your skates on. I feel a beer coming on!'

The Big Smoke

When the time came I had no difficulty at all getting out of bed at two in the morning. In fact, I got a big burst of self-righteousness knowing I was going to work in the big city while everyone else was having a snore. Although I fairly quickly lost my righteous feeling in the following years, I really preferred what most normal people would call the night shift. It was quiet and there was very little traffic about. Most of all it was tranquil. There was time to enjoy the sunrise and the early dawn. There was more opportunity to take in the beauty of it all. You didn't have to concentrate so much on not being killed by motorists who, incredibly, had managed to pass the driving test. Of course there were many days when the weather was really bad and nothing could be seen beyond the windscreen wipers, but at least there were fewer commuters to avoid in the early hours.

'Hugh, we'll skip breakfast till we get there, because firstly, I don't want to be caught in the rush-hour and secondly, there's a really good café next to the delivery. It'll be your first London breakfast for nearly 20 years. You must be really gagging for it.' Jack laughed.

'Yeah, you're right, but you're going to drive it in, right?'

Yes, yes, I don't want to waste time while you fight with the map and make mistakes. You can do the rest of the day's shift after we're empty. Got it?'

'I've got it.'

The last part of the M4 going into London is the Brentford flyover. It would present a beautiful view over Kew Gardens if it wasn't obscured by the massive office building of Brentford Nylons. Next up was the Chiswick roundabout with an old iron flyover passing over the top. It was only for eastbound traffic approaching from the south. We followed the Great West Road into town and did a right down Earls Court Road which was one way. Warwick Road runs parallel and one way in the opposite direction. I often wondered why Earls Court Stadium was on Warwick Road and not the other. Jack knew his way perfectly and we went this way and that for a half hour or so, taking in the Thames and the Houses of Parliament as we raced along. It was very confusing for me.

'You need to buy yourself an A to Z of London like this, mate. Most of the places we go to are regular, but from time to time we get a new one or you might have a delivery from somewhere else. I know my way around pretty well now, but it's easy to get lost if you don't. You'll need to get loads of maps of the whole country really and some city plans too, but all in good time.'

'I've got maps but I haven't got one of these. Where are we? Where are we going?'

'We're going to Joan St, just off The Cut. I'll show you on the map when we get there, but Michael says you're better at maps than me.'

'I think he was taking the piss Jack, but yes I want to take a look.'

'Here we are Sir. We've arrived.'

'Christ in heaven man, you'll never get it down there!'

'Well I really hope you're wrong cos I got it in there before at least a dozen times. But yeah, it is very tight. Always bear in mind the artic driver's rule. Never drive in where you can't back out. I know you can't back out, and I also know it's even narrower to get out forwards. But you'll be driving then, so who cares?'

He gave me a huge grin.

'There's a great café on the other corner. Don't look so worried. Here we go, hold on tight and don't shout.'

From Google maps I notice the lay-out of Joan St has changed mightily in nearly 50 years. There is now a café where we used to unload called Jack's Café. How ironic is that?

We parked up alongside a row of arches, which I supposed supported the railway line running overhead. Each arch had a big wooden door. It was quiet, apart from the noise of the trains and no one was about.

'Great, they're not here yet. Come on Hugh, let's get the ropes off and loosen off the sheet, but don't take it off till they get here. They should be in at about 7.45.'

A group of blokes turned up at 7.30. One of them greeted us.

'Mornin' drive. Oh, there's two of yer.'

'He's a learner.' Jack said.

'What's to learn? It's only a fucking lorry.'

'Yeah, true enough. Can you drive one?'

'It's too early in the morning for a fight. Get your sheets off and we'll get on with it.'

They all worked hard and with good humour despite the bad start. It was sweaty work as we all had to muck in off-loading by hand. Cork is not heavy, but there were a lot of boxes on a 40 foot trailer.

'Drive, take your mate and get some breakfast. We'll finish off and put your sheets on the trailer. When you come back you'll probably want to use the 'phone. You can use this office one if they're all local calls.'

'Thanks. Yeah, they're all local.'

We walked over to the café and I tucked in to my first London breakfast in nearly 20 years.

'How come they'll all be local calls?'

'Every driver has to find his own loads when he's away. Sometimes though, Michael has got something lined up for an export load for Watchet. So we can go wherever we please provided we have a load on. Where do you fancy?'

'What? Anywhere? How do you find a load?'

'Well, anywhere within reason. I don't want to go to Scotland because it takes so long to get there and it's really difficult to get anything to come back with. So Manchester or Leeds is about the furthest north I'd aim for. Or we could go west, like Cornwall or south Wales.'

'I'm not fussy, but how do you find a load?'

'We all got a list of numbers of other transport companies or clearing houses which are local to wherever we are. If they got anything surplus, they'll give it us. It's how Michael gets the cargo shifted from the dock if he hasn't got any of his own lorries at home to do it.'

'Where do I get a list?'

'I'll give you a few numbers. Some of the other drivers will give you a few and the rest you find on your own by using your gob and keeping your eyes and ears open. It takes time, but you'll get there. Come on, let's pay up and get to the phone.'

It's a good breakfast in there.' Jack said to the foreman.

'Yeah, it's a very popular café. Phone's over there.' He pointed and then turned to me.

'You sound more like a lawyer, son.'

'I'm trying to change my appearance.' I said.

'Are you happy in your work?'

'I love it.'

'I wish I was.'

'I expect you'll feel better by lunch time.'

Jack interrupted.

'There's one for Anglesey or one for Stockport. Where do you want to go Hugh?'

'Wherever you like, Jack. It's your bonus.'

'OK. Stockport is better for a load back. We'll go there. It's reels of paper which is more work, but there are two of us.'

'We'll take Stockport mate,' he said into the 'phone, 'What? Yeah I got a learner with me.' A pause, 'Purfleet wharf, yeah OK. We'll be there inside an hour. Thanks.' He hung up.

'Thanks mate.' He said to the foreman, and then to me,

'Come on learner, get behind the wheel. Let's see the sights.'

Leaving Joan St was indeed considerably more difficult than getting in and tested my scant abilities to the limit. I had to practically put the cab through the café door in order to allow the trailer to cut the narrow right-angled corner on my blind side. I made it and got a round of applause from my passenger. Then it was out into the mad traffic of central London. In the 70s there were very few places you couldn't go with a lorry, but I remember Jack saying

'I'm not sure if we're allowed over Tower Bridge but we'll go anyway as it's the quickest route. Right, do a left at these lights, down to the roundabout and go right. Right? When you see the bridge, aim for it. Don't let anyone cut you off or we'll be stranded in the middle of something. Yeah that's it. Just keep going. They'll blow their horns, but they won't ram us unless they've got a death wish. Keep your eyes open because I don't want another car stuck under the trailer. Oh yes, good man, we're on the way over the water.'

It was a splendid view. There was no London Eye in 1977, but from high up in the cab and on top of Tower Bridge we could see quite a way down the river. On the other side was the Tower of London to which my Dad had taken me. We could see the dome of St Pauls and the City, or financial district. We couldn't see the Houses of Parliament because they were round a bend in the river. Anyway, I had seen them on the way in. There was no 'Gerkin' or the high-rises of Canary Wharf because it was still a working wharf. It was exciting but it was all over in minutes, and I was busy negotiating the route to Purfleet under Jack's directions. From the centre of London we always used the route which took us past the East End docks to reach the ports of Purfleet or Tilbury.

I professionally pulled up at the entry barrier to the dock alongside an empty glass office. I turned to Jack. 'There's no one here.'

'I noticed.'

'He'll probably be back. He might have gone for a shit or something.'

'If he has, he's got a problem because he hasn't been back in three years.'

'Really?'

'Yeah. It's not in use. Back up and go round it. There's a caravan down there to check in next to the loading shed.'

'I'll do that then. Why didn't you say so?'

'It was a joke. Not funny?'

'Great, keep them coming mate.'

Portakabins were very modern and rare, so most temporary offices were caravans embedded permanently in the ground. They served the same purpose and sometimes, in quiet periods, happy drivers got offered a real tea or coffee made with boiling water from a recognisable kettle. We checked in but didn't get offered refreshments. Perhaps we didn't qualify by conveying the correct level of happiness required. We were directed to the loading point in a specific shed and waited in position for our turn. It came and I moved the lorry forward.

Roll up, roll up

The reels of paper were about the width of the trailer, but not quite. They were loaded with a giant forklift which had rounded-off forks so they didn't damage the paper. They picked up one at a time and lowered them on to the trailer. As the forklift pulled out we had to push the first reel tight up to the headboard and then knock two wooden chocks into position at the bottom so they didn't roll back. For our load we didn't have to supply our own 'scotches', as they're called. When the back reel was put on they gave us a 'back scotch', which is a long version of the small door-stop type. It got tapped in along the whole length of the reel and we tied a rope over it to stop it coming loose. Next they put about two or three on the top tier sitting between the reels on the bottom level. We were loaded.

'Right, up you go Hugh, you're the learner. Get the first sheet spread out to cover the back part, and when it's done spread the other over the front of the load.'

It's the way it was done because the two sheets will overlap. The wind will be coming from the front as we drive. If you do it the other way, the wind and weather will get under the back sheet and give the appearance you're driving a hot air balloon.

Tying the sheet is a bit like wrapping a parcel, except it's 40/45 feet long, 8 feet and a bit wide and in our case, the reels reached nearly 9 feet off the trailer floor. Additionally, the bottom tier covered the whole of the trailer bed and there were only two on top, so it was a bit of an awkward shape.

There were no ladders or safety lines supplied in those dark ages, so you just had to be young and agile. You also had to be very careful you didn't fall off and die, or worse incapacitate yourself for the rest of your life. I was always very careful when climbing about on a high load, despite being carefree and sometimes reckless in my approach to life.

We completed the job quite quickly as there were two of us. It normally took about 30 to 40 minutes on your own. Then we threw the rope over and pulled it tight between the reels.

"What a pretty sight Hugh. You've done a good job. We'll park it up and use the wash room here 'cos there won't be anywhere clean on the road"

We grabbed our wash kit and followed the signs marked TOILETS. Inside the shed there were two doors. One was marked 'PRIVATE' and the other, 'DRIVERS'. The door to the private one was open and it too was a washroom. It looked to be about the same as most factory washrooms, not immaculate like home, but almost acceptable. Beyond the door marked DRIVERS my first impression was of a swamp. We waded in to get a better look.

'Hey Jack, I don't think this has been cleaned since last year.'

'The one before more like. But look mate it's what there is, and it's a lot worse on the road. You just got to get used to it.'

'Oh yeah, I know, but putting the mop round once a day shouldn't be too taxing should it?'

'Why don't you go and tell them?'

'Oh I can do much better.'

There was a mop near the door and I swept most of the water out. Then I stuck it in a couple of basins and had a swab around. The porcelain didn't exactly shine but it was a great deal better.

'Well done mate. That's an improvement. You're a 'Hugh-of-all-trades' ain't you?'

'That's about the whole of it Jack.'

We had a strip wash because there were no showers. You can get very dirty sheeting and roping, hence the need for overalls. You didn't want to carry all the muck into the cab. Well, most drivers didn't. So the need for washing facilities was imperative, for me at least. In the middle ages of the 1970s, it was almost impossible to find places to wash properly, and encountering a shower was like finding bananas growing wild in your garden.

'Why do you think these toilets are segregated from the dockers' ones?'

'Oh that's easy. They don't want to get contaminated by the transport industry.'

'There're no toilets for the girls either.'

'Yeah, more's the pity. They'd be spotless and smelling of roses, but it's because girls don't drive lorries. Again more's the pity, and I've never seen a girl working on a dock. It'll never change Hugh. It's how it is. On the bright side we have hot water.'

We finished and were soon on our way north. Driving is a mostly solitary occupation which you get used to and for the most part enjoy. We talked very little on the way out of the 'smoke' apart from Jack giving me directions, however he did tell me about the expenses.

'Whenever you tip south of the river and load north of it, as in today's case, you should always claim the Dartford tunnel toll whether you use it or not. It's only 50p, but 50p is 50p. They never question it, but if they do just say it was because of traffic or road works. Right?'

'Right,' I said. It seemed to make sense despite being a lie.

We travelled up the M1 for a couple of hours before either of us spoke. 'You got a girlfriend Hugh?'

'Not right now no, but I know what you're asking. It's going to be very cosy sleeping in here with two of us. I'm not going to put my hand on your knee, I assure you.'

'Yeah, that's what I meant.'

'Good. You have anyone?'

'There's no-one at home but there's always someone available when I'm away.'

'What always?'

'Well, nearly always.'

'No girls in the cab Jack, I like to turn in early-ish.'

'It's agreed. It's a sensible rule while we're working together.'

'I'm not against threesomes, but this is a very small space to enjoy it.'

'I'll tell you a joke, if you like, about two blokes living in confined spaces.' I said.

'Go on then.'

'Well, there were these two friends who went on a camping holiday together in the jungle. They only took one tent to reduce the weight they had to carry. One evening they passed a tribal village and set up camp about a mile away from it. They cooked their food and drank a few beers and then went to sleep.

In the morning one of them went out to take a shit. Within five minutes he'd returned screaming in pain and clutching his cock.

'What's the problem?' said his mate.

'I got bit by a snake. On my cock! It hurts like fuck. What am I going to do? I'm going to die, I'm going to die.'

'Calm down mate. It'll be alright. Put this ointment on it.'

'Ointment's no fucking good. I'm sure it was a venomous snake.'

'Oh shit, really? And you really got bit on your cock?'

'I said so, didn't I?'

'OK look, I'll go down the village and ask the witch doctor. I'm sure he'll have some natural remedies. Don't panic. I'll be as quick as I can'.

So he left. He found the witch doctor and put his question. The doctor told him that the only solution was to suck the poison out.

'And if I can't?' the lad asked.

The witch doctor shrugged and said,

'Your friend will die.'

He returned to his mate who said,

'Did you find him? What did he say?'

'Yes I found him. He said you're going to die.'

'Yeah, very good,' said Jack, 'I don't think there're any venomous snakes in Birmingham so you should be alright.'

Later Jack wanted to know why I was driving and not working in an office. I told him all of it but added he was not to tell anyone else.

'I definitely wouldn't do that. Drivers are like old washer women. As soon as they stop they tell everyone all the bits of info they have. If they don't have any, they make it up. I tell a lot of stories myself. It's why Rodes' drivers call me 'Jackanory', but I never say anything private. You can count on me. But fuck me Hugh. You've had 50 fucking jobs in five years!'

'49 jobs, and it's 7 years.'

'I had six before my dad lent me the money for the test. It was only because he was sick of me coming back with no wage in my pocket. I've stuck this one for three years, and I love it!'

'I love it too, so far. Yeah OK then, I think we've covered that, right?'

'You don't want to tell me about your other jobs?'

'Oh, it's not that. I'm happy to talk about what I've done, but the history thing of 49 jobs is not something I'm particularly proud of. It just turned out that way till I found what I wanted to do.'

'I still don't understand and despite what you'd call your long CV you sound well educated. So you're still a Toff. I reckon you'll find it really difficult getting to know the others. You ought to try dropping your accent a bit. It might help.'

'I've already encountered a similar problem with Arnie.'

'You don't want to worry yourself about him. He's a prat. It's the other slightly brighter ones who could help you with stuff like numbers for 'back-loads'.'

'I'll practice. I like languages but I know they'll see through me.'

'They will, but it don't really matter so long as you sound like you're making an effort to join in. Like everything really.'

We finished for the day and parked for the night in a small town south of Birmingham. Jack showed me how to fill in the drivers' hours log book. They were all hand written then and we hadn't filled one in every day, so we had to play catch-up. We referred to them as the 'Book of Lies'. They were vaguely accurate, but it depended if the following day was a Friday or not. Tachographs weren't used until later. We went in search of beer and food.

Our lorry was a Volvo F86. To me it looked like a Fiat 500 which was raised to a height of about ten feet. It was small by lorry standards even then, and inside it was even smaller. There were the standard two seats which were rock hard and without suspension. It was similar to travelling swiftly up and down the motorways on a park bench. But I should point out there were much worse.

Cab-over or bonnet

Instead of having the engine under a bonnet like so many American 'trucks' the engine was underneath the cab. So the F stood for forward control. It meant the rods and cables for clutch, brake and accelerator went down and back to the engine. It put the driver forward of the power plant. In between the seats and marginally higher than the seat level was an engine cover, which continued to the back of the cab rising all the time. An inspection plate could be opened and was used for checking the oil and water levels. But many drivers put an extra tube down it at night so you could have a pee without having to face the elements. It was very convenient if it was freezing cold or pissing with rain. Of course, to do your heavier business you'd have to make a run for it to the toilets, or take one in the bushes.

It was a very similar life to camping but with worse facilities, unless you camped in the wild. As lorry development continued it became more like 'glamping', but the facilities provided by society never kept pace. Some modern lorries now have proper loos and even showers, so the driver can be wholly self-contained, provided he remembers to carry enough water. The days of it being standard were still years away.

Sleeping arrangements

Behind each seat there were two voids divided by the raised part of the engine cover. They were there to store stuff like sleeping bags, pillows, maps, flasks or anything else which would fit. It was not a good idea to keep ropes, chains or straps there, because of the dirt element. Those were generally stowed outside and behind the cab. If the voids were adequately filled there was then a level space behind the seats to lay a bit of foam rubber as a mattress. It wasn't very long and only 18 inches wide. It was perfect for a good night's sleep. In our case, the second mattress was laid out across the seats and gave an almost standard size bunk. Perfecter! I got the small bunk even though Jack was vertically challenged. Learners got to learn.

Both of us did sleep well on our first night after a surfeit of beer in the pub and excellent fish 'n' chips from the chippy.

I spent a bit less than the three months I was promised working with Jack. He taught me a good deal and we got on well. It was a good thing because an F86 is a very small place to live.

The only other thing which springs to mind about that period is a trip we did to Golbourne. As usual, there were at least 50 vehicles waiting in line to unload.

We spent the time chatting, cleaning the windscreen and lights, tidying the cab and taking short walks. I got out to check the lights while Jack operated the controls.

'Tail lights?' he hollered.

'Yep, all good.'

'Indicators, left?'

'They're working, they're not working, they're working, they're not working.'

'Indicators, right?'

'They're working, they're not working, they're working.'

'Brake lights?'

'We got one out on the trailer. Look out a spare.'

I returned to the cab.

'Hugh. You are a fucking laugh a minute.'

'Yeah OK, it was just a joke. Got the brake light bulb?'

'We've run out. You'll have to nick one. One of the Mostyn blokes has just gone for a walk. Have one of his,' he instructed.

'Then he'll be short of one. There is another way. I'll show you.'

'What you going to do? Make one?'

'Watch and learn son.' I said.

I wandered over to the two blokes from Mostyn who were having a chat.

'Hello lads. I got a brake light out and I've run out of spares. Have you got a spare bulb you could let me have?'

'Yep, I'm sure I have.'

He rummaged in his spares box, came out with one and gave it to me.

'Many thanks mate, that's kind.'

'It's nothing mate. See you later.'

I took it back, fitted it and went to the cab again.

'How ingenious and effective Hugh.'

'Yes. I thought so, and I see you're learning more words to experiment with. We've taught each other a lot in a short time haven't we?'

'Cheeky bastard!'

What I forgot to mention was, at the end of the first week with Jack, Harold stopped to have a word with me while we were swapping trailers at the dock.

'I spoke with Cathy, Yooee, and she said for you to go and see her on Saturday if you're home. I writ the address down 'ere. She's called Mrs. Baker to you. About 10 o' clock's best before she goes down the shops.'

He passed me a note.

'Thanks a lot Harold. I'll go and see her tomorrow.'

'Let me know how it turns out. She's a nice old girl and she'll have plenty of stories to tell. Everyone likes her.'

'That's a stroke of luck mate.' said Jack. 'Good of you to help my pupil out Harold.'

'No trouble to help a mate, even you Jackanory!' he laughed.

I knocked on Mrs Baker's door the next day.

'Good morning,' she said 'You must be Hugh. With an Haych. I'll try and get that right. It's nice to be called by your right name, I know. Now come in and have a look at what I can offer you.'

'Good morning Mrs Baker. Yes it's all correct. Harold sent me.'

'Yes, yes, I know. He's a good old stick is Harold. Come on, come on in.'

She ushered me in and then led me up the stairs. There was a door right in front and she opened it. Inside was a small but utilitarian kitchen. To the right was a larger room which served as a small bed sitting room with a single bed against one wall. The furniture was basic and next door was a bathroom without a shower, but with a shower head attached to the bath taps. The colour scheme throughout was bland but certainly not frightening. It was perfect, and I said so.

'This is perfect Mrs Baker. It'll suit me brilliantly. It's comfortable and I can do my own thing without bothering you. It's great. How much do you want in rent?'

'£20 per week. Can you afford it?'

'Well I'm only getting £60 at the moment because I'm learning with Rodes, but I'll be on their normal wages in three months, so yes I think so.'

'Look, you seem like a nice lad and Harold's recommended you, so I'll charge you £15 to begin with and when that stingy Michael Rodes gives you a proper wage it'll be £20. I can't be fairer than that.'

'Goodness, thank you. That's wonderful. It's a deal.'

'And Hugh, I don't have a car any longer so you can put your motorcycle in my garage. There's nothing in there.'

We shook hands and I went to tell my present landlady. I certainly landed on my feet there, thanks to Harold.

I lived there for a few years. Mrs Baker and I became as good friends as was possible. And my bike was safe and dry. Result.

On my own at last

My time with Jack was rewarding and I learned plenty, but of course I'd got used to having someone else in the cab to correct my mistakes. Now I was going to have to do it on my own without making a fool of myself. I'd manage, I told myself. As it turned out, when Michael presented me with the lorry he told me,

'Jack has given a good report of your progress and I'm happy. Even so, I'm going to put you down the dock with Harold for a week to help him get trailers up to the yard. We've got three ships in this week and it's busy. You're the only one I can spare, added to which Harold can make sure you're quick and efficient with sheets and changing trailers. After we're done, you're up the road on your own. We'll have another chat before it occurs. Understood?'

'Yes Michael.'

'One more thing, Hugh, don't tangle with Arnie. He's a difficult bastard. He could give you problems, but don't let him bother you. You're on £90 per week flat rate from now. It'll change again when I let you loose.'

With those words, he was gone. Hey, hey, 50% pay rise in the space of five minutes. Things were definitely looking up, and Mrs Baker would have a smile as well. Further, Michael never charged me for the garage in the yard. I only used it for a couple of weeks and I might still have the keys. I'd have to check.

Some people enjoy shunting or moving trailers very short distances. You certainly don't have to go very far and you're home every night. It doesn't tax your brain, but it is very, very boring. By lunch time on Monday I really could not wait for Friday night to arrive. It did give me the opportunity to put some personal touches to my new working home and clean it a little. It was new to me but it was in fact the oldest lorry on the fleet, first registered in 1971 I think. It was another F86 so there was nothing different to get used to. I fixed up my bunk and it looked sort of permanent. By the time I'd fitted the carpets it was just like home. Well, that's a bit over stated.

I managed to get some more maps, including a large A to Z of London and a big book of listings of UK transport companies and clearing houses. Later they came in really useful. I fitted some curtains, which might have been better described as window coverings. Anyway, come Friday I was very pleased with my efforts. I managed to get a second-hand radio from the workshop where they had a selection of used ones. It actually worked, which was a surprise.

I worked hard with Harold and we got on well. He told me lots more stories of his driving life in the 1950s and 1960s, which were truly eye-opening to a youngster like me. Some of them could have been from the period directly following WW2, but I still wasn't sure of his age.

Harolds' tales

'Twer much harder back in the 1950s, Yooee. Lorries were slower with no comfort at all. None had a bunk. Weren't no radios. They all had gaping holes in them especially round the foot pedals. In winter we wore bicycle clips to stop the cold air rushing up your legs and freezing your bollocks off. You lads don't know you're born.'

'It took days to get anywhere. Weren't no motorways then. We never came home except Saturdays, and only then if we were lucky.'

'I remember my old lorry had a top speed of 28mph. That were flat out and screaming. They all had hydraulic brakes so you could never stop them unless you had time to make a plan.'

'You know that long sweeping bend, t'other side of Flaxpool with a layby they got on it now?'

'Yes, of course.'

'Well, that there layby was the old road and the bend were pretty steep. Often when we came down the hill we couldn't slow down enough to go round the bend, see? So rather than lose the load we just drove through the gate into the field. That gate got busted so many times, in the end farmer just took it off its hinges so we could run in.'

'We used to go up north a lot. Right up north, Carlisle, Penrith, Whitehaven, and plenty went into Scotland. It took a whole week to get to Glasgow. Can you imagine that? No 'course you can't. It'd only take you a day now.'

'Anyway, when we went up there we used to stay in lodgings in a little village near Kendal. You know, where they make mint cake? Kendal is not far from the bottom of Shap Fell. God Christ that were a long steep hill.'

'After breakfast, all of us who were staying in the boarding house set off in our lorries, one behind the other. The landladies would make packed lunches for all of us and all the townspeople would walk up Shap, alongside the lorries. 'Twer a sight to behold.'

'It were hard work but I were a young man then. No more than 25 tops, probably less.'

I calculated I'd got his age wrong. He couldn't have been more than fifty-five but he looked older.

'We had to put them in first gear at the bottom and stick a wedge of timber under the throttle pedal. Then we could get out and chat with the ladies till we got to the top. I got a picture Yooee, of me looking like I'm pushing the lorry up the hill from behind. I'll look it out to show you. We even had trick photography back then, see?' He laughed.

'Who steered them while you were practising your chat-up lines?'

'Oh, we all had trailer boys in they days. We didn't actually have trailers and the boys were just learning till they was tall enough to see over the steering wheel. Then they'd get a job. No licences then, boy. You had to have a car licence of course.'

'You know Haydock Park, near Liverpool? Racecourse? Horses?'

'I know of it but I've never been there.'

'Yeah well, back along, before the shipping company had lots of Portuguese work, we used to do a lot of loads for the paper mill, see? There was a whole crowd of us delivering in Scotland together and we knew there was a big race at Haydock, same week. We arranged to meet up there on our way back, Yooee.'

'We all managed to get there about a couple of hours before the first race. The marshals let us park in their yard. So we nosed up to the railings in a line and settled back to watch the gee-gees. Good job there was no telly back then cos the boss, who were Michael's dad, would've turned it on and seen his whole fleet with their feet up watching the horses! Lucky really 'cos he were a hard bastard and we would certainly have lost our jobs.'

'Did I tell you about young Jimmy what was getting married?'

'Tell me another time Harold. I've got to go up to the yard. They were great stories though and I really enjoyed listening to them.'

'Yeah, 'course you have. I'll tell you another time then. Get on your way."

"Before I go, Harold, and just out of interest, how much were your wages in those days?'

Without hesitation he said,

'£3 and 10shillings a week plus our lodgings. There weren't no overtime. It were just work time.'

He wished me well and later gave Michael a glowing report of my efforts that week.

Released into the wild

On Saturday morning Michael collared me while I was filling up with diesel. He gave me some delivery notes.

'Hitch up to trailer 44 for Golborne, get it ready for Monday, clean up for the weekend and then come and see me before you go home, Hugh.'

'OK Michael.'

I did it all it as quickly as I could and went down to the office. It was about lunch time and I was looking forward to a pint. The words he spoke to me then stayed with me all my life. I've never forgotten them and I used them as a benchmark for all my working life. Well, all of my life actually. They've been very useful except for the last rule regarding cats.

'Right Hugh, let's take a stroll in the yard. Come with me.'

As we passed the trailer workshop Michael noticed a driver who had the workshop foreman by the neck and up against the wall. His fist was raised as if to hit him.

'Driver!' Michael shouted. 'Don't do that there please. I only had the walls whitewashed yesterday. Come on Hugh, come with me.'

We went and stood at the bottom of the yard looking up at all the lorries which were parked up and ready for the Monday morning start.

'Now then,' he began 'I just want to go over the rules before I set you free. Jack will have taught you the basics, so you know you will be rewarded with instant dismissal for thieving, fighting or drunkenness in the yard or while on duty. That will also occur if you lie to me. I will always know the truth so don't.

You now know you are responsible for everything on your vehicle while you're away from base. Everything! Except the road tax and the insurance which the office will make sure is legal and up to date. Any faults you must report to the workshop and if they do nothing, tell me.' He paused then followed with the most important bit.

'When you leave this yard on your own in my lorry, you are my ambassador. Be polite. It costs you absolutely nothing to be civil. Make sure you are. Secondly, never, and I mean never, stand around with your hands in your pockets watching someone else struggle. It doesn't matter what you might think of them. One day you could easily find yourself in the same position. Lastly, my cats tend to take a walk in the yard very early in the mornings. Sometimes, but by no means always, I go with them. Do not under any circumstances run them over or there'll be hell to pay. Those three rules are gospel while you work for me. OK Hugh, I wish you well. Work hard and you'll be well rewarded. Oh, did Jack explain how the pay and bonus work?'

'Yes Michael.'

'Good, well nothing has changed since he told you. If nothing goes wrong you should have another pay rise at the end of next week. When you search for a back load you may go anywhere you please, so long as each night you ring me and tell me: who you were working for, what you carried, where to and what the rate was. If there are any export loads required to be brought back to Watchet, I will tell you in advance.'

'Good, that's it. Enjoy yourself. Please give my regards to your landlady Mrs Baker.'

'Yes I will. Thank you Michael.'

Away we go

It would be very dull to tell a story of travelling countless hours on millions of miles of tarmac. I know it would bore you all to death before we got five miles up the road. So I'm going to tell you about the various things which happened to me and others, and what I heard about over the years. I remember things which were said and amusing anecdotes which were recounted to me.

I've calculated I journeyed at least one and three quarter million miles in lorries during my working life as a professional driver. I drove my various cars and rode motorbikes in my few leisure times as well. When you consider insurance companies believe private car owners notch up approximately 8,000 to 10,000 miles per year, you will appreciate the distances covered in the service to business and individuals throughout the beloved UK and Europe. I seldom took a holiday especially in the early years and had little or no home life, although I didn't miss it at all. Driving lorries was my leisure as well as my work. Some of the stories of our activities might suggest reckless or dangerous behaviour, but you have to bear in mind it was over 45 years ago. There were fewer heavily policed laws and much less traffic. The majority of my work companions were young and barely more than three of us on the company payroll were over 35 years old. Most of us were less than 25 years old. Through both uncomfortable and happy times, it was a grrrrrr8 life.

Although the lorry I started solo with was old, slow and uncomfortable, they did get better gradually, and so the work became considerably less tiring. I only had the F86 for a couple of years as it broke down almost continuously and was eventually relegated to the docks. On the first day it behaved very well but it soon turned out to be a real pain-in-the-ass. Mechanical repairs were never my forte but we all have to learn the basics when we're on our own. In the end I learned quite a lot, despite disliking the delays. Very soon I knew intimately nearly every yard of every hard shoulder on all UK motorways.

My first breakdown was between Bristol and Birmingham on the M5. I noticed in the mirror there was a rope which had come loose. I pulled onto the hard shoulder and stopped. I retied the rope and then went to start the lorry, but I was rewarded with just a click when I tried the ignition. I tried it several times and then realised I'd have to investigate. I checked the battery terminals. They were tight so I had to walk to the nearest emergency 'phone. We didn't have mobile 'phones. It was a good 1200 yards. I picked up the 'phone and was greeted with,

'Police emergency.'

'Hello. I've got a breakdown.'

There was a pause and then he asked me for all my details. I mean all. They included those of the vehicle and a contact number for Rodes.

'OK, we'll get in touch with your boss and call you back. Please wait.' So I waited, and waited, and waited. Suddenly it rang.

'Yooee, what's the problem?'

I explained.

'OK, so the battery terminals are tight. Good. It could be a fault on the starter. Tip the cab, make sure the lorry's not in gear, and find the starter. Do you know what the starter looks like?'

'Is it the thing which looks like the front of an aeroplane engine and has a winding handle hanging off it?'

Pause.

'For Christ's sake Yooee, don't fuck about! I'm really busy and if I've got to come out to you, you'll be there for hours.'

'Yeah, yeah, OK. I can find the starter motor.' I thought I could anyway.

'Wonderful. On top of it there are some electrical connections what are soldered on. Get a piece of metal and rest it between two connections at a time until you get a reaction from the engine. Leave the ignition turned on throughout. Got it? If you don't call back we'll know it worked. In any case find a load for home and we'll fix it when you're here. Got it?' I got it and it worked. I was on my way again.

As the weeks passed I learned to work out ways of temporarily fixing things till I got home. I'm glad I did as it was really useful in the future. It saves so much time. I was able to do most of the simple things myself and it gave me a basic understanding of how the lorry worked. However I was never entrusted in changing a clutch or a head gasket on the side of the road. Thank the lord.

Years later I met a bloke who'd been sleeping in his car in the lorry park at Heston services near London.

'Christ man, you look knackered,' I said. 'Have you just driven all the way from Reading?'

'Yeah sort of.'

'You look like you could do with another day off. What are you up to?'

'I'm what they call a roaming mechanic.'

'Well, I hope I break down in a minute. How far do you roam?'

'I've just driven out to Turkey to fix a gearbox. Change one, actually. Then when I rang back in they told me there's a lorry in Hull with an electrical problem. So I drove all the way back from fucking Turkey to Hull. Turned out the driver had a wire loose on the fucking trailer lights.'

'You drove all that way just for that?'

'Yeah exactly, so I floored the cunt. I told the boss what I'd done and all he said was he'd send another driver out.'

'You must be on superb wages.'

'Let's not talk about it. I'm going to Paris now to replace a clutch, which might be more rewarding.'

'And all the time you have to sleep in the car?'

'No, I don't have to, but all my tools are in it and the overnight expenses don't run to hotels, even in Turkey.'

There you are you see, the driver's lot is not as bad as some others have it. I bought him a cup of coffee.

Returning to the F86, we used to do quite a lot of what I called fleet deliveries to the same place. The whole fleet would deliver to the same address for about a week, or longer if Watchet dock was in a position to take another ship load. Later on we called it group therapy. On those occasions we generally returned to base without a load, which meant if the destination was Golbourne, we could do one and a half journeys a day. Therefore, if we set off on Sunday we'd have every night away from home. If you went on Monday you would have almost every night at home. But only if it worked out right, (NB Murphy's Law!). I always chose to leave on Sunday along with several others who were young, free and single. During the week we'd get separated by waiting times, queues and traffic. The fleet was expanding quite quickly then and I knew several of the others who joined up. It was good to be able to spend the evenings with people I knew.

There were two overnight stops we used when we went north. One was at Sandbach and the other at Worcester. Which one we stopped at depended on the driving hours we had left each day. As there were no mobile 'phones and still no one had a CB radio, we devised hand signals when we passed each other on the road. A hand held flat but making the movement of waves signified The Dolphin at Worcester. Two fingers in the same manner as the bowmen at Agincourt meant The Military Arms at Sandbach. Both towns were equally good. Sandbach had a parking area in the centre of the town which was surrounded by pubs and take-away shops. It was never too far to stagger back to the lorry. Worcester was a beautiful city and we used to park underneath the railway arches, but it could be noisy at night because of the trains. It also had a disco boat which went up and down the River Severn. I never went on it because it got back at 2am, which was almost the time to start work again. We had a lot of raucous nights. Neither of the towns had public wash houses or toilets near the lorry parks, so we had to do ablutions beforehand in some dubious places. Finding a place to wash at the end of the day was one of the most time-consuming tasks. In the end I used to carry a camping stove, saucepan, washing-up bowl and five gallons of water. It wasn't a perfect solution but at least I could always get hot water.

After three or four months of working solo at Rodes, I was becoming better accepted and the others would spend more time chatting with me. It was still a real uphill struggle. I sometimes thought it would be easier for a woman to become a coal miner or a fireman. Prejudice was rife, but gradually life got better as I learned more and stayed longer. For the most part, the drivers seemed to forget they thought I'd been born and brought up in the 'Grand Palace'.

Don't shoot!

I was in the yard with Ray, one of the drivers. Michael came out of the office and told us to do one load each to Barnstable. We decided to go together. There was no Devon Link Road then. We could either go all the way down to Tiverton and along the main road to the north Devon coast or take one of two alternative routes which went over the hills. Those were considerably more arduous with a lot of really steep hills and tiny little villages. The advantage of the latter was they knocked a good half hour off the journey, so we took the country route. On top of Exmoor it is truly beautiful, and with the added height of the lorry you could see over all the hedgerows. Quite often at the right time of year you could spot stags or foxes. On our day the weather was good although the hills were very taxing for my old lorry. There are a few which are 1:4 and exceptionally narrow so if you meet anyone on the incline you are screwed. You can't go back and if you stop you'd never get it to pull away again. Great fun! Anyway, we never came across anyone and went through two tiny fords as well. I knew the country well but I'd never thought hulking great lorries could go that way.

We unloaded and headed back to Watchet. Somewhere on top of the hills we were passing a field and suddenly Ray stopped in front of me. He ran back to me.

'Yooeee, tip the cab and pretend you've broken down.'

'Why? What for?'

'I'll tell you in a minute. Just do it!'

I did it. I watched Ray jump the barbed wire fence and run across the field. He picked up what looked like two heavy sacks and ran back. He chucked them over the fence and then climbed over himself. At the same moment a bloke appeared from behind the hedge carrying a shotgun.

'Oi, bastards! Bring back my swedes you thieving cunts.'

Ray panted up to me and chucked one bag in my cab.

'OK mate, drop the cab and let's fuck off.'

'I don't like swedes.'

'So what? Let's go. NOW!'

The bellow came again.

'Bring they fucking swedes back or I'll shoot.'

Yes, I thought, I bet you won't. I was just getting in the cab when there were two loud reports, a small cloud of smoke from the gun and a mass of pellets hit the cab. Oh, he has shot at us. I was terrifically happy the lorry started straight away, and I swiftly followed Ray. I heard two more shots but luckily we were out of range. We arrived back at the yard without further incident.

'I don't like swede Ray.'

'That's not the point. I don't like carpentry but you must never leave a building site without enough timber to rebuild your kitchen. It's an opportunity see?'

'There's shooting evidence on my cab.'

'It won't be noticed, believe me. Some one likes swedes. Sell 'em.'

I went to the diesel pump to refuel and Michael came out. Jesus Christ! He was quick, I thought.

'Hugh, do you remember what I said about thieving?'

'Yes Michael, but I haven't stolen anything.'

'I know, but you could be described as an accessory after the fact, or even receiving stolen goods, could you not?'

'Well, ah, errm.'

'Hugh, I know the farmer involved and now I have to drive all over the hills to buy him a pub lunch to keep him quiet. For God's sake don't be led on by these blokes. Be your own man. Now get on with it and pick one up for Birmingham. I hope you like swede because you'll be eating it for weeks.'

'Oh Hugh, I love swede. Well done.' said Mrs Baker, my landlady.

'Jolly good, enjoy them.' I said.

'Don't you want to keep even one for yourself?'

'Er, no thanks Mrs Baker.'

'I think you've been here long enough to call me Cathy. Do that, will you?'

'OK Cathy. I'll be away early again tomorrow, so good night.'

'Of course, Hugh. You shouldn't work so hard. Pop in and have a drink with me at the weekend.'

'Thanks, I will.'

Hiding

Following the swede incident I decided it would be for the best if I spent a bit of time away from home and went tramping, (loading to different parts of the country without returning to base). With that in mind, I managed to find a load for Kings Lyn in East Anglia after I'd unloaded in Birmingham. I'd only been to the area once before so it would be somewhere new. I knew of a company in Boston which I'd used in the past to help out with the next leg.

I was still on my way to pastures new at around 7pm. I was looking out for a quiet village with a pub and a lay-by close by in which to park for the night. I was looking forward to an uninterrupted night. I was cruising slowly along a country road in Rutland when I came across just the place. It was a small village with an attractive looking pub on the corner of the main cross roads. In fact, there wasn't much more than the centre before I was out into the countryside again. Yes, a lay-by, and only 100 yards out of town. Ideal.

I set up my 'bedroom' and had another wash, changed into my glad-rags, attached the 'curtains', locked up and set off for a pint and a bite to eat. The inside of the pub is what my mates would have called posh, but I described it as well appointed. There was a middle aged man sitting on a stool at the bar. There was no one else around. I went to the bar and sat down. There was no barman so I waited but no one came. Suddenly the man said,

'What would you like?'

'A pint of the best beer would be a good start.'

He went behind the bar.

'They're all the best there is in these parts. Which one do you fancy?'

'I'm not from these parts, so surprise me.'

'OK, try this one.'

I tried it.

'Yes, very tasty. Thanks.'

'We don't get many strangers here. Are you just passing?'

'I'm a driver, so yes. I saw the pub and thought it'd be ideal. Do you serve food?'

'It's good to see someone new. No. We only do snacks at lunchtime and evening food at the weekends. There are other pubs nearby who do food but you'd have to drive.'

'That's a pity. I've run out of driving hours and I'm fairly hungry now, but I expect I could skip it and get an early breakfast.'

'You sound too well-spoken for a driver. Are you filling in for someone?'

I told him most of the story whilst trying not to bore him or myself. Then I asked him about the pub.

He told me he'd worked in London for years and got bored with it. He'd made enough money to try doing something else but on his own. He had family in the Rutland area, so he and his wife had decided to buy this pub. It had turned out to be really quiet without the mass of passing crowds which they'd anticipated.

'Our customers are mostly local farmers, and then only at the weekends. They work so many hours, you see? In the City I'd thought everyone finished work at five in the evening and then headed for the drinking trough. Not here. More isolated pubs get better business in the week. I'm thinking we might have made a mistake, but nevertheless it's a beautiful place to live.'

'Don't you miss the City life?'

'Not at all, but I think Mary does sometimes.'

Mary appeared behind the bar and gave me a disdainful look but didn't say anything and returned to the kitchen. It looked like there was an argument brewing.

'Well, my name's Mike. What's yours?'

I told him,

'Look, Hugh, you can't go hungry. There's a pub down the road which serves food. What say we go down there and get you fed? We'll go in my car and afterwards I can show you some more of the county social life.'

'Are you sure you don't mind? I could certainly do with a bite.'

'Not at all and I should get out a bit more anyway. Got everything? Let's go.'

'Mary.' he shouted in the direction of the kitchen, 'I'm going to show Hugh a bit of our countryside.'

'The Oak Tree you mean.'

'Yes that as well. See you later.'

Mike's car was not a landlord's country runabout. It was an almost new sporty type Jaguar, probably with a mammoth engine and with the most luxurious seats. I sank in to my position murmuring something like, 'Very nice Mike.'

'I bought it just before I left London. It's probably not best suited for the country but it's a lovely motor. It's only about five minutes to The Royal Oak. Hang on.'

It wasn't long before we were sitting in the pub. Mike bought me a drink, gave me the menu, and I chose.

'I'll pay for that.'

'You don't have to, I get an overnight allowance.'

'I'd like to. Come and meet my mates.'

Mike made the introductions. They seemed a friendly bunch and probably successful farmers or early retirees. They were interested in my choice of job and seemed almost envious. We chatted a bit until my food arrived and I started eating. One of them told a joke which was greeted with guffaws of laughter.

'You must know some good stories, Hugh, with all your time on the road'.

'Yes, I know one about lawyers and farmers.'

'Let's hear it. It sounds like a good topic.'

'OK, well there were two young and inexperienced lawyers who weren't doing very well. So the chief partner told them he was going to send them to the country. To a bull farm to understand how other people lived. They'd never been to the country before.

They arrived at the farm where the owner greeted them and invited them in for a drink. As they were chatting the farmer asked them if there was anything they wanted to know about bulls in general. They said they'd seen a few bulls on the approach to the farm and had noticed some had long horns. Some had short horns and some, no horns at all. Could farmer explain those differences?

'Well,' he said, 'It's all to do with breed. Some breeds have different horns to others but it's quite a complicated subject. It's best explained by my cattle man who you'll meet tomorrow.'

They went to bed after eating and the following day they were introduced to Bert. Bert had a large animal on a rein with him and they all set off for the fields, together with the animal.

Bert asked them if there was anything they wanted to know before they got started and they repeated last night's question.

'Ah yes,' said Bert. 'The boss is right, it is quite complicated. He's right. Some breeds do have long horns and some short ones and then again, there are those without any at all. I'll explain the differences of breeds through the day.'

'OK Bert,' said one of the youngsters, 'but beforehand, could you just explain why the bull you've brought with you today, doesn't have any horns at all?'

Bert looked very pleased and said,

'Yeah, well that's an easy one to answer. The reason this 'ere bull don't have no horns at all is because…it's a horse.'

My new drinking buddies creased up.

'Very good Hugh, that's made my day. A clean one as well. Perfect. I can tell it at the Round Table dinner.'

Mike wanted to make a move and show me some more pubs but we'd already drunk quite a lot. I wasn't sure about him driving me anywhere. I mentioned it to the others while Mike was settling up.

'Oh don't worry about Mike's driving. He's perfectly safe. The more he drinks, the slower he drives. You'll know when he's blind drunk because he'll come to a complete stop.'

There was more laughter from the group. I thanked Mike for his generosity and we set off on our country pub crawl. He wouldn't let me pay for a single drink. He drove us back safely and I rolled out of the car, thanked him again and weaved my way back to the lorry.

Nowadays it takes me 48 hours to recover from a good night out, but I was much younger then. I woke at 7am to discover it had rained in the night. I hadn't shut the door properly and my pillow had fallen out. It was resting in a muddy puddle. I thought a cat had nested in my mouth, but after a hasty cup of coffee I was feeling ready to face the world.

I'd fully recovered by the time Kings Lynn hove into view. I was hoping to arrange another load before lunchtime. You had to carry a huge bag of tuppenny coins with you because sometimes you could spend hours occupying a public phone box. I was lucky and discovered the company near Boston had loads for Watchet. It was steel wire. He said there were already several of my mates waiting to load. I wasn't planning on going home but it would have been not only churlish to turn it down, but I would probably also have got a bollocking for not taking it. So I went over there.

'Yoooeee!' Dave greeted me, 'How did you get here? No one said you'd be coming.'

'I drove, Dave. You?'

'Always the comedian, ain't you Yooeee?'

'I hate steel wire.'

'Why's that? It's an easy load.'

'It's because I can't do what allegedly all men are born to do.'

'Tell me.'

'I can't knock lots of six inch nails into four inch pieces of timber.'

'Fuck me Yooeee! It's easy.'

'You keep saying that, but nothing in life is easy until you know how to do it. Not even tying your shoe laces.'

'Yeah, I suppose you're right. Are you any good at sheeting?'

'One of the best, as it happens.'

'Right, I'll make a deal with you. I'll nail your timbers down and mine and you sheet both loads. How's that sound?'

'That, my man, sounds like a fucking good deal. Agreed. Let's go to the canteen and get some lunch.'

For transport and storage purposes steel wire is made up in coils or wheels. When they're loaded they stand on edge and lean against the trailer headboard. To prevent them rolling sideways off the trailer, lengths of timber are nailed into the trailer floor in two parallel lines creating what looks like two tramlines. With that part taken care of by Dave, we both went to the works canteen.

The food, despite being very inexpensive, healthy, and swimming in gravy, was not what could have been described as Cordon Bleu. Nonetheless, I was ravenous and ate greedily. I noticed there were reasonable washrooms with showers which even we, the filthy drivers, could use. I made a note to avail myself of them after I'd completed my side of the bargain with Dave. As we were leaving I saw a small box on the wall with a posting slit and a glass window. You could see the contents. It was marked. 'Suggestions for the Canteen'. It was full of half-eaten pasties and some other food detritus. It's made me laugh for years. Why didn't someone just sack the cook?

Mach 1

Until almost the end of the last century, lorries were amazingly underpowered for what was to become a large motorway network and heavier gross vehicle weights. They needed a great deal of speed to power them up practically any hill in order to come over the crest without having to engage crawler gear, which is the one below first. Actually the crawler gear wasn't fitted in my F86 and so speed was even more important. Lorry engines got larger and larger as the years passed. Even so the engine design still didn't give them much more power to pull up the hills without the speed at the bottom.

While I was searching for something at the front of the engine I discovered by chance the accelerator bar, (which connected the throttle pedal to the diesel pump), was slack. Instead of reporting it I made an amateur repair by simply putting a kink in the bar. To my joy the lorry travelled much faster and soon became the fastest on the fleet.

Some of you may think speed is an obsession of young males driven solely by testosterone. Amongst young lorry drivers at the time there was fierce competition in the workplace and a desire to earn more money. I'm sticking to my theory.

One sunny afternoon I'd been designated to take a load of corkboard to Preston for a 7am delivery the following day. It was quite a light load, (about 10 tonnes), so there wasn't a lot of gear work to enjoy but it was a longer journey than usual, being some five and half hours driving. The lorry was travelling well and I was starting to get a bit bored, so as the speedometer only registered up to 70mph I decided to calculate how fast my modification had made my flying camper. I owned a stopwatch which made it easier, and measured the distance over five miles. I did the calculation from that.

Everything was going swimmingly. I flew past all the traffic, the sun shone brightly and all was right with the world. I pulled in behind another lorry which was a half mile ahead. As I drew closer his trailer obscured the view but I could see we were approaching another motorway bridge. I glanced down at the odometer and stopped the timer. When I looked up we were passing under the bridge and the other lorry was slowing down rapidly. I had to throw the anchors out of the window to stay behind it. When we emerged from the bridge it was black everywhere. I have never since experienced such a sudden change in weather. One side of the bridge was summer and the other side it was heaving down with rain and strong winds. I could see nothing except headlights. The good thing was I survived despite my foolishness. No-one was hurt but it taught me the lesson of constant vigilance. During a stop for a nice cuppa tea it also transpired my lorry was capable of 97mph. Whoopee! My lorry came to be referred to by the rest of fleet as the 'Flying Wreck.'

I found the delivery point in a small industrial estate close to the city. The gates were open so I drove in and parked for the night. I had already eaten and washed on the road. There were dozens of crates and packing boxes stacked in every available space, so I parked somewhere in front of the only roller shutter door in order to be first in the queue if there was one. There's nothing quite so irritating as arriving the night before and finding you're last in the queue to unload in the morning.

A grumpy, late middle-aged man arrived at 6.30am and nodded at me. He went inside and the roller door opened magically without the use of chains. I examined the entrance and decided the lorry was not going to get in there without moving a lot of the crates.

'Right driver,' he grunted at me, 'back the lorry in here and don't hit the roller door because I only had it installed last week.'

I had become pretty good at reversing an artic even after only two years or so. I'd had plenty of practice when I worked with Harold on the dock and I'd had much more time to improve the technique whilst I'd been on the road. Even then one could say I knew what I was doing. 'I'm not going to be able to reverse in there, Sir, without you moving a lot of these crates outside.'

'Of course you can. You're a driver aren't you? Just put it in there before it rains.'

'That's just the point. I am a driver and I'm telling you it won't go in there.'

'Oh, for Christ's sake we've had bigger lorries than yours in here. Loads of times, and they all got in.'

If I'd had a pound for every time someone had said that to me in the first ten years of driving, I could have retired as a millionaire at 30 years old.

'I'm telling you it won't go in there.'

His helper arrived just then and exclaimed 'We won't get him inside the shed boss.'

'Shut the fuck up the two of you. Now driver, reverse in the shed.'

'As you wish, but there'll be damage.'

'There better fucking not be.'

After a lot of manoeuvring, I would have managed to get it into the shed but the new roller-shutter door got in the way. No one shouted any warning and I was blind to the impending disaster because the lorry was at right angles to the trailer. I hit it. My realisation came more by sound than from any other sense as I heard the one week old roller door come crashing to the ground. I feel there is nothing to be gained by recounting the following sequence of events and expletives. However, during my telephone call to Michael I was exonerated, especially as the helper had agreed with me.

Driving lorries is tiring but not as much as waiting and loading. During actual driving hours we normally survived on endless cups of tea and adrenalin and never seemed to notice. So really the driving part is not the part which wears you out.

In the 70s and for much of the early 80s mechanisation was not a top priority for many customers. Lots of cargo had to be loaded and unloaded by hand. We were lucky at Rodes Transport because all of our outgoing work was loaded for us on the dock. Still in quiet periods or when we were tramping there was a lot of manual labour involved.

We used to load fertilizer in 50kg bags from Avonmouth. It was partly mechanised to the point where the bags arrived at shoulder height from an extending conveyor belt, but the driver still had to lift them into position onto the lorry. We loaded peat from the Somerset Levels. The bags arrived at the side of the lorry on pallets with a forklift, but the driver had to manhandle each bag directly onto the lorry. At tile companies the driver, with help from the customer's employees, had to load all the tiles individually onto the lorry. There would be thousands to a 21 tonnes load. I was in Surrey one day doing just that. The foreman came up and spoke to me,

'Where's your gloves driver?'

'They're worn out.'

'Here cop these ones, mate. Make sure you wear them. You'll cut your hands to shreds without them and then you'll be no fucking use to no one.' Then there were bricks and concrete blocks and sometimes even lengths of timber. It was very hard work. Luckily, these days almost everything is loaded by forklift or crane.

After a load was finished we were usually offered a cup of tea, and then,

'Right driver, that's your lot, hop in and fuck off. And don't be late.'

The work was constant and unrelenting until the weekend arrived which could be Friday night if you were lucky but often it was Saturday. The most tiring part of the job was the endless waiting. Waiting in a queue to load or unload, waiting for someone to return your call or waiting for paperwork. There was a lot of waiting. Driving often came as a relief.

Siesta

I hadn't taken a holiday in almost two years and most working days I clocked up 15 hours. I began to notice I was making silly mistakes. They often happened during routine jobs like picking up or dropping off trailers. They were simple errors like forgetting to collect my delivery notes when I'd already been told my destination. They weren't particularly dangerous mistakes but potentially they could have been. I was young then and still relatively inexperienced. I hadn't yet settled in to the gentle rhythm of driving continuously which comes with time. I probably hadn't taken rest periods when I needed them.

One day I was again on my way to Chard and went through Taunton as usual. I stopped at the first set of red lights and promptly fell asleep. Suddenly there was a knock on my driver's door. The public were very polite in those days. I sprang awake.

'Yes mate?' I said.

'Are you alright driver?'

'Yes perfectly. Why?'

'It's just there's a long queue of cars behind you and we've sat through nine sets of traffic lights waiting for you to move.'

'Oh, I'm so sorry. I'll move on right away.'

'NO! No no, not now. They're on red again.'

'Thanks. I'll choose the next green one. OK?'

'Fine driver, but I think you ought to see someone. You might be unwell.'

'Thanks for your concern. I'll do that.'

I did do that. On my return I reported the events to Michael and he sent me home with instructions to visit my doctor and let him know afterwards. I never saw a doctor regularly enough to say he was my doctor, but I did know what he looked like. When I visited him he didn't look anything like he should have done. It turned out the one I saw was a locum as the regular man was away. The new doctor was very pleasant and French. He examined me after asking various relevant questions. In the past my father had told me about fatigue and warned me of the consequences of ignoring it.

'Fatigue,' my French doctor told me, 'is a very serious condition. It affects all the things you do and makes you appear an idiot, which you are obviously not. Fatigue is not just a matter of being over tired. It also attracts other underlying problems you might have. The treatment I recommend is probably to you, as a young man, quite enjoyable. However, you must do precisely what I say for a period of 14 days and then return to see me again.'

I reported the doctor's words to Michael and he signed me off until the doctor said I could return to work.

The treatment was enjoyable and I soon felt it could be a condition I could live with comfortably for the rest of my days. I was instructed to:

Go to bed each night at 10 pm. Get up each day at 7am. Take a substantial breakfast. Go for a walk for about an hour. Do normal household duties until noon. Go to the pub and drink no more than three bottles of Stout.

'Like Mackesons?' I said.

'Exactly.'

To return home and eat a good lunch, but not too much. Take a siesta for about an hour. Take another walk for the same period of time. At 6pm, drink another 3 bottles of stout. Eat a light supper and go to bed at 10pm. Repeat for 14 days.

'We'll make another appointment for you to see me in 15 days to see if my treatment has worked. Is that alright?'

'Perfect. Thank you.'

Sick pay wasn't going to be quite as much as I'd become accustomed to. Even so I was sure it would stretch to 6 halves of Mackeson a day. Michael actually wrote it down as holiday, so I was saved.

I returned to work fit, well and once again raring to get into the routine of 15 hour days. During my absence Michael told me the fleet was being updated.

There were some new lorries coming, and a batch of second hand ones as well. I was to be given a second hand one, which was still excellent news for me. I wondered what it would be but assumed it wasn't going to be anything which was top of the range. It wasn't. Although it was much bigger, higher, more comfortable and had a radio as standard, but it still had no bunk.

There was to be a wait of a few days while the newer lorry was serviced and checked for the road. I was told to empty my own vehicle of my personal stuff, plus ropes, straps, chains etc. and to work with it for the remainder of the week on the dock with Harold. I was to leave the lorry in the dock overnight and walk to work each morning. It was no hardship as it was only 200 yards.

On the second morning I arrived at the dock and got into the lorry. I started it and let it warm up while I had a mug of tea with Harold and the dockers. There was a very nasty smell inside. It smelt like a mixture of cat's piss and week-old dead fish. I opened all the windows and put the cold air blower on to try and clear it, and went for my tea. I got the feeling everyone seemed overly happy, but I put it down to a joke I hadn't heard. I returned to the lorry and with the engine now warm the smell was truly over powering. It was revolting. I checked under the seats. Nothing. I checked round the outside and underside. Nothing. I tipped the cab and looked round the manifold. Nothing. There was nothing for it but to start work so I coupled a trailer and pulled it on to the weighbridge. Harold was there.

'It smells a bit fishy since you've arrived Yooeee.'

'It's bound to. We're on the dock.'

'It's not the smell of the dock or even the open sea, Yooeee. Have you thrown up on the lorry?'

'Of course not, I've only just got here.'

There was now a small group of waiting drivers and dockers looking for something to do. I was sure they were all sniggering. Anyway, I put up with the smell through the day and it was still there several days later. I was pretty sure I knew what had happened and who was behind it, but it wasn't worth picking a fight. I've always enjoyed a good practical joke, and to be honest it was a pretty good one, especially as I never got to the bottom of it. To this day, I've no idea how the smell was created or who the real culprit was, but I still laugh about it.

Three star comfort

I finished at the dock on Saturday about lunchtime. I spent the afternoon cleaning my new lorry and fitting my stuff into it. Afterwards I secured my load for the Monday delivery. I didn't need to mess about with my window coverings because real curtains were already fitted, complete with a curtain rail. I'm not sure why they were there because there was no bunk, but anyway, it was going to be real luxury, I told myself. It was a Deutz 232.

All vehicles have a built-in design fault and the Deutz was no different. It was one of our routine jobs to check the wheel nuts were tight at least once a week. The Deutz had much smaller wheel nuts than is usual and the wheels came loose much more frequently. We had to check them at least twice a day. It was a bore, but we got used to it. It was just another job to do.

Monday's delivery was bound for St Austell with timber and English China Clay in big bags for return to Watchet for export. It was a four hour journey because the motorway only went as far as Exeter. The remaining part of the trip was on the old road. In those days it had not yet been upgraded to a dual carriageway. It was a long, hard road to drive in a lorry. There were five of us together. We stopped once for breakfast and again for a cuppa-tea. Both stops were longer than usual because drivers chat like pensioners when they get together. Finally, we were on the last stretch before dropping down to the town when we got stopped by Her Majesty's Police force.

'Just a routine check Sir.'

But it wasn't. It was a driver's hours' check. I realised what was going on when I saw the driver in front handing his log book out of the window. I scrabbled about in the cab to find my book and was busily updating it when my turn came.

'Good morning driver,' said the officer. 'Show me your log sheets please.'

I was still shakily filling them in so he opened the door and stood on the footplate.

'You're meant to fill them in throughout your working day, driver.'

'Yes, yes I know officer. It's just I've been on the sick and then only did a couple of days shunting on the dock before I got started on the road again.'

'Ah well, you still have to fill them in when you're on the dock because it's a public place you see.'

I thought it was a moot point as the public can't enter the dock without permission. However I didn't say so.

'Really? I wasn't sure about that.'

He had a look at my scribbled efforts.

'You are also required by law to carry the last 5 working days of log sheets with you at all times.'

'Ah, er, yes OK.'

'How long have you been driving?'

'Well, about four hours this morning.'

'No driver, I mean in this job.'

'Oh, about a couple of years I suppose.'

'Alright, look these appear almost the same as the others for today, although the lines are a bit wobbly. You know in the London area breaking drivers hours laws is considered a capital offence?' He smiled, but I didn't.

'But down here in sleepy Cornwall we don't consider it so badly. Just keep them up to date and think yourself lucky. OK driver, on your way'

'Oh thank you officer, thank you.'

In fact, not much changed until the introduction of tachographs. Log sheets were really no more than a small matter of trust between government and individual drivers, and in practice were un-enforceable. Even those who were paid by the hour filled in an equal amount of fantasy. They put in more hours than were achieved. Others, like us who were paid a bonus, put less hours. My new lorry did have a tachograph fitted, but they weren't a legal requirement at the time. I spent some of my waiting hours inspecting it to see how it functioned. Just for fun really.

The next trip was to South Wales. Several of us were destined for different delivery points but we all had to load from the same dock. We were to load orange juice for a cold store in London. The rules still hadn't changed so it was still possible to load foodstuffs on an open trailer. Loading took hours as usual but there was enough time to make the delivery the same day. We left individually. I arrived in London in the evening about 7pm and thought I'd be turned away until the following day. However, I pulled up to the gate and wound down my window. The gate man spoke first.

'Good evening Sir.'

I glanced quickly round the cab for someone who could have been addressed as 'Sir' and then quickly replied,

'Good evening.'

'You look a bit concerned Sir.'

'I just wasn't sure to whom you were referring. We don't usually get spoken to as 'Sir'. It's normally Driver, or Oi, or You.'

'That Sir, is because this is a forward thinking company. Anybody who visits is important to us. You, for instance, have brought goods which will make this company a profit and in turn will keep us employed. In any case a basic courtesy goes a long way.'

'It may well be the case and I agree with you but it doesn't normally happen anywhere else.'

'In that case I think they should drag their employees kicking and screaming into the 20th century. Now then, your delivery notes please.' I passed them over.

'Very good. You see those sheds for unloading over there on your right? Please reverse onto number 26 in a straight line. Leave your load secured. Give your notes to the foreman. When you look straight ahead of you from there, you will see a tall building with lots of windows. That is the canteen. All the meals are free. If you want to wash there are showers in the same building. Feel free to use them. Lock your cab before you go up. Should you wish to park for the night, ask in the canteen. If I may say so, you've made a very professional job of covering your load.'

'Well, thank you very much Sir.'

I followed his instructions and found the canteen. It was clean and tidy without dirty plates lying around uncollected. The smell of the food was scrumptious.

'Hugh mate, the grub's fantastic. Grab yourself a plateful.' It was Doug. We used to call him the 'corpse.' I'm not sure why.

'Yeah, I will Doug, but I'm going to get a shower first.'

'They're first class too. It's like a five star hotel.'

I glanced out of the window and saw they'd got my sheets off and were folding them up in the proper fashion. There's a special way to do it so when you open them up on a new load they just fall open as they're needed. And they'd coiled all my ropes professionally.

'Will you look at them. They're folding the sheets and ropes like proper drivers,' I said.

'Yeah, I reckon they are drivers.'

I went in the direction of the shower rooms. Well, strike me down. I thought this was heaven. It was a real shower room with individual high pressure showers and drying rooms. There were even hooks to hang your clothes on and real soap. If you've never experienced the facilities lorry drivers have to put up with at the end of a long, dirty and sweaty day, you wouldn't understand the joy of being offered those conditions. I was speechless and spent a good half hour under the shower. When I emerged my mates were on the coffee course and a couple more had turned up. They passed me on the way for a shower. I looked out of the windows again and saw the blokes had lifted my sheets and ropes onto the empty trailer bed. I could get used to this, I mused. The food was excellent and the servers were cheerful and chatty. They asked me if I was staying the night and I replied in the affirmative. I was given a note and told to fill in my registration number and present it to the exit gateman. He would direct me to a parking slot.

'Fill it in whenever you like, Sir. Take your time. There's no rush.' In the following 1000 years of driving lorries, I was never to be treated so well by any customer in the UK, and it was pretty early on in my career. My signed delivery notes were left under a windscreen wiper in a plastic envelope. It's a pity I can't remember the name of the company, but I do know it was a cold store in Leyton, East London. By contrast during my driving time in Europe if I ever asked a customer if I could use their showers I was always invited to do so. Bloody 'forriners' are so welcoming!

Back to school

A few more months passed and life was truly looking up. I had more comfort in the cab than in the first lorry. I received better wages as my knowledge increased. The work was still hard, but enjoyment was greater as I made more friends amongst the other drivers. The fleet was increasing and ships were arriving more frequently at the docks. There was a move towards taking on some owner operators to work on contract for the company. Soon the offer was made to the existing employed drivers. Those who took it up would be funded almost entirely by Street's Transport. There was quite a large take-up, probably 25%. But in order to get started an operators' licence was required which meant going on a course. I was drawn by the idea although I felt it was too soon to be self-employed. Even so, if I had the licence I could start when I pleased. I signed up for the two week course and soon found myself back at school in deepest Shropshire. It was a bit dull but I learned a lot, and if I passed I'd achieve both a National & International permit for life. It was funded by the company so I had nothing to lose. I went with another driver called Tony who was serious about starting on his own straight away. We returned and went to work as usual while we waited a few weeks for our results.

One Saturday morning I was sitting in the cab waiting for the crowds of drivers to disperse, so there would be room to pick my trailer up for the following week's work. I was trying to catch up on my drivers' records when Michael arrived at the window.

'Hugh, how many times have I got to tell you to do those records each day? Never mind, I've got some good news for you.'

He passed me my certificate for an operator's licence through the window. 'Well done Hugh. You've passed. Think carefully about being an owner operator with me. I believe you'd do well.'

'Oh, brilliant. Thanks I will.'

But I didn't think for long. I knew it was too soon. There was a lot more to learn yet and I had a good job. I was getting paid an average of £190 a week after deductions and I really didn't have enough money to invest in lorries, equipment and stuff. Plenty of the drivers did take it up though, and it made the job much more competitive for the rest of us.

It was the beginning of a new era. A new type of management thinking was being tentatively introduced to encourage more efficient working practices and better profits for the companies. Some new faces arrived with their own lorries. We thought most of them came from rich families or well-paid jobs with which they'd got bored. For the most part their lorries were brand spanking new. They were equipped with what in those days were massive engines and their cabs were filled with all sorts of gadgets to make their travelling more comfortable. We used to laugh at some of the drivers for thinking they were a new sort of folklore hero. They knew very little about the severity of hard work and weren't used to it. 40 years ago a new tractive unit cost around £30,000, which for us was a fortune. Of course, compared to today's prices of £150,000 and more, it was probably manageable. The economy was different. Anyway we saw them come and go over the months and our own fleet grew swiftly. You really do need to know what you're doing before you embark on living the dream. Even then it doesn't always turn out well.

I had met a bloke in my home town who was looking for a driving job and we became friends. Red or Reddy was a Mancunian and he told me he'd been made redundant 17 times in the north. He came south to find more constant work. He got himself a coach licence and was on the buses for a year until he managed to obtain a HGV licence. He asked me if I could put his name forward for a job at Rodes, which I did.

Different lives

Michael came back.

'Hugh, I forgot to say you'll have a newer lorry soon. It's being prepared in the workshop but it won't be ready for next week. You remember the boy whose name you put forward? I've offered him a job. There's a demonstrator vehicle here now. I want you to take Red with you next week to Golbourne. Let me know what he's like, and what you think of the lorry. Take the demonstrator. It's a 310 Deutz. You'll like it. It's much more powerful. Move your stuff over to it. Red will be here soon and I'll tell him what's to happen. Good, we'll speak on Monday.'

Whooopee! Reddy showed up soon afterward looking really pleased with himself.

'Red mate, got your kit for next week? Let's load up for a fun week.'

'Yep, it's in the car. Give us a 'and. Where're we goin?'

'North. Hurry up and we can get back for a pint.'

"Wonderful. We can see mother on Monday. I haven't seen her in five years.'

The 310 was outstanding. It had a full sleeper cab with twin bunks and it was comfortable. By comparison to previous driving experiences it was immensely powerful and went up hills almost as fast as it did on the flat. It was a pleasure to drive. As far as gadgets were concerned there weren't many differences, except it had an overnight heater. These were later added as standard and actually required by law. It was a mammoth step forward for driver-kind. It was winter and on Monday we set off in bitterly cold winds with sleet falling. I did the first stretch before breakfast, not because I was senior driver but because I was so excited to try out a new lorry.

'We'll see Mother tonight.' Reddy repeated it all the way to the north.

The top speed of the 310 wasn't anything to write home about. It only managed about 65mph, but it continued the momentum up most inclines. It did away with having to use the entire gearbox to reach the summit.

We stopped at the 'smokey hole' café near Worcester for breakfast. It opened at 5am daily and they cooked on a solid fuel cooker. The chimney was designed before the end of the first century. The result was smoke covering a radius of five miles around the cafe. Inside visibility was down to about six inches for the first hour. Even so, the breakfast was always excellent although the tea tasted of coal fumes.

Reddy drove the rest of the way. We stopped again for a nice cuppa tea at Lymm and arrived at the delivery point bright and early, and on time. It was the first time I'd ever been at the front of the queue.

We unloaded and then I got a shout from the forklift driver,

'Hughy,' we were on first name terms by then, 'there's a message for you to phone your office.'

'Thanks.'

I went and used the phone and returned about five minutes later.

'It's bad news for you Red. Change of plans. We have to go to Newcastle to pick up paraffin wax for Watchet. We won't be seeing mother tonight.'

'Never mind, we'll see her tomorrow night then.'

I took over the driving again and we set off, west to east on the M62. It started to snow as we climbed the Pennines. On top, the snow was settling and the road and getting pretty slippery. Visibility was very poor and soon we were crawling along at very slow speeds. The snow eased up a bit around Leeds and soon we picked up the A19 to go north. We stopped for a lunchtime snack near York and afterwards changed drivers again. I was getting a bit bored being a passenger but Red seemed to be coping alright, so I decided to try one of the bunks and lay down. I was fast asleep in seconds.

Red hailed me from the forward position after what I thought was only ten minutes, but it must have been longer.

'I'm running out of driving time Hugh. What shall I do?'

'Well, we'll have to stop. How much time do you have left? Where are we?'

'About twenty minutes and we're a bit north of Thirsk.'

'OK. Don't know it. Take the next on the left. Any next on the left you fancy.'

He did so and we found ourselves driving down a very narrow country lane. The wheels were almost running in the ditches. Then we came to an even narrower bridge, but we squeezed over it.

'What happens if there's nothing down here, Hughy?'

'Well firstly, all roads lead somewhere and secondly, most roads have a pub on them. If by some far flung possibility I'm wrong we'll be, as you're obviously inferring, completely fucked! Drive on, my man.'

'I think we ought to stop and ask someone.'

'Brilliant, who do you suggest? Ah look, there's a bloke up there hiding in the bushes. Stop and I'll ask him.'

We really were in the middle of absolutely nowhere. I wound down the window as Red stopped and turned off the engine.

'Good evening Sir. Excuse me, but could you tell me if there's anywhere down here where we can park?'

He was quite young and looked astounded. He was covered in hedgerow but smiled winningly.

'I'm awfully sorry,' he said with a foreign accent, 'but I really have no idea. I've just flown in from Pakistan this afternoon to see my uncle, as he's quite ill. I've never been to England before.'

'Oh OK. We'll ask someone else. I hope your uncle recovers soon.' I turned to Red.

'Put your foot down mate.'

'Ask someone else? You're dreaming, Hughy.'

'All will be revealed, oh ye of little faith. He spoke good English didn't he?'

In a short moment we came to a T junction and there, in front of us, was a wide open cobbled space and a large stone building which was all lit up. It had a big sign over the door.

'What does it say Red?'

He pulled up in front and stopped.

'It says, THE CAT AND BAGPIPES. Christ, you're a lucky fucker!'

'I have to give credit where credit's due, mate. You were driving.'

Within seconds the front door flew open and a very agitated landlord came rushing out flapping his arms about. I wound down the window.

'Good evening Sir.'

'You can't park thic bloody great thing here. This is a pub. I've got four darts teams coming tonight.'

'Look, I can appreciate this is a massive inconvenience for you, and we're really sorry it's happened.'

Red whispered, 'I'm not.'

'But the thing is we've completely run out of time. We can pay if you like.'

'No, we can't,' hissed Red.

'We drink copious amounts of beer and we're so hungry we could eat a horse. Maybe two. We could back up a bit, away from the front door. We won't be a nuisance I promise.'

'Oh well, you seem pleasant enough. It's just there are a lot of people coming. It's going to be a busy night. Well, OK then. Just back up a bit so there's room for them to park. I can't do you any food till gone eight o' clock. That be alright?'

'Perfect.' I said, 'Do you have anywhere where we can wash?'

'Oh yes of course. There are showers out by the games room. Get your kit and I'll show you. Come in when you're ready. The big rush won't be till after 7.30 pm.'

'Many, many thanks Sir. It's really kind of you.'

He turned round and went inside.

'You have a silken tongue, Hughy.'

'Oh indeed, Red. I'm self-taught you know.'

It wasn't a legal requirement to use tachographs to record drivers' hours in the UK until about the middle of the 1980s. But Rodes used them from about the end of the 70s in the lorries which had them fitted. To be honest it was easier for both the company and the drivers and there was less paperwork to store. Neither Red nor I had any idea about the rules for double manning in those days, (two drivers sharing the driving in one lorry), so we just used one card each and changed them over as and when. There were easy ways to be dishonest, but unless your mother was dying and you had to be home, fifteen hours work seemed plenty each day. We thought so. So we completed our cards, put in another for the following day, grabbed our wash kit and made our way to the showers. Obviously we went via the bar for a well-deserved beer.

'Two pints of your finest ale please, landlord,' said Red in his rich Mancunian accent.

'Straight away Sir!'

'I'm sorry about arriving so unexpectedly,' I said.

'It's absolutely no problem lad. I'm used to it already.' He turned to Red.

'You're not from round here son, are you?'

'No. Other side of the hills but I don't bite.' He laughed. We all did. The differences between Yorkshire and Lancashire are tangible in a pub, but that night we were friends already despite me being a southerner. In fact my antecedents came from Aberdeen.

The showers were out at the back in what was more like a village hall than a games room. There was no heating and it was freezing cold. At least the shower room was clean although the water only trickled out and it was none too warm.

'Christ alive Red. I suggest we make this a very short shower.'

'Why's that? …Aaarrrhh it's fooking cold.'

'Yeah. You got it in one.'

We washed and changed quickly, and went to put our stuff back in the cab. 'I reckon we could try this 'ere night heater,' I said. 'I'll turn it on now and put the thermostat on what? 10°? And then it'll be toasty warm when we go to bed.'

'Sounds good.'

The darts teams started arriving.

'They're all women, Hughy.'

'So they are. Time for another pint then.'

We went in again and the bar was heaving with people. It really was going to be a busy night, probably a rarity for such an out-of-the-way place. We made a few friends almost immediately and soon they all started their matches. The landlord spoke to us from the bar.

'Steak, chips, mushrooms, egg and tomatoes alright with you two?'

'Fine thanks.'

'It's too busy for us to offer the whole menu, so it's all we've got.'

'Perfect mate.'

The food arrived ten minutes later and we ate in between gulps of beer. We got steadily drunk as the evening wore on. The girls formed orderly queues at the bar in between matches and everyone had a good time. Reddy fell in love with all four darts teams, but was eventually unable to progress with his intentions as it all came to an end. We said our goodbyes and thanked the landlord profusely. He even invited us back in the future but the opportunity never arose. Such is the life of the nomad. He drew a map to show us an easier way out on to the A19.

We returned to the lorry to sleep. It was snowing heavily and it was windy and bitterly cold. The night heater had done its job and the cab was lovely and warm, so we brewed a cup of tea, drank it and climbed into our respective bunks. We decided to leave about 6 o' clock. Red, on the top bunk, woke up about 3am.

'Christ Hughy, it's fucking hot! Can you turn the heater down, or off would be better?'

'Mmmmm what? OK, yeah I'll give it a go.'

I fumbled around in the dark for the 'off' switch, located it and moved its position. Nothing happened. I moved my arm to the thermostat and played with that. There were no clicks signifying a change of temperature. We waited about ten minutes and still nothing had happened. It really did feel hot.

'It's not responding Red. Still it's no worse than Benidorm in July.'

'Maybe so, but there's no sea to take a cooling dip in either.'

'You could slip outside and roll in a snow drift.'

'Just open the window a bit more.'

I did and the icy wind howled through the cab.

'Oh yeah, much better Hughy.'

It certainly wasn't. The north winds raced through the cab at 100 miles per hour and I was soon reaching for a woolly jumper.

'What you doing you southern softy? This is the lovely ambient temperature of healthy living.'

'It's not healthy, I'm going to contract pneumonia or something worse.'

'I can live with that. Just don't die.'

We set off in the morning more or less as planned. Reddy drove again. We stopped within an hour for breakfast. With the warming food inside us we took deep breaths outside in the fresh air. I say fresh, but although the snow had stopped there was still a biting wind. We crunched our way to the lorry, and climbed into our very own mobile sauna. We still could not turn the night heater off.

Newcastle came into our sights quite soon and we managed to find our way to within a mile or two of the loading point. Reddy stopped when we saw a likely looking chap, and I got out and asked him for directions. He beamed straight away which suggested he knew the answer to the question. Then followed the difficult bit. He said a lot of things while he gesticulated with his arms and fingers and then completed his oratory by looking directly at me and saying,

'Did you understand all of that?'

'No.' I shook my head.

'Any of it?'

I shook my head again.

'Yeah, it's alright mate. I did. Thanks for your help.' Red shouted.

I thanked the man again and got in the cab.

'Did you?'

'Yes, of course I did. Geordie is not as difficult as you southerners make out.'

I can assure you the Geordie dialect is very difficult to understand and in time I found it easier to understand a strong Scottish brogue. The people from Newcastle became known as 'Geordies' in about 1745 during the Jacobite Rebellion. They were accused of being supporters of the Hanoverian King George. Hence 'Geordie.' Another theory is that in the 19th century it was believed nearly everyone from the region was called George. Choose whichever you're happy with.

We loaded the wax and headed south. Red started singing again,

'We'll see mother tonight.'

That time we did. I've never been a fan of family reunions, especially after a lot of time has passed. They weren't my family either, but I can recall practically every word which passed their lips. I continue to find it heart breaking although it wasn't my world, and our brief meeting made it all the more poignant.

Reddy's parents lived on a council estate. It was very airy and the houses were well spread out. It was built in a large circle and in the centre there was a bit which was like a roundabout. There were about two or three extra houses built on it. They seemed quite big. There was no suggestion space had been compromised and everyone seemed to have a garden and a small drive. The estate was at the top of a hill with a wide road leading to it. It wasn't far from the town which was on the outskirts of Manchester, but not in the bustling centre. It was quiet, peaceful even. Reddy drove up the hill singing his now boring tune, and we parked facing downhill so as to be ready for the morning. There were very few cars suggesting most people didn't have one or they were still at work at 7pm at night.

'Come on Hughy. Let's go and see mother.'

We walked in. It wasn't locked and we wandered through to the kitchen. His mother was there busying herself with this and that.

'Hello Mother.' She looked up without showing emotion.

'Hello Red, I wasn't expecting you. Look, if you want something to eat there's very little in the fridge but help yourself. I'm off to play bingo and I'm late already. I'll see you in the pub afterwards. See ya.'

'OK, thanks. See you later.'

'Yeah, your father's on 'lates' this week so he'll be there 'bout 9.' She left.

My mouth was hanging open. I was speechless.

'There's only half a slab of cheese Hughy. We'll share it and go down the pub for a real pint of beer. Boddingtons! We can go to the chippy after, alright?'

'It sounds good to me.'

The pub wasn't far away and we were in from the cold pretty quickly. Neither mother nor father had arrived. Red got us a couple of pints and we sat down. It was a pleasant little place, warm and lots of people chatting. Red's mother arrived within half an hour and was very keen to tell Red she'd won at Bingo, but then chatted on with her mates. A little later his father came in. He saw Red but walked past him to the bar and then turned and said,

'You finally come back then. Well, Godstruth.' Red went to the bar.

'Yeah dad, I got a good job now. Driving lorries.'

'A fooking lorry driver, eh? Is that the best you could come up with? I told you, you should have stuck to your trade. I heard your mate talking to you when I came in. He's a toff. Who is he?'

'He's a mate. He's a driver too.'

'He won't last long with a voice like that.'

'You're probably right, dad. You usually fooking are.'

'OK, so if you got a job you'll be earning money. It's your round. Get 'em in.'

Red bought a pint for his father and his mates and then brought back two more for us. Just then his mother got up and said,

'Cheerio lad, I'm off down the club with the girls. You'll have to stay in your lorry tonight. I've let yours and your brothers' rooms out to lodgers. See ya.'

…and she was gone. I didn't say anything to Red. There wasn't much to say. His father left without saying anything more. So we sat in silence and then I ventured,

'That went well, then.'

'Yeah. Look, leave it be Hughy. It's how it is. Come on. Let's go down the chip shop.'

We mounted into our hot house once more and after a good sleep we set off early in the morning. An early start in driver-speak means anytime from midnight to 3am. It was 3 o' clock.

I never mentioned anything about the previous evening to Red. Neither then, nor in all the time I've known him, though despite knowing him for over forty five years I have to admit we haven't spoken in probably fifteen.

We stopped for a cup of tea on one of the motorway services and then didn't stop again until it was breakfast time in Gordano, near Avonmouth.

The interior got hotter and hotter while outside the icy winds blew snow everywhere. We tried dropping the windows a bit but that forced outside air across the tops of our heads. The end result was we had to strip down to our underpants and sink down in the seats to avoid the cold air. It worked for a while but when we arrived at Gordano we were sweating. Benidorm-on-wheels!

The big transport fleet from Shepton Mallet was already there. I'm sure they had the most archaic lorries in the whole of the West Country. It wasn't so much the age of them as the fact they were littered with holes in the cabs. They were just like the lorries Harold had described. The drivers were even wearing bicycle clips! The windows didn't shut properly and I don't think they had heaters. There were gaping holes where the foot pedals come through the floor. The list goes on. The point of this description is it was snowing with a freezing wind blowing. The drivers were stamping their feet and clapping their gloved hands together to get warm. Some of them were wearing two overcoats. Then we rolled in. We couldn't wait to get out of the cab. We opened the doors before we'd stopped and we both jumped out in nothing but our underpants and let the healthy wind blow through us.

We arrived at base in time to tell Michael the Deutz 310 was the hottest thing on eighteen wheels.

'Be more specific, Hugh.'

I gave him the notes I'd made en route. Fuel consumption, power, comfort, (ergonomics isn't it?), and a glowing report of Reddy's performance. At the weekend we were both allotted different vehicles. Mine was a second hand sleeper cab, similar to the 310 but a 232 but Red got something a bit older.

Top deck

The same winter we had a lot of deliveries to Telford and on one occasion there was a crowd of us heading up the motorway together. We were planning to stop for breakfast at Frankley, just south of Birmingham. There were more new faces joining the fleet every week. There was a bloke from Cardiff who we unimaginatively nicknamed Taffi. He did talk a lot and he had more stories to tell than Jackanory, although they were predominantly less believable. He'd been everywhere and he'd done everything. I expect you've met somebody like him. He said he'd been doing a lot of international work and told many stories of his travels to Norway. It was something new to me and to begin with I was agog. I quite fancied driving lorries in foreign lands. After further investigation it turned out that he'd only taken one load to Oslo dock on the ferry from Hull, dropped the trailer in the dock, picked up another and returned to Hull. Anyway, he was a nice enough chap but clearly not the sharpest knife in the drawer. He did have a good sense of slapstick humour and was prone to pulling practical jokes.

We were nearing Frankley services and I could almost taste the approaching breakfast. It was snowing very hard and the wipers weren't coping with it so it was building up on the windscreen. Taffi was in front of me. Boredom had obviously started to set in for him and he was sticking his arm out of the window to collect snow from the windscreen. He fashioned it into snowballs which were actually more like iceballs. He started chucking them back at the drivers behind him. I was first in the line of attack but most of them missed. Then suddenly there was a loud crack and my wing mirror completely left its mounting, followed closely by a taffi-iceball. We had words…

When it had warmed up a bit later in the year we began delivering pallet timber to a place in north Wales called Ruabon. It was a new destination and to begin with there was a whole ship-load to deliver. We employed the same plan as we used at Golbourne and we returned empty from Ruabon. Later Michael made an agreement with a Welsh haulier. We used their loading ramp to load one vehicle on top of another for our return. It saved the fuel costs for half of the lorries.

We had to drive one vehicle up onto another's trailer. Obviously, one lorry and trailer is longer than just a trailer but precisely the same width, which made it very exacting. It's very difficult to have to put your own lorry on top so we used to draw straws to see who'd be upstairs. One day I got the short straw. It's quite frightening driving the lorry up because your vision is restricted. The height aspect adds another dimension to the terror. If you made a slight error you could easily be off the side in a heap. Anyway, I accomplished it and then had to climb down. There were no useful tools like ladders.

Now we had one lorry sitting on top completely flush with the carrying vehicle and with one trailer axle hanging loose and unsupported at the back. I supposed the total length of the load would have been about fourteen meters. It might even have been a notifiable load but we never told anyone. Sometimes we even tied a bit of rag on the back as a warning. We strapped the loose axle to its trailer body and secured the rest of the lorry with rope around the wheels. Absolutely safe!

I travelled with the 'corpse' and prayed he'd drive sensibly. It was too far to get all the way home, so we stopped for the night under the railway arches in Worcester. We washed, found something to eat and drank some beers. At bedtime I had to do some mountain climbing to get up to the bunk in my own lorry. Doug said we'd leave at 6am and he'd wake me beforehand. I slept soundly.

A stationary lorry tends to rock and sway to the outside movements. Depending on where it's parked during the night it might react to trains passing by, passing lorries and sometimes just windy weather. It's something a driver gets used to, similar to a sailor on the open seas. In Worcester I was lulled through the night by the rumbling of overhead trains. I became aware of a more severe rocking. I looked at the clock. It was 6.30 in the morning and I thought it must be almost time to make a move.

I leaned out of my nice cosy bunk and gently parted the curtains.

'Christ Almighty!' I shouted out to no one in particular. There was a motorway bridge hurtling towards me at 60mph. It woke me up instantly. The bastard didn't wake me up, I thought. After a moment to collect myself, I realised it couldn't be any less or more dangerous had I been downstairs. I settled down to doing the mornings' tasks before I attempted to make contact with my runaway driver. I managed the ablutions part and only spilled a little water. I wrestled to get my clothes on while the cab rocked considerably more than usual. I drew back the curtains and made everything ship-shape for the days' proceedings.

I really did have a bird's eye view of the passing countryside. Making up a cup of coffee was a bit more complicated. The camping stove wouldn't stay where I put it but it settled down after it had a pan of water on top. I drank the coffee with a bite to eat, cleaned up, stored the equipment and thought about how to contact the "corpse". I turned on the ignition and pressed the horn which was less noisy than a bicycle bell. No response. I had recently fitted a pair of air horns so I gave them a pull on the cord. Not enough air in the system. I fired up the engine and waited for the air to build up. Then I pulled the cord again and got the required response. A thumbs-up appeared out of his drivers' window and I guessed we'd stop at the next motorway services, which was Strensham.

We sailed passed Strensham at top speed and the next opportunity would be Gordano, because it was more popular than Michaelwood in those days. It was about an hour and a quarter away. I amused myself by trying to take some aerial photos, but it was too bouncy a ride so I went back to bed. Finally we arrived and I did a rather wobbly climb down.

'Doug, why didn't you wake me up you bastard? You could've killed me if we'd had an accident,' I said indignantly.

'I thought you could do with a lie-in, mate. And we didn't, so stop fretting.'

'What've you been doing up there?'

'Oh I did my ablutions, made a cup of coffee. You know, the usual.'

'How did you get a piss? Hope you didn't try leaning out the window.' He laughed.

'That's what the bucket's for, so I don't have to go outside stark bollock naked in the night.'

'Oh Christ, a bucket? I wear pyjamas so I just get out, but it can be chilly in winter.'

'Pyjamas? You wear pyjamas in the lorry? You are kidding me.'

'Yeah, I always have. There's nothing wrong with pyjamas.'

'Perhaps not. But in the fucking lorry? No, you're having me on.'

'Look, I won't say anything about your unhygienic piss pot if you don't talk about my pyjamas.'

'It's a deal on condition you buy me a full breakfast.'

'Fuck me Hughy, that's a bit steep.'

'Breakfast? Pyjamas? Breakfast? Pyjamas?'

'OK, OK, it's a deal.'

North of the border

For a while business was quiet at the docks. Although there were no incoming ships, a few loads remained on the quay. I often spent those periods tramping around the country. Sometimes I spent two or three weeks away without going home. I discovered all sorts of places I would probably never have come across in a normal life. I went to the far reaches of Kent and then over to the west coast of Wales. I saw a lot of East Anglia and down as far as Penzance. I visited the north-west and north-east of England and sometimes I'd go to Scotland if I was lucky enough to find a reasonably paid load. I had never managed any forays as far as the west coast of northern Scotland or even north of Inverness. There are so many places throughout the UK which are absolutely beautiful. I especially liked the mountainous regions of North Wales, where later I would spend weeks on end delivering to farms from a sugar factory in the Midlands.

It was during one of those quiet periods I was offered a load from London to go to Sterling in the 'neck' of Scotland. It was for a Friday afternoon delivery so I obviously wasn't going to be home at the weekend. It paid quite well because the customer was in a hurry for it. All the Scots who had delivered to the South-East had already begun their return journey. The rates were nothing special in those days but anything over £200, (of which I got paid 20%), was a good earner for the likes of me. Despite the distance I accepted and set off on Thursday afternoon. I made a few phone calls on the way north to try and organise a return load to the south. I struck lucky with a Scottish clearing house just after lunch on Friday, which was good because by then I had spent a lot of 2p coins in phone boxes. I couldn't load it till Saturday morning but I was assured the factory was open 24/7. I completed my delivery at about five in the evening, confirmed I'd load on Saturday and then called Michael.

'You're a long way away for a Friday night lad.'

'Yes, but even in Scotland they have Fridays.' He laughed.

'Have you found anything to come back with? I'm going to forget what you look like if you're not home soon, Hugh.'

'Yes. I'll be loading from a chipboard factory tomorrow for a Monday delivery in Newcastle. The rate is almost the same as it is to go to South Molton at £70, so I thought it was for the best.'

'Yes, completely right. And as it happens, we've got another batch of paraffin wax to collect and bring back here. You remember the load you did with Red in the hot demonstrator?'

'Yes of course.'

'Right, do another one then. There are others going up either on Sunday or Monday. Noddy is going up at the weekend so you might bump into him. Have a good weekend Hugh, and well done boy. See you Tuesday morning probably, but remember to call me on Monday.'

Michael was always quick to remonstrate with any of us if we did something wrong, but if we did what was required he never failed to praise our efforts. Those little things go a long way in developing trust, and I tried to repeat the attitude during my time as an employer in later years.

On Saturday afternoon I managed to squeeze into a car park near the centre of Edinburgh and parked for the weekend. Years ago there were very few restrictions for lorries and the parking was relatively cheap. I picked a spot at the back, out of the way but with clear sight of the exit. I didn't want to get boxed in on Monday morning.

I can't remember having a very meaningful weekend, but I did manage to do a visit to the castle. I like castles. Years later when I was on holiday in Scotland I visited Sterling Castle. I saw Mel Gibson's sword, well, Sir William Wallace's. It's over six feet in length, and most people in the 14th century seldom measured more than five foot six inches at most. It must have been a hell of a thing to wield in combat. I tried a few Scottish beers and sampled the whisky. I ate and slept very well. The Scots are a very friendly people on the whole, so I reckoned I'd go back whenever I had the chance.

On Monday I left late as there was no real hurry and it wasn't very far to go. I made my delivery to somewhere where they made kitchen cabinets or similar, and then found my way to the collection point for the wax. Noddy was already there.

'Nod, you must've left early, or did you fly?'

'Yeah I reckon, Yooeee. I had a delivery to a farm warehouse in Yorkshire. I got it off last night and came on up 'smorning.'

'You obviously found it alright then?'

'Yeah, well I had to ask. They don't 'alf talk funny in these parts.'

'I reckon we'll help each other with the sheets and run down together, yeah?'

'Nice one. We could make it to somewhere round Birmingham. What do you think?'

'That'll do it.'

Bogged down

It had been raining for days all over the country. It was drizzly, fine, drenching rain which is not so much a downpour but the really wet stuff which gets into your bones. It soaks into the earth gradually to make everything sodden. It was depressing. We were away to the south fairly soon. Visibility was poor and it made the journey very dull as there was nothing to see except low cloud and more water. Towards six o'clock we were near Coventry but still in the country. We would never have got home within our time. I was leading so I turned off onto smaller roads to look for a reasonable pub with parking nearby to accommodate us. We passed through a quiet and attractive village with a brightly lit pub. Noddy flashed his lights in my mirror and I started looking for a suitable place to park two long lorries. Just beyond the village there was some farm land with two rows of trees creating an avenue between the road and the fields. In the half-light between the rows of trees there appeared to be a sort of service road or track where we could park in line. I turned in towards the field gate and then did a hard right into the avenue. Immediately the wheels started to bog down. I kept going but soon the lorry started to sink. I signalled to Noddy not to follow and continued to plough through the mush to try and get out the other side. I almost made it, but finally everything came to a full stop just before getting clear. Noddy hadn't taken any notice and followed me in. I was stuck and the lorry was sinking. Noddy was directly behind and he too was embedded. The good news was we'd found somewhere to park and not far from what looked like an inviting pub.

'I don't think this is ideal, Yooeee.'

'No, you're probably right.'

'What we going to do about it then?'

'I'm not going to dig it out now in the wet and the cold. Let's hit the pub. See if we can't find some useful help and a calming pint, eh?'

'That's the first sensible thing you said in four hours, Yoooeeee. Let's go.'

The pub was very welcoming with an equally friendly landlord. The place was dimly lit with a big open fire burning brightly. There were several beer taps along the bar with unrecognisable names, but I was sure there'd be one we'd like. The barman was chatty from the outset.

'Are you the two drivers who just parked in the old drove?'

'We just parked in a wet field, if that's what you mean.'

'Easy mistake to make but nobody has made it in ten years. You two might win a prize.'

'Great. What is it, the prize?'

'Well your lorries might sit there forever and become a monument to the village.'

'Wonderful. So to start the evening off, what super delicious beers have you got on offer, and have you got any food to sell us?'

'Take your pick, and yes we can offer you an excellent supper. Welcome. I only know because one of the farmer boys saw you struggling in the mud. Don't worry, I've phoned the big farmer round here and his son Bob is coming down for a few. He might be able to sort you out with his mammoth tractor.'

'That's thoughtful. I think we'd enjoy meeting Bob.'

'I'll point you out to him when he gets here. Now then, what do you fancy?'

We chose and sat in front of the fire clutching our pints in a friendly manner. It was best to forget our dilemma for a while, so we talked about home and work, but not about the weather. Bob arrived inside half an hour and didn't need to have us pointed out. Strangers were rare in any village and news travels very quickly in the country.

'You the two what gone and parked in our attractive drove?' He greeted us.
'Yes, the very same.'

'It used to be the old drove to run the cattle through to market or other grazing, but then came big lorries and stuff so over the years it got filled in bit by bit. It's become a good shady place for people to take a family picnic in the better weather. You two gone and fucked it up now.'

'Yeah, we're sorry but we don't want to become a living monument like the landlord suggested. You got any ideas?'

'Oh yeah. It's no problem. What's your weight?'

'We're at 32 tonnes a piece.'

'OK, easy. Well, easy-ish. I got a big enough tractor to pull you out but I'm not going to do it tonight, so I'll be round at 6 o'clock in the morning. You both manage that?'

'Yeah Bob, it sounds grand, but will you be able to give us a bill as we won't have enough cash to pay you.'

'I don't want your money. What say you keep me in dark-splits for the night and it'll be done?'

'Excellent mate, many thanks.'

'Line 'em up landlord,' shouted Noddy.

There's an entertaining pub game in the Midlands although I've only ever seen it the once. Bob said it was played all around the region in the pubs. Noddy was a keen skittle player so he liked it immediately. In essence Skittles is much the same as ten pin bowling, but with slightly different rules and only nine pins. It's a Somerset pub game historically. The game near Coventry was similar to skittles but in miniature. The skittles sit on a plate in what can only be described as an oversize leather padded desk chair. The players stand about two meters away and throw a wooden discus to knock them down. It's livelier than it sounds.

The morning came round quite soon with a weak sun. The rain had stopped but the ground was still sodden under foot. At exactly 6am Bob's tractor growled into sight with clanking chains hanging off the back. He reversed into position and we got to work digging the excess mud out from underneath the lorry axles. I lay in the dirt and wrestled to get the chain fixed around the front axle.

'Right mate, I'll pull up the slack and get it moving. You get ready, and as soon as we've got movement put it in gear and we'll pull together. When you're out, park it on the road and come back to give us a hand with the other one.'

By the time we'd finished both Noddy and I were caked in mud from head to toe. Bob laughed and said,

'You even look like farmers now. There's nowhere here to wash the lorries, so you'll just have to drive the muck off. There's not much traffic about at this time in the morning, so by the time you reach the motorway they should be as clean as whistles.'

We thanked him profusely and he roared away to the fields. The muck flew off the lorries in all directions and was mostly gone within half an hour, but we were still caked in it. We stopped at the first available place to get a personal wash off.

'What a stroke of luck meeting Bob,' I mentioned to Nod.

'Yeah, but ten pints of dark-split was a bit pricey.'

'On the other hand, if we'd had to call Michael to get a crane out we'd have no job.'

'Point taken.'

Changing places

There were changes afoot at Watchet. Although we drivers didn't know it, it seemed Rodes had been in talks with the council for some time about reducing the amount of heavy traffic in the town. The first sign of an agreement having been reached was when a piece of land was bought on the other side of the hill. It was to be the site of the new lorry park. The workshop was to stay where it had always been, but in time another diesel pump would be installed in the new yard. Michael's office would be used for all business apart from day to day traffic planning. A new man had been hired to be our transport and traffic manager and a portakabin had been set up in the new place for his use. As I knew only too well new faces always took a lot of getting used to, so there was some bad feeling to begin with. He was called Gerry and we'd learned he'd had no driving experience. It didn't fill any of us with confidence.

There would clearly have to be lorries going through the town, but not so many. Someone was taken on to haul the trailers from the dock to the lorry park, and when sub-contractors were used they would load directly from the dock. Street's drivers were not allowed to pull loaded trailers into the town. We could only go to the workshop without a trailer. It was a compromise but it worked reasonably well for a few years. Gerry was gradually accepted and he started making a few changes. Those included the office finding a lot of the return loads on our behalf. It saved time and increased revenue for the company. It also gave us a better wage because the office would be getting better prices than we could manage individually. To begin with it was much the same as before but in time tramping would come to an end.

Before it all kicked in the cargo on the ships started to change. To begin with, enormous toilet rolls started arriving and one of the destinations was a small factory near Northampton. It was imperative to keep the paper dry so the loads were also covered with a fly sheet on top of the big sheets. The factory would cut the paper into rolls for domestic use. The owner had storage space scattered around the same industrial estate. The warehouses were spread out and he didn't have any means to move the paper from one to another.

There were lots of little scams which drivers got involved in. None of them added up to very much and they were difficult for the office to discover. If they did, and no one ever mentioned it, they were generally overlooked.

The factory owner was a pleasant chatty Asian. It looked like business was good and one day he approached a group of us who were waiting to unload.

'Good morning lads, did you have a pleasant trip up here?' We mumbled agreement.

'If you'd like a nice cup of tea, I'll put the kettle on.'

'Yes please.' We all said together and shuffled into the warehouse. While we drank, he explained his dilemma.

'Look lads, as you can see there's not much space here and I have to get some of the older rolls of paper down to the factory. It's only couple of hundred yards away but I haven't got anything to do it with. It'll only take about twenty minutes a load. Do you reckon you could help me out?'

There was a bit of mumbling amongst us and someone said,

'You ought to phone our boss, mate. We might be able to.'

'Yeah, I know, but I just thought you'd like to make a few extra quid.'

'Well,' I said, 'how many extra quid are we talking about?'

'I could pay you a tenner a load, how's that?'

'Er, no, I don't think so. But we could probably give it a lot of consideration if it was £15 a load.'

'No I can't run to that, but I could meet you somewhere in the middle like maybe £12.'

'It sounds OK to me. What do you blokes think?'

There was enough nodding of heads to clinch the deal and I said, 'We'll still have to phone the boss and say we've been delayed. If he calls back, you Sir, will have keep the story alive. And it's cash, yes? We won't be able to spend more than an hour at it.'

'Yes, cash of course. An hour altogether is fine. Thanks a lot.'

So it was. It became quite a regular occurrence but finally it came to an end as all good things do. None of us ever got questioned about the regular delays, because delays were commonplace in haulage. In that era, in some places like Liverpool docks you could almost set up camp for days on end.

Deepest Devon and colourful Scotland

I was only in Liverpool docks just the once, probably as a penance for some misdemeanour. I'd only been waiting there for five hours, but I was getting marginally bored and quite sleepy. There was an Irish driver in front of me in the queue. I'd had a brief chat with him earlier but he wasn't wholly communicative. He'd told me he'd been waiting for two days, which brought our chat to an end. I tried amusing myself with my book. Then I was catching up on my drivers' hours stuff and sorting out the old tachograph cards. I'd been for a couple of walks but I'd been told to get back in the cab, probably because I'd been suspected of being a spy. Then suddenly something caught my eye. There was a great flurry of paper from the Irishman's cab. It looked like rubbish. On closer inspection I saw he was chucking hundreds of tachograph cards out of the window. I had plenty which I needed to lose but I just didn't have the nerve to simply throw them away. Eventually we both got loaded together. I'd only been there all day.

Shortly afterwards I found myself in the Liverpool region again. It was a bit quiet on the return load front, but eventually the office found me a half load of bees' sugar to go to somewhere rural in Devon. I found the place and the forklift driver started loading my ten pallets almost immediately. He was half way through and I was manhandling my sheets up onto the load when he put a pallet directly on my foot. It was obviously a mistake, so I said,

'Take the pallet off my foot mate, would you?'

He laughed and shrugged like I was joking, but it was starting to hurt.

'Take the fucking pallet off my foot. Now!' I shouted.

He moved it straight away and was suddenly all apologetic,

'Christ mate, I'm sorry, very sorry, mate. You alright? Does it hurt? Do you want to go to first aid? Christ, I'm really sorry.'

'No, no. Calm down. I'm OK. Just keep your eyes open next time.'

I don't know why I remember it, but his face was a picture when he realised what he'd done.

Devon here we come.

The load was a sugar feed for farmed bees, and interestingly the destination was called Beaworthy. It's not spelt exactly the same as the insect but it's pronounced the same. I arrived around seven o'clock in the morning after a six hour journey. It was a bright sunny morning with clear blue skies and not a breath of wind. Beaworthy was not very big, in fact it was tiny. Within a blink I was passing through the other end and heading for the open countryside. There was an old chap sitting on what appeared to be the only village bench taking in the tranquil beauty of it all. I stopped and turned off the engine. He didn't seem perturbed by seeing such a large vehicle in his home town so early in the morning and looked up enquiringly. I got out with my delivery notes in hand and said,

'Good morning Sir, I wonder if you could help me? I'm looking for this place.'

I showed him the address. He looked interested and replied. 'Morning lad, let me get a closer look. Arrh yes, I knows exactly where that be. I'll direct ye.'

'Oh that's good. Thank you.'

'Now boy, you see that bit of grass yonder? That's what we call the village green but it's just the grass triangle for the T junction. You turns right there and goes up the short hill. At the top there's a telegraph pole with a crow sitting atop of it. He never moves. Then you turns another right. It's very narrow and you'll probably be running in the ditches. Go down there aways and you'll know you're on the right path when you sees an apple orchard over to your left. There'll be an Alsatian dog lying in one of the tree branches and howling like it's a full moon. You goes right on down to the end. It's about a mile and a half. Follow the lane round to the left and the archway to the house is on your right. You can't miss it lad. I've no idea how you'll turn round, but you can't back out so I expect you'll find a way.'

'Well, thank you very much Sir. You've been very helpful.' I said it while thinking why me, God? The only living soul in the village is a sandwich short of a picnic. However, there was no one else about so I set off again hoping for the best.

There certainly was a crow on top of the telegraph pole. Perhaps someone had nailed it there. But most bizarre of all there really was an Alsatian dog lying on a branch in an apple tree and howling! So I knew I was on the right lane. No one ever believes me but that story is absolutely true. I bet someone else has got a dog which nests in trees.

The bee lady was waiting at the gate when I arrived and had a big smile. 'Hello,' she said. 'What a lovely day. You found us alright then. I'm glad.'

'Yes, I asked an old chap in the village for directions. They were very accurate.'

'Excellent.' She said and nodded at the load, 'could you just put them in the hay loft please?'

'Er, no madam. I've just done a six hour journey to get here, and unfortunately I'm not paid to go hiking with hundredweight bags up into lofts. I will gladly hand them off the lorry but that's as far as it goes.'

She looked crestfallen but resigned.

'Oh OK, yes. I'll have to phone for some help, then. Would you like a cup of tea while we're waiting?'

At least she didn't lose her temper as many customers do, which was a relief as it was clear I'd need a hand to find a way to turn round later. As luck would have it, her neighbour arrived within half an hour on a tractor.

We unloaded and he pointed out what I'd been thinking earlier.

'The only way to turn you round is to tow you around that there mountainous, bumpy field in front of you. What you reckon?'

'Doesn't look the best, but it does seem to be the only way.'

'Yeah it is. Let's get the chains on yer.'

The brief journey was like a ride on the fun fair but without the fun. I thought the lorry would fall to bits at the speed we went round, but everything survived without damage and I was away again. I howled at the dog on my way out.

We didn't often get loads for Scotland from Watchet dock. We normally had to find them when we were tramping. Not all the drivers were happy to do the distance, because it was too much time away from home. Furthermore, you couldn't earn very much bonus because of the time involved. On the other hand I loved to go, so I was told to pick up a trailer loaded with cricket bats bound for Glasgow. I had never thought cricket was popular north of the border. It obviously was as there were literally thousands of bats in hessian sacks on the trailer. Another one to unload by hand, I noted. They weren't on pallets.

With those old lorries you couldn't get to a delivery point in Glasgow in one day's driving period. Additionally, there was no M74 in the early 80s, so you had to be extra careful about speed limits. Normally it took nine hours or more to drive to the outskirts of Glasgow from Watchet. It was plenty of work for one day.

It was a beautiful journey once you got passed the traffic in the midlands. The views were splendid and the different sorts of lives people lived became apparent the further north you travelled. From the main roads you could see tiny farms and smaller crofts, small villages, and sometimes just a pub on its own standing in the middle of nowhere. If you're a country person it brings great happiness on a long journey. I adored my travels to Scotland, primarily because there was no particular rush. There was always plenty of time to sit, dream and take a look about. There were no time schedules and no likelihood of getting a bollocking for not being on time, which I liked to be if I could.

I've had to look at the map to remind myself of the place names. The searching flooded my memory with the places I'd visited up north. Scotland is such a beautiful country and I remember now how much of it I really travelled in the lorry. We'll come to that later, but on this particular journey I'd decided to stop short of Glasgow in the country. So it was I discovered Crawford. There's a good pub there. The parking was full so I had to find a lay-by on the edge of the village. It made it a half mile walk back to the pub. I was lucky it wasn't raining as there's quite a lot of wet stuff north of Hadrian's Wall. The bar was full of people with a sprinkling of drivers from different places. The beer was good, as was the food, but understanding the language was a challenge. Anyway, it was a pleasant evening after a long journey.

My destination in the morning was the Gorbals in the centre of Glasgow. Luckily it was not far from the A74 which runs through the city. Despite all the deliveries I've made I've never been very good at pinpointing the exact place I have to go to. I can always find the area, but then I just fail to see the address, even if I drive straight past it. So I drove round in circles for half an hour before I eventually found the store. I had probably driven past it half a dozen times. To be fair it was a very small store. The owner was a street trader who had a little warehouse to keep his stuff. We had to unload the cricket bats on the side of the road.

While we were wrestling all the bags off the lorry, a small child of about 8 or 9 years old came alongside and shouted.

'Do you want a hand to get those off mate?'

'No! Fuck off you little cunt before I smack you senseless.'

He took off, and I said to the owner,

'That was a bit harsh wasn't it? We could do with a hand, couldn't we?'

'Yeah we could. But those little bastards will take off a bag or two and then when you're not looking, they fuck off with three and sell them. They can't be trusted as far you can spit.'

'You're the boss.'

'Don't leave your lorry unattended for a second round here mate, and make sure it's locked even when you're in it.'

I took his words on board and kept my mouth shut. We finished unloading within a couple of hours. I got the paperwork signed and headed off for breakfast. Gerry had said he'd find me a load, because otherwise I'd find something which wasn't worth doing. I doubted he'd do any better, but I was paid to drive not think. I found a café outside the city with plenty of parking and phoned in. Then it was time to wait. 50% of all driver duty periods are allotted to waiting. It was worse when the office was looking for the work, but anyway I waited and rang in every 30 minutes.

Just before I felt lunchtime calling, I got my instructions. I had to load six new Cummins engines from Cumbernauld for Exeter, and eight pallets of paint from Dunbarton for Liverpool. I never thought of the mixture till later in the day and decided to load the engines first. It was a lucky choice, as it turned out.

I rolled into the factory in time to grab some lunch in the canteen and then they directed me to a very clean and dry loading space. I was loaded with six brand new Cummins engines on custom-made pallets. Each engine was covered in tight fitting plastic and then the entire pallet assembly was shrink-wrapped. Lastly, a large sheet of thick plastic covered the entire load which was almost 10 meters long. It left a little space on the end for my second collection. I approached the foreman for my delivery notes and asked him,

'Can you tell me the value of this lot, please mate?'

'Why? What do you want to know for?'

I was a bit taken aback, but then realised he thought I wanted to sell them.

'Well, it's for Goods-in-Transit insurance purposes. We normally do general haulage and we're only insured to about £1000 per tonne, so if the load is worth more I have to inform my office. They can arrange greater cover for the duration of the journey. If you can sign to say it's not worth more, it'll be fine but...?'

'Oh right, I thought you were trying to be funny. OK, so you've got about fifteen tonnes and the value of each unit is about £9000.'

'Thanks. In that case could I use your phone please?'

'Sure driver, come with me.'

I organised it with the office and returned to cover and secure the load. They wouldn't let me do it outside, which was great news as it looked a bit on the chilly side. I had a high value load which was very carefully packaged, and later very carefully secured. I set off for Dunbarton and arrived towards the end of the day.

By comparison to the Cumbernauld factory, it was like a shack in the garden. There were old wooden doors to the store and a forklift which was coming to the end of its days and pushing out clouds of smoke. The lads were very cheerful, but it was the end of the day. They wanted to get me loaded and out of the way. The paint was in very old tins, and I later learned it hadn't been moved since 1945! Fortunately there was only one layer on each pallet. But after they'd loaded four pallets, they started putting the others on top.

'No, no, no mate! You can't stack the pallets. They'll all break.'

'They've all got to go on, driver. That's the deal.'

And so it was. They stacked them up two high and I figured it would probably be OK. I made sure they were properly separated from the engines and put a separate sheet on to keep them apart and self-contained, so-to-speak. I wasn't very happy about it but it was how it was and I set off for the south. It wasn't long before I'd forgotten all about my precious load as I took in the scene over Glasgow. Firstly from the Erskine Bridge over the Clyde and later as I motored along the M8 motorway through the centre of Glasgow. It was a lovely but cool evening with hardly a cloud in the sky. I still had plenty of time to get a good way on my journey. I might even have been able to reach Carlisle and get to sample a rare single malt whisky I'd heard about. It was from a distillery which closed down years ago.

Life was good.

Some cars came past me blowing their horns, and some drivers were even shouting out of their windows. A few had their windscreen wipers working, which I thought was a bit strange on such a nice day. It continued for a while, so I looked in the mirrors and saw my nightmare had just begun. The paint tins had started to split and colourful drops were flying through the air. They were lovely colours like those ones you never see in paint shops any longer. It looked quite serious though, so I slowed down. I decided I could probably get to Hamilton services if I wasn't stopped by anyone official. I was in luck, so I found an out-of-the-way place and backed up on the grass to disguise the colour loss. On closer inspection it seemed the engines were unscathed, but the trailer was now very brightly coloured, especially over the axles and wheels. A show-stopping design, I thought. It had certainly brought my show to a stop. I went in search of a telephone. Originally there was only one phone at Hamilton and it was on the north-bound side, but to my relief they'd just installed one on my side as well. I explained the situation to Gerry and in true transport manager mode, he said,

'Can't you just wrap the sheet round it a bit tighter?'

'Watch my lips. This is now a bulk liquid load. I need a tipper or a skip lorry to transfer it into. The paint is all over the trailer. Top and bottom. It's very pretty, but it's a fucking mess. I can't continue with it on my lorry. Do. You. Understand?'

'Alright, I'll get another lorry sent round.'

'Thanks.'

I hung up. I went back to the lorry, made a nice cup of tea and settled down to another long wait.

I was just finishing my fourth cup of tea when a lorry turned up, so you can imagine how long I was waiting. Of course it wasn't a bulk tipper or a skip lorry. It was a ten tonne flat bed. I decided to be cheerful and optimistic otherwise I knew the driver would just get aggressive and leave.

'Hello driver, you didn't take long to get here.'

'Helloooo there. Boss said it was a rush. So what have we got?'

'Well mate, there's some paint tins on the back which probably won't make the journey, but they should do a local trip to a skip.'

'OK mate, I'll pull up tight alongside and we'll hand them across.'

'Grand. OK driver.'

He parked his wagon very close to mine and we started. I grabbed the best looking tins to begin with and we got them on to his lorry without fuss. Then we got to those at the bottom, and nearly every one I passed over split or the bottom of the tin fell out. Within five minutes we were awash with colour. There weren't many left, but he started grumbling and saying he couldn't carry it.

'I did say the same to my boss, but obviously he didn't believe me.'

'Look,' he said, 'I'm not happy with this at all. Don't move any more. I'm going to call my boss and tell him we need a tipper. Where's the phone?'

'There's only one and it's on the north-bound side.' I lied breezily.

'OK, I'll be about five minutes. Don't move any more over and I'll be back right soon with news.'

'OK driver, make it swift.'

I reckoned it would take him five or six minutes to cross the bridge and locate the phone. Probably another three or four minutes to put his case to his boss and four minutes to get back. He disappeared out of sight and I thought I'd have between ten and fifteen minutes to shift the remaining twenty odd tins. I set about it quickly but it was like throwing water without a bucket! I got them off in about five minutes. I then swept the excess paint off as quickly as I could and retied the sheet over the remaining offending parts. I rolled up my overalls and gloves tightly and chucked them under the front sheet, but without touching the engines.

I leapt into the cab, revved up and rushed off. I never saw the other driver during my exit, or in fact for the rest of my life. It was probably a bit unfair, but he did live within a stone's throw and it would take me a day and a half to get anywhere near home. Anyway, it was a needs-must occasion. I drove for about an hour and found a lay-by which was right off the road, shaded with trees and with plenty of undergrowth. There was no one else in sight so I parked up out of view. I set about cleaning up the kaleidoscope of colour as best I could. My broom would need replacing so I put it in the waste bin provided. I spread my overalls out on top of the load to dry and roped them on. It was probably a bit of a give-away, but I doubted they'd be searching for the 'roaming painter' by helicopter.

So there was no need to go to Liverpool and I set off for Exeter. I did get to Carlisle the same night and managed to find the rare whisky.

It was a wonderful whisky called…I'll look it up. No, I can't find it, but it was from a distillery which closed down and reopened several times. It's a very smooth dram and it's classed as a Lowland Whisky, even though Carlisle is not in Scotland. I did have a wee book of Scottish whiskies but it's missing - in action I would think.

They were very pleased with the engines in Exeter and made no comment about the multi-coloured trailer. I had just enough time to get back to base and rolled in about 4.30pm. I reported to the office and Gerry went out to inspect the damage.

'Yes, as you said, it's very pretty. I had a call from the Scottish haulier. He's none too pleased, so I've passed it on to our insurers who at present are having a laugh about it.'

'It's not as if you weren't given all the information, is it?'

'Well, drivers are prone to exaggerate.'

'Oh right. I hope you don't get any calls from irate Glaswegian car drivers.'

'Why would I?'

I told him.

'Oh shit!' He said.

I never heard any more, but the trailer remained brightly covered in many colours for years and was referred to as 'The pretty trailer.'

Searching for sanity

Later the same year we had loads and loads of waste paper to go to Ramsbottom, north of Manchester. One miserable and dark winter morning several of us arrived together. We had to wait in line before we could get under cover to unload. It was raining, well soft drizzle really. It was an uncomfortable rain which usually hangs around for days. We prepared to unload by loosening the sheets on each load, but kept them on so the rain didn't dampen the paper. There wasn't a lot of space and six of us had more or less filled up what was normally the entrance road. Meanwhile, one lorry was under cover unloading. We chatted amongst ourselves, brewed up several cups of tea and waited and waited. Some bloke in a suit came out of the warehouse and said we had to make some space to allow his own lorry to get out. He told one of us to back up a little way and move into the car park. Ken was chosen, but he said.

'I can't see to reverse with the sheets hanging loose, mate'

'Right, well you'll need a sane adult to direct you then.'

We looked at each other.

'There's no one like that here, mate.'

He seemed to accept our response without question.

'OK, I'll send one of our blokes out.'

A man came out, but he really didn't seem to fit the required description. Anyway he was cheerful and greeted us all. He went to the back of the lorry and started waving his hands about and shouting but Ken could neither hear him nor see him. The chap was directly behind the load so obviously out of sight in the mirrors. After a while, one of us said,

'Look son, you'll have to stand where the driver can see you in his mirrors or you'll be a waste of space.'

'OK OK, I'm just trying to help.'

He moved a bit to the right and started hollering.

'Alright drive, come on back, come on, nice and steady.'

Then he started waving his arms about like a windmill. Another driver spoke up.

'It's no good going through your dance routine chap. He still can't see you for the sheet blowing in the wind.'

He stood a tiny bit more out to the side where Ken could eventually see him and he started reversing very slowly.

The man kept doing his dance movements, which no one could understand. The lorry was getting closer and closer to the parked cars. The sane adult did not put his hands up in the 'stop' motion, or shout at the top of his voice to 'stop!' Instead, he suddenly stopped dancing and threw his arms across his eyes in complete silence and shock. Ken's lorry continued its slow reverse movement. Ken failed to see any change in the messages and the lorry gently rolled over the managing directors' brand new Mercedes convertible. It was reduced to a length of about three feet as Ken pushed it into the boundary wall.

We had never seen anything quite so comical in years. It could have been because of the speed. There was nothing sudden about it. It was just a relentless push the driver was completely unaware of because of the weight of the lorry. The sane adult then collapsed onto his knees and wept like a baby. None of us actually laughed out loud but there was plenty of quiet sniggering. It was time to make a swift exit and see if the canteen was open.

I was quite fond of my lorry by then, and it didn't look like I was going to get anything newer for a while. I had been passed over several times when new ones had arrived on the fleet.

So I'd invested in some extras. One was a completely pointless fibreglass sun visor. It never kept out what little sun we ever got in the UK and it made it more difficult to see out of the windscreen, but it did look pretty.

Then I added a night heater, which really was a good investment as I've never got used to the cold, especially when I'm in bed. I put another useless item inside the cab which was very heavy and cumbersome. I'd personally designed it to store things in different compartments. It was a real struggle to get it into position on the top bunk, but once installed it was solid and didn't move. I've no idea why I carried so much junk with me, although the lorry was home for a good part of my life. I seldom went to my real home unless I ran out of driving hours in Watchet. I can remember having nights out no more than 15 miles from base.

I just loved the lorry driving life and I couldn't get enough of it. They paid me a night out allowance even if I was within walking distance of the yard. That wasn't the reason for staying out. After all, it was still only about £8 per night.

When it started becoming popular I bought a CB radio but I never really enjoyed it much. If you had a long trip to Scotland you could pick up with someone on the CB not far from base. Then you might be stuck talking absolute drivel with them for hours. My 'handle' was Moonshine. Sometimes when I couldn't put up with it any longer I just had to be rude and say,

'I'm bored now mate. I'm going to sign off for a while.'

I didn't make many extra friends.

I put in custom made curtains and special cushions and bought various stickers for the screen. I might even have put my name up with sticky letters. I hope I got that wrong, but I can't remember. Personalisation was important then, but those ideas wore off after ten years or so. Although wholly unattractive, one useful addition was to tie old strips of rag to the mirror arms. They flapped about in the wind and kept the mirrors clean which is very useful in wet or damp weather. Without them you had to keep stopping to clean the mirrors by hand in order to have constant clear vision of where you've been.

Ah, but the night heater. It was just perrrrfect. I really didn't know how blokes shivered their way through every night and then spent the next day driving vehicles which were like wind tunnels with all the holes in them. It just wasn't right and there should have been a law against it. There was later, much later.

Drifting

A very cold winter descended on us. 1978 or '79. One or the other, or it could have been both as winters seem to span two years at a time. I don't remember it being really cold although there was a lot of snow, ice and freezing fog and all the miserable things which come with extreme English winters. It wasn't desperate like the winters of Russia or Alaska which they're accustomed to every year, but it wasn't very pleasant. Driving in those conditions doesn't take the fun out of it, but it does make it slower and gives you much more to concentrate on. It's not a time of year to practise your 'Jack-knife' stopping methods.

In those years diesel wasn't treated to prevent freezing to the same extent as it is now. The best method to stop it happening was to add about a gallon of petrol to the tank whenever you filled up, or to keep the engine running at night. Diesel doesn't freeze like water. What I mean is it doesn't solidify, it turns to a sort of treacle and the viscosity increases. Which means it won't pass through the various filters and pumps correctly, and it won't fire the engine on ignition. Basically if your diesel freezes you can't start the engine. If it did happen you had to warm the entire fuel line from tank to ignition before it worked. Heating the tank was the easiest part of the job and sometimes fixed it. I remember seeing many lorries with make-shift camp fires burning underneath the diesel tanks while the driver went for breakfast. It might be a worry for the layman, but it is also true diesel doesn't ignite as quickly as petrol. In fact you can throw a cigarette end in a diesel tank and it'll just go out. Of course, if there had been another flammable liquid in there before it might well explode. Lesson 1: Don't try this at home.

Right your tech data on frozen diesel is now over. As you can imagine, I wasn't at home when the snows started. It was cold and it was wet, but it wasn't white when I left the balmy temperatures of Costa del Somerset to head up to the frozen wastelands of the north. It was somewhere near Leeds.

I did the unloading and loading stuff which was required of me. Then I set off to find somewhere congenial to park for the night, with showers, a five star restaurant and a convivial bar to relax in. I realised within thirty minutes it was going to be like searching for a palm beach with deckchairs. Then I had my first experience of freezing fog. I put the wipers on which just smeared the screen with ice, bringing visibility down to two feet. It was quite interesting because whilst it swirled about as rain, the moment it touched the screen it turned to ice. No matter how snug you might feel in the nice warm cab. Through the occasional gaps in the windscreen I spotted a car park and slid in there. It had a sign which said 'Lorries Prohibited'. I was prepared to talk my way round the potential problem if challenged, which luckily I wasn't. I set off for food and a bevy.

Until recently I've never found other people's misfortunes remotely funny. I always used to feel sorry for them and tried to help. Since I've gained a few more years and considerably more experience, things have changed. Frankly I can't tolerate a fool. They don't upset me but they do make me fall about laughing.

I'd found my fish and chips, eaten them and then found a happy bar where I downed two or three pints and spoke with a few people. I walked back to the lorry. Obviously the roads were wet, and most of the people I saw were wearing some sort of waterproof or carrying an umbrella. There was a Zebra crossing ahead of me. On the road immediately before it was an enormous puddle. By city standards it was vast, albeit not quite a lake. A man was standing there looking to see if the road was clear to cross. I imagined he must have noticed the puddle. He saw a car approaching and edged closer to the crossing in order to cross immediately after the car had passed. I was going to shout a warning to him but I was transfixed. How could anyone be so stupid? The car actually sped up just before the crossing and as it passed it sent up a tsunami of a wave and the pedestrian was engulfed. At the time I felt incredibly sorry for him, but as time has passed I just roll about laughing. Of course, if we could all see into the future we wouldn't be slaving away at our daytime occupations. But for goodness sake a little forethought never goes amiss does it?

If you're lucky enough to take the car number plate you can prosecute the driver and get damages and your dry cleaning paid. Did you know that? I didn't either, until later.

The following day it started to snow in earnest before I set off for a delivery just south of Birmingham. It was quite slippery getting out of the car park but the roads had been gritted overnight and were slushy. Within an hour it was snowing hard and settling. It was worse on the approach to Birmingham. The dual carriageways were reduced to one lane, making for very slow going. I arrived before lunch and the place was like a winter wonderland. They were clearing the snow by pushing heavy pallets along the ground with forklifts. They made lots of noises about not being able to unload me, but eventually a manager got things organised and a smallish space was made available for the forklifts to work. It was what could best be described as hazardous, but after a couple of hours I found myself with an empty snow covered trailer. I called the office for the next assignment but they said most places had closed down early. It was best to return to base empty. Apparently it was very white in the south too and several roads had already been closed.

'Just do the best you can to get home Hugh and on Sunday we'll assess the situation for next week.'

I really didn't think I'd have much trouble once I'd reached the motorway but I'd never encountered extreme weather conditions before. I could remember bad thunder storms and torrential rain, and on several occasions deep floods, black ice, fog etc. Santa Claus weather was a novelty. The snow kept clogging the wipers so I had to keep stopping to clear it with a long handled broom. The traffic was almost at a standstill although it kept moving gradually. When I eventually reached the motorway it had been reduced to one lane and there was very little movement on it apart from the odd snowplough. I thought it should be just about three hours to get within twenty miles of base. But no, it took more than four hours to do what normally took 45 minutes. I had got as far as Michaelwood services when I was directed off the motorway. They'd closed the motorway which was unheard of unless there was an accident. There weren't many lorries in the services. I found an out of the way spot where I wouldn't bother the others by running the engine overnight.

For those of you who have ever taken a holiday at Michaelwood services, I know you'd be able to report just how disappointing it was. I was there for almost forty hours, but within twenty hours I was in the mood for writing a letter to the travel agent. The washing facilities were flooded and in much worse condition than usual. They were filthy dirty. The heating was on low and it was a mite chilly. They almost ran out of food. It was all getting a bit dire and they said,

'You might have noticed there's a lot of snow about and it's why we haven't got enough supplies.'

OK fine, but given all the weather forecasts you'd think they'd have planned ahead. Some water pipes had allegedly burst and it was causing havoc with the heating. There was no one on site to fix it, and all the other rubbish you get told by people who don't care. To be fair, the car drivers had it worse than us because our cabs were mostly all-year-round living accommodation. Suffice it to say there was a lot of grumbling, but interestingly no-one lost their temper. What do they do in Norway, Alaska and Russia in the winter? Give a shrug and a wan smile and go home? The UK has always been hopeless at customer service for travelling professionals. It never improved in all the time I was driving and I very much doubt it ever will. It's really no wonder only 3% of lorry drivers are women. I grant you it was an extreme situation, but cleaning the toilets can't be any more taxing whether there is snow outside or not.

I got home on Sunday morning. There were some hills on the last stretch which were very tricky. The snow had drifted and the snow ploughs had piled it up in great walls above the height of the hedges. It was beautiful, but I couldn't remember it being that deep since the winter of 1963, when I went tobogganing with my dad in the country. I had to walk home from the yard, which was about six miles. I'd moved from Cathy's house and I wasn't used to hiking.

Of course 1978/9 was not the only snowy year we had, but it was the worst and went on for weeks. The roads weren't closed all the time, but it was about a week before we could regroup and get going again. When they were sufficiently clear for heavy vehicles we had a group therapy trip to St. Austell. Five or six of us I think, with timber on board.

In the late '70s the A30 was not the same as it is now. The motorway ended at Exeter. There were very few by-passes on the trunk road and the most direct route for us was through Okehampton and Bodmin, and later to dive south to the coast. Including re-loading we could just manage the round trip in a legal day, but only if there were no delays. After negotiating Exeter the road took us towards Okehampton, and we had to go via Whiddon Down and through a tiny village called Sticklepath.

There was a steep wooded and narrow winding hill which descended into the village. The built up area was only about 100yds long. It had a few cottages alongside followed by another very steep climb to exit onto the moor. We'd all caught each other up by then and were crawling down the hill when everything came to a stop. I sat there waiting in the queue for about ten minutes. Nothing happened so I put on my warm jacket and went for a wander to investigate. The rest of my group were standing at the bottom gazing up at the outgoing hill where there was a 'forrin' lorry. It was completely stuck in the slush and ice.

'What's the hold-up, boys?' I asked.

'It seems a "forriner" has got stuck on the hill.'

'Aren't we going to help him?'

'Not much to do really is there? He's stuck. We're not going to push him out are we?'

'Perhaps a bit of shovelling might help?'

'Need more than a bit. Anyway we're in the middle of the nineteenth century. Council will be along soon.'

'It's the twentieth century.'

'No it's not. This is 1979 mate!'

'Have it your own way Billy. I'm not giving classes before breakfast.'

'Mmmm, breakfast is a good idea and we're not far from the café.'

'We'm far enough.'

'Where the hell is the council? I'm hungry.'

Instantly the front door to one of the cottages opened and out stepped a man with a shovel and a set of keys. He was dressed in a fluorescent yellow jacket and trousers.

'Right gents,' he said, 'what's all the noise about? I can't get a wink of sleep with you lot hollering outside my bedroom window.'

'There's a lorry stuck on the hill and we can't get to the café. We got to wait for the council.'

'You're in luck, I am the council.'

'What are you doing lying in bed for when there're all these roads to clear then?'

'I'll have you know, I been up all night clearing roads from 9 o'clock last night till 5 o'clock this morning. Anyway, I'm here yet again to save you all from the 'Big freeze.' The Mrs is brewing up some teas and making toast for you. Get them down you and come and give me a hand with Jonny Forrinner.'

He shouted up the hill,

'It's no good putting chains on, chap, there's grit and salt under and you'll just tear up the tarmac.'

He started coming down the hill and we said,

'He won't understand, he's not English'

'Of course I fucking understand, I've only come from Dover with an Italian trailer.'

'Why did you put chains on? Just because you have them?'

'I thought they'd help.'

'This isn't the Andes mate. Have a cup of tea with us and then get them off. We'll have it all clear in a while and we can get on. I'm starving!'

We drank the tea and ate the toast, thanked his wife and mucked in with shovels. Mr Council got his van out with the salt in the back and we threw it around a bit. Just as we'd finished off, the council team from Bodmin showed up.

'The cavalry's here lads, after we shot all the Indians and captured the fort. Where the fuck have you lot been?'

'It's a long way from nice warm beds to freezing countryside but we're here in time to wave you off.'

Finally we were under way. Those sorts of incidents don't often happen now, apart from possibly in northern Scotland or the mountains of Wales where snowploughs are about as frequent as unicorn sightings.

It could have been the same winter or it could have been another cold one. I can't remember but there wasn't any snow in the yard when we started the journey. It had been a really cold day with a bitter wind and I could feel it beginning to bite in my feet and the tips of my fingers, despite heavy socks and gloves. There was a rush on at the end of the day for several deliveries to go to the north. Some drivers had decided to wait until the morning, but a few of us wanted to get up the road before the blizzards started. The Taunton police had reported the motorway was still flowing freely, but they couldn't predict the state of the roads in the countryside for the coming night. Four of us said we'd set off straight away. We swiftly secured our trailers and left. It was about 5pm. The road to the motorway was fairly easy going but there was just one village which is a bit like Sticklepath with two really steep hills on either side. It had just started to snow but only a little was settling on the road. We reckoned we'd make it to the outside world.

We reached Flaxpool and it didn't look at all good. I was leading and I stopped at the top of the first hill. Looking down and it seemed a bit slippery. We all peered down into the valley.

'What do you think boys?' I said.

'It looks fairly white but I shouldn't think there's any ice underneath yet.'

'Oh well, that'll be absolutely fine. Thanks. I'll give it a go then, but I suggest we do it one at a time. I can't deal with a pile-up just before opening time.'

'Good plan. Off you go then.'

I mounted up and gently eased the lorry down the hill. It seemed fine so as is usual I gave it a little more throttle just before the upward turn. At the first corner it slewed across the road, lost all its traction and the wheels spun to a stop. It wasn't the most graceful of turns but it was the last one of the day I realised. By chance, there was a bus stop at the bottom of the hills, which provided a very suitable parking bay. With much difficulty I managed to reverse it in quite neatly. I dropped the trailer and set off up the hill I'd just come down. Obviously, I didn't want to be stuck down in the valley for the night with the pub only two miles away. I got back up with ease but it was by then snowing heavily and there was already an inch on the road. I was greeted by my mates with mixed feelings.

'What're we going to do now?'

'There's nowhere to park up here.'

'That was neatly done, Hughy.'

'We're not going anywhere tonight then'

'Gentlemen, what I suggest is, we spin them all round here and take the whole lot down to the Carew Arms. There really won't be many cars about in Crowcombe tonight. We'll get the proverbial pie and a pint and sleep in the street. Anyone offer anything better than that?'

Chorus, 'That is a splendid idea.' Robin was the lead singer. And that's what we did. The landlord was very welcoming and understanding, but in any event knew most of us from other visits. Robin was partial to dark splits. Manns Brown splits by preference, but it wasn't a beer which had gained much of a foothold in the south. As he said, after you've downed four or five pints it doesn't make much difference what you prefer. We had a lot of beer and home cooked pie between us. It was a good evening. At the end the landlord said,

'Sleep in as long as you like boys. I'll wake you up when I know the road's clear. There won't be any cars about tomorrow. I can guarantee it.'

We left about mid-morning to head north.

Cats

Like me Robin was marginally over educated and I think he told me once his father was a Lord. He wasn't into any of that and did his own thing. He might have been disowned by his family. He'd done a little driving for supermarkets but he'd got bored with all the waiting, which still happens now. He said there was too much manual work so he started with Rodes to 'see the world'. He was heavily into motorbikes so there was common ground there for us both. He became quite a good friend until Rodes closed and then I lost track of him. He had a small flat which was not much more than a motorbike workshop with a mattress on the floor. I suppose his cab was five-star luxury by comparison. He was a grass-track fan and during the season he raced his own motorbike with a sidecar.

He was the driver who picked up a load of cork board from the yard at 3 o'clock in the morning and set off for wherever. When he got to the first village and had to do a sharp left turn, he looked in the right hand mirror and discovered on top of the load one of Michael's cats was making a getaway on his trailer. He knew the cat law was rule three of the Rodes' gospel, so he had to do a hasty about turn and get back to the yard. He said Michael found him there at 4am trying to coax the cat off the cork,

'Hey kitty, kitty, kitty come on down off my very urgent load. Come on kitty kitty.'

He said Michael told him,

'Robin. Stop that kitty, kitty stuff,' looked up at the cat and shouted, 'Jonny come down off that lorry immediately. You hear me? There'll be no breakfast for you! You understand?'

Robin said he was dumbfounded as Jonny immediately scrambled down the ropes and went to his master.

'Right Robin, thanks for coming back. Now, on your way and don't be too late. I'll make your excuses.'

Oh yes, 20th century industry has to make you laugh.

Hillbilly

There are some hills which a lorry literally cannot climb and there are some hills which cannot be descended safely. Road builders often build in escape roads on steep gradients. If you lose control of your vehicle, there will be a place into which you might be able to steer. This could avoid a nasty incident or even death.

There is a very steep hill in my neck of the woods which now prohibits heavy vehicles but it didn't in past years. The hill in question has a gradient of 1:4. I don't know how you calculate inclines but I've discovered you need a degree in pure maths to do it. Nevertheless, 1:4 is fucking steep, even on a bicycle. They built an escape road on it and put it on the "S" bend. The first part of the S is a sharp left hand bend and the second is a sharp right hand bend. The escape road is on the second bend at right angles to the direction you'd be travelling on the downward journey. If you were out of control or without brakes you'd need super-human powers to get into it, especially with 'Armstrong Steering', (ie not power-assisted), and the weight of your load would very probably take you over the 500ft cliff to the bottom. It was mostly used for picnics. What was the council thinking of? Whilst pure maths degrees are something to study for, common sense comes at a very low value. Anyone can acquire it, even councils. There was an alternative route which was a toll road. It was very narrow but not so steep. It had a lot of very tight hairpins on it. In fact, they were so tight you'd have difficulty getting a camel caravan round them. However I don't have any lorry stories of either hill, whereas there is one about some hills in North Devon which are equally steep.

If you don't know the region, on the northbound approach right at the last moment it truly appears you're going to drive off a cliff. The road just disappears out of view and then suddenly you are plummeting over the edge. There was a haulage company in the region which operated bull nose Mercedes lorries. In the main they hauled forest logs. One day, a driver who was new to the job and travelling north was unaware he'd been advised not to use the route while he was loaded. The road probably disappeared sooner than usual because of his bonnet. Without warning he was diving downhill at great speed. He could well have reached terminal velocity. At the bottom there is barely enough space for a large vehicle to straighten out before going uphill again. It was at this point he embedded the bonnet in the up-going hill. The whole lot snapped in half and there were logs everywhere. I believe he survived, but it must have been very frightening.

The arrival of springtime

The snows came to an end and spring sprung. Everyone was happier and life became easier. New deliveries started, which was always good as it distracts from the boredom of going to the same places all the time. I don't know how tipper drivers put up with it. Load from the site, deliver to the tip. Load from site, deliver to tip. It must be soul destroying, but I never did it so who knows?

In the spring we were given timber deliveries to a place called Duckinfield, near Manchester. I was aware some of the guys had been there before me so it was prudent to see if I could get sensible directions from those in the know.

'Hey Rob, have you been to this one at Duckinfield?'

'No mate, but Rick has. Ask him.'

'Rick. You've been to Duckinfield they say. Can you give me an idea of directions?'

'Get your travel brochure out and take a look. I know where it is but I'm not very good at giving directions. Ask Rod.'

'My map's not very good. Roddy, you been to this one?'

'Yes mate. I'll show you.'

We spread out my ancient map and had a study. Most drivers are partial to a drink after work, but for some reason my mates thought I was more partial than most, which was not the case. Roddy pointed out the way for me and then described it in some detail. I retained most of the salient points and thanked him. I left after lunch. It should have been about four or five hours driving. Roddy had a bigger smile than usual on his face.

So it was M5, M6, M56 and exit at junction something. Then it was up that road for a couple of miles, right at first big cross roads, fifth set of lights do a left. Follow that road till you see a huge sign which says Leeds to the right with a set of lights. You'll recognise it because there's a big pub on the corner called the Flying Star, or something like that. Don't go right. Go straight over and take the very first on the right, etc.

I was doing fine. Rod's directions were spot on. I saw the Flying whatever, went straight over and turned right immediately. It was very narrow and it was a dead end with a very busy off licence at the bottom. Ah, very funny.

'You brought more supplies mate? Hope so, because he's going to run out soon.'

'Er no mate, it was a wrong turn.'

'You'll have fun backing out of here.'

'I'm sure. I'll try and make the most of it.'

After I'd managed to back out and find the delivery point, I supposed it was quite amusing, but obviously I needed to get my own back. It could be months.

Loads for life

On rare occasions, drivers find they've collected a load they can't deliver. There are plenty of reasons for it. It could be an office error or it could be a price scam by a broker. Later on it could have been a computer glitch. It could have been a mistake in stock control. It could have been anything, but mostly the reason was not part of the drivers' remit so he just got stuck with it.

Rodes started hauling waste paper out of south Wales for all parts of England. I loaded one for west London on a Monday morning. Waste paper is usually used for making new paper, although there are other uses like making compressed logs for burning and also I believe for insulation, although I might be mistaken. The majority goes for paper production and the manufacturing process includes it being immersed in water and saturated. However, it was still necessary to cover it and keep it dry in transit. I think the reason was because it was bought by dry weight. I duly arrived in west London and waited in the queue to unload. I was told to loosen the sheets but to keep them on. I did so and continued to wait.

'Alright driver, pull it forward to there.' He pointed.

I did so. A man came along with what looked like an oversize thermometer. He stabbed various bundles and looked at the result on his gadget, frowning each time. It didn't seem good. He went round the other side and repeated the process.

'There's too much water content, driver.'

'You mean it's wet?'

'Yes precisely, driver.'

'Well it's as dry as it was when I loaded it. It's probably drier.'

'It's not the point mate.'

'What is the point then?'

'The point is, driver, we won't accept it which means you got to take it somewhere else. I suggest you phone your boss.'

'Good plan. I'll do that then.'

Gerry didn't seem too worried. It was almost as if he knew it would happen. I phoned back in 30 minutes and he gave me another address in Birmingham.

'But Hugh, don't tell them what happened. Just tell them you've brought it from south Wales where you got it. OK?'

Off I went to Birmingham. I got there the following morning. The same thing happened again and the office gave me another address in Leeds with instructions to keep to the same story. Then they sent me to Preston, then Norwich, and then down to Southampton and then up to Wrexham. It was a pretty good series of loads for me, with minimal effort and lots of travelling. I was sure the paper would have been bone dry by Friday if I'd been allowed to take the sheets off. I imagine it sweated up quite a lot of water with all the exercise.

It was refused in Wrexham as well, and so I was instructed to take it back to where I got it from in Wales. The story was to change. I had to tell them I'd loaded it in Newcastle the night before. It was Friday. They believed me. Of course I'd had to make up my own delivery notes. Amazing! And they unloaded it. It was quite clear to me someone was getting conned. I got paid my bonus for each non-delivery. I thought it was a pity I couldn't have kept my load on for a year or so. Everything is finite.

Soon afterwards I was near Leicester looking for a likely café to get some breakfast. I spotted a place with a collection of lorries outside, which is always a good sign. There wasn't a lot of space left but I managed to squeeze in towards the back. I went inside and up to the bar. There was a large lady behind it shouting orders. She was probably the owner. She certainly didn't look like anyone to mess with and the food smelt good. The menu, such as it was, was chalked on a blackboard.

'Good morning.' I said.

'Good morning lad. What can I get you?'

'A full English without the black pudding please, and a mug of tea.'

'And what's wrong with my black pudding then?' She bellowed at me.

'I've no idea. But I don't like black pudding.'

'You'll like mine.'

'My mother always said the same about her spinach, but I never liked it.'

'You don't like a lot of things, do you?'

'I reckon I'll like everything else in your breakfast but I don't like black pudding and I don't want any, thank you.'

She stood as tall as she could, which looked like well over six feet, put her hands on her hips, puffed out her ample chest and walked round to my side of the bar. She addressed her customers in a loud voice. It was a very loud voice.

''Ere, you lot. This lad don't like my black pudding. What do you think of that then?'

'He'll probably like your bacon and eggs Margy, but if you don't hurry up and cook them he'll probably get bored and fuck off,' offered someone. 'Well, I've never heard the like of it before! Here's your tea. I'll bring your special breakfast over to you when it's done.'

'Thank you.' I said in a shaky voice.

'How much is it?'

'I'll tell you when you've finished it.'

I went over and sat opposite the driver who'd come to my black pudding rescue.

'Thanks for helping out.'

'Oh Margy's alright. She's just a bit proud of her cooking.'

'You're a regular then?'

'I stop here nearly every other day. Are you tramping?'

'Yes, more or less. Sometimes we do and other weeks the office finds the work. Just depends how busy we are.'

I told him about the load of waste paper which went round and round. 'Yeah, it sounds like a scam by a broker to me. I'm glad I don't do general haulage anymore. It's too much hard work with ropes and sheets. Added to which you never know when you're going to be home. But then, some blokes love it.'

'Yes I do, but I've never done anything else. What do you do?'

'I'm an owner-driver mate. I've got a bulk tipper.'

'I've been told they don't pay very well.'

'No, you're right. Normally they don't, but I picked up this little number, years ago. It's a bit like your load of waste paper. It pays well and always on time.'

'Tell me.'

'I haul coal from the stock yards in Newcastle. I take it down to Kent. It's called stock transfer. They load me up with a certain type of coal and I take it down south. Tip it out and go for a rest period. Then an hour later I come back and they load me up with exactly the same type of coal I brought down. Then I take it back to Newcastle. I think it's an office error, and one day someone's going to work it out. Then I'll have to look for something else but I've been doing it for eight years.'

'It sounds perfect.'

'Yes it is, up to now. You see, there's never any rush apart from clearing the stock. They can't wait to get rid of it out of one yard and the other one doesn't really want it. So once I'm loaded I can take as long as I like, but obviously time is money. I do three round trips every week and they pay me on the last day of the current month. You can't beat it really. All the yards work 24/7.'

'You could just keep the same load on all the time.'

'In theory yes, but I've got to be seen to deliver and seen to load again. Then there's the paperwork. Each ticket is marginally different, as are the weights and I need them to send in my bill and get paid.'

'You need a sensible lorry for that sort of mileage.'

'I've been doing so well I bought a new one last year. It's the blue one out there. Transcontinental, with a 350 Cummins. Bloody excellent. High, comfortable and powerful, but if there were a complaint, it's a bit heavy on the fuel. I'm still getting about 6mpg.'

'Lucky chap you are. We're still design testing Magirus Deutz!'

'Life will improve son. It's only the 1980s and most of us have got inside toilets in our homes already.'

We both laughed and my breakfast arrived. It was very tasty. I thanked Margy and apologised for refusing the black pudding. Perhaps she charged me £1.10? It was very cheap. She laughed loudly again and told me to come back.

Hands up!

During the time we were delivering to Ruabon in North Wales Michael had managed to secure some work from Chirk. Chirk is just across the English border north of Oswestry. A large company called Kronospan had a chipboard factory there. We collected the occasional load from them and the arrangement continued for several years.

One late afternoon I found myself in the chipboard factory collecting a load for delivery to London. After I'd secured my cargo I ran out of working hours and arranged to park on the company site for the night.

The town was not what could have been described as the centre of Welsh night life. After a lot of searching I discovered there was a pub. It was devoid of human life when I entered. In fact, the whole time I was there nobody else showed up for a drink. The girl behind the bar was chatty from the start. After a couple of beers she asked me who I was and what I was doing in Chirk.

I was still very young in those days but after some time as a driver I had developed a serious case of overconfidence. I was often boisterous, loud mouthed, and some people may well have described me as irritating. So to reply to her I dreamt up something wholly ridiculous.

'I'm an itinerant murderer. I'm also a lorry driver in my spare time. I'm parked at Kronospan for the night.'

She gave a light laugh and disappeared into the kitchen. She returned shortly after with the hamburger I'd ordered, but didn't say much more. I had a few more beers and probably outstayed my welcome and then struggled to get back to my cab without falling over.

I climbed into bed and considered I'd made a particularly stupid comment to a complete stranger and then fell asleep.

In the middle of the night, there was loud knock on the door. I'd no idea what time it was. In fact there were several urgent knocks. I rolled out of bed, drew the curtains back a little and peered outside.

'Fuck me.' I shouted.

There was a small collection of heavily armed policemen pointing some very dangerous looking guns at me. One of them wrenched the drivers' door open. Stark naked, I froze in my seat.

The sergeant recounted my entire evening to me in some detail. Then I was told to account for my whereabouts on a specific day, two weeks previously.

'Can I put some clothes on officer?'

'No, we've all seen a naked man before.'

'I was driving on the day in question and nowhere near Wales. But I don't carry my drivers' records for so long ago. They're held by my transport manager. This is his home number.'

He radioed his station for them to get Gerry out of bed. Things were not going at all well, I thought. They kept their weapons trained on me throughout. One of them had a shotgun, but I don't think it was sawn off.

Fifteen minutes passed and then the sergeants' radio crackled into life. There was an exchange of words.

'Right driver. Your whereabouts have been accounted for and you were not in Chirk.'

'Where was I?'

'Shut up! It's now clear to us you had no idea there was a murder in this town recently. I will now give you some advice.'

'Yes officer.'

'The next time you go into a bar in a town where you are unknown think very, very carefully before you open your big gob.'

'That is sound advice.'

The weapons were lowered and they left.

I've done and said some remarkably stupid things in my life. Fortunately I can't remember them all. I should never have done them but I can't regret because a mistake made is a lesson learned. Nevertheless, the Chirk incident was a monumental error.

It was very frightening. It certainly put me in my place and took me down a peg or two. I resolved to quieten down and keep my trap shut in future.

However, it wasn't the reason I never spent another night in Chirk. It was because I could only find one bar!

Physics class

(This was more than a year after the naked gun incident)

When I'd been working on the boats in Nice in France I'd bought a Swiss watch. It was quite a fancy one for those days. It was an Incabloc for anyone who's interested. I'd seen it in a jeweller, and it was discounted from some fortune which I'd never have been able to afford to the paupers price of only 330 Francs. Even so, it was a lot of money bearing in mind I earned about 9 Francs a day. So the value in my terms was more than £35 or five weeks' work. It was still a lot of money at the time and I can't think how I had so much. Anyway I liked it so I bought it. When I came home I took it to be cleaned. I was told it would cost £25, but it was well worth it because it had a value of £300. Each time I took it to be cleaned the man told me the same thing except the value increased each time. The last time I took it in, it had reached the princely sum of £1500. My word! I never thought I was capable of making such a worthy investment. I wore it every day and I was very proud of it. It was attached to my wrist as usual when I went to load chipboard again at Kronospan, in Chirk.

In case you're wondering why I'm telling you this, it's because it's a physics class. Partly.

I loaded the board. They were always quite quick there. I was in a bit of a rush to get away because despite Chirk being a pretty and picturesque tourist village, socially it was as dead as a morgue in the evenings. Chipboard is a difficult load, or it was back then. It looked really neat on the trailer but it had a tendency to slide about in transit because all the boards were melamine-topped. It's a nice rectangular shape and easy to cover but you had to use every strap and rope you possessed to stop it from moving in transit. I flew around it and over the top, covering it with the sheets and put all my ratchet straps on it. While I was working someone brought me a cup of machine coffee, which was kind. I took a sip and put the remains on the fuel tank for later. I finished securing the load within an hour.

I used the wash room to clean up and returned to the lorry. It was only then I realised my watch was missing. I hunted all around the trailer and under the lorry. I looked under the sheet as far as I could see. I searched the cab, but it was nowhere to be seen. I went back to the washroom but it wasn't there either. In the end I reported my loss to the Kronospan office and left my details in case it turned up, although I wasn't hopeful. You win some and you lose some. I put it to the back of my mind and set off. I reckoned I'd stop for a snack and a tea on the other side of the aqueduct. It's the one which spans the gorge between

England and Wales. It's part of the canal which runs out of Birmingham. It's impressive, I can tell you.

There was only one other lorry in the park and it was a fridge trailer. I went in and got my tea.

'You just loaded out of Kronospan, mate?'

'Yes.'

'I saw you go in. They're pretty quick in there aren't they?'

'Yes. It makes a change from having to spend your whole day waiting.'

'Oh I know. Cold stores are terrible for waiting.'

'You loading or delivering?'

'Ah well, it's like this see. I've got a pallet of cheese on board. Only one, and I've had it on the trailer for three months so far.'

'It's a tidy little job for you then.'

'Yes and no. Everywhere I take it I have to wait for a couple of hours before they'll open the doors. Then they take it out, give it a good looking over and then put it back in again saying they don't want it. I've taken it to Chirk twice in the last month. I've no idea why they have to look at it each time. They know precisely what it is.'

'Rules is rules I expect. It's probably run out of sell-by date by now.' I told him about losing my watch and he said,

'You'll probably find it on the trailer under the load in the morning, if you're lucky. Where are you off to?'

'Sevenoaks.'

'Good luck. Safe journey.'

I set off on the short journey down to Hollies café between Cannock and the motorway. It was a big lorry park but without any marked out parking spaces. It was more like a lunar landscape. It had vast deep craters and lots of long ruts. You just had to find a relatively level place to park the lorry without preventing anyone else getting out earlier in the morning than you wanted to go yourself. It was popular. It's still there but the lorry park is very different now.

I got to my destination in Sevenoaks at 8 o'clock, which is customary and sometimes even obligatory, despite the often requisite amount of time you might have to wait. This time they were champing at the bit, revving up their forklifts and ready to unload. It was off in no time and then one of the drivers said,

'Look driver, there's a watch on the trailer. Is it part of the load? Because if it is, I'll have it. I collect watches.'

'Well spotted. No, it's mine. I lost it last night when I was loading.'

I picked it up and it was still working and even telling the correct time. What luck, Mr Cheese was right then.

'Can I have a look, mate? It looks like a pretty rare and expensive one. Oh, it's Swiss. You can't beat the Swiss for clock engineering. Do you want to sell it?'

"No mate, thanks. I'm quite attached to it. Well, I was till last night.'

I told him its history.

I was very lucky and I thanked my stars. The forklift driver confirmed it had a value of over £1000. However, when the time came to sell it, the best offer I could get was £50. I've still got it now although I've never worn watches or rings or bracelets since the early 1980s. Harold told me they could get caught up in ropes or other equipment and could pull your hands or fingers off. It was sound advice and I did hear tell of other drivers who had had those sorts of accidents.

The fact it was still on the trailer was not the important part I was going to tell you. What was truly fascinating to me, and still is, was the half-drunk plastic cup of revolting coffee. I'd left it on the fuel tank and it was still there without having spilt even a drop. How could it be? It had travelled about 200 miles at speeds of 60mph on the motorway. It had suffered the parking lot of Hollies Transport café. It had careered over speed bumps, done tight turns to the left and to the right. It had suffered the indignation of being bumped around while the lorry was unloaded, and it was still waiting for me to sample the delights of its remains.

The latter was the physics class. Explanations on a postcard please…

Itchy feet

There came a point when I began to feel a bit disheartened. I'd been driving lorries for about five years. There was no getting away from the fact I loved the job. On the other hand, things had changed a little. I didn't have the same freedoms as I had when I'd started with Michael at the helm. From the business perspective the new man was definitely good at the job, but from the drivers' point of view it was a lot more organised. This meant we couldn't go where we pleased any longer, unless of course there was no work passing through the dock or from the few outside contracts which had been arranged.

The money was considerably better but there was always a huge rush to get to destination and wait for hours before unloading or loading. When I'd been left to my own devices, I'd made lots of contacts and learned to avoid a great deal of the hanging around. This often resulted in the prices being less for each journey. Unlike management I wasn't hugely motivated by the profit side of things, or by earning big wages. I often thought back to the job at the garage and my wage of £21.87 per week. I knew driving was not only better paid, but also I was really happy in general.

I was disgruntled. It was nothing more than that. I had learned a lot and I suppose at the age I was I felt I knew it all. I was beginning to think I could do the management job as well as my own and still be back for teatime. I got a bit boisterous in the office and was continually answering back and sometimes not doing what I was told. It was ridiculous and childish behaviour and I started losing friends with the paper-pushers. However, I did know it was time to start searching for job No.50. I asked at various different companies but without success. Then I thought perhaps I needed a change from driving and could maybe try my hand at lorry traffic management. I hadn't got very far with that perceived change of direction when a massive cargo arrived for delivery to Merthyr Tydfil.

I got busy, along with all the other drivers. We were going to Merthyr in the morning and reloading out of Cardiff with steel for export. Financially it was going swimmingly. We could do the round trip easily in a day. I did a daily round trip for a week or more and it was starting to get a bit boring.

One morning I was thundering up the Welsh roads to my destination and I began to experience some extra vibration which I hadn't encountered before. The sun was out for once and all was well with the world. I continued without giving it another thought, apart from reporting it upon my return to 'technical control', or the workshop in normal speak. I was just passing a small industrial site and was enjoying the view when suddenly the lorry just sat down on the floor. The experience was like having to sit down in a chair unexpectedly or as if you were pushed backwards. The front axle lifted up in the air and when I glanced in the mirror I saw sparks racing up the road. Immediately afterwards a full set of wheels and tyres flew over the cab and raced up the road ahead of me. I could only assume I'd lost my drive axle wheels. Indeed I had. The whole outfit slewed to a noisy stop and I leaped out to see if I was right. The inspection didn't take long. I walked up the road in search of the missing bits, but for some reason I couldn't find them. There was nothing for it but to report to base. I found a phone on the industrial estate.

'Hello Gerry. It's Hugh.'

'What's the problem Hugh?'

'I've lost a set of wheels.'

'Shit! Can't you just tighten them up the best you can and come on back gently?'

It was a reasonable question because they were always coming loose and you just had to return slowly and get the hub changed.

'Certainly, but only if I can find them. I've already searched but they've disappeared.'

"Oh for God's sake. I'll tell the workshop and they'll have to go out with the low-loader and the spare lorry. Where are you? Precisely, please?' That was that. I just had to wait for the rescue crew.

When I finally got back it was quite a subdued meeting in the office, and I was very surprised to discover I still had a job. Nevertheless, job No50 was beckoning fiercely.

Within a couple of weeks I had another mishap. I was carrying only five plastic drums of some gunge for the paper mill in Watchet. I'd loaded them from Manchester and I stopped for the night in Worcester. Normally steel drums don't need much securing because of their weight. They dig into the floor boards and stay in place. You could be extra careful and put a sheet over them if you were a worrier. On the other hand, plastic drums behave quite differently. The bases of them dance all over the place in transit. The smaller the number, the more difficult they are to secure. I should have covered them with a sheet and roped the whole lot in place as if it were a single package. On the occasion in question I was lazy and just roped them on by winding the rope around the neck of the outside two and knotting it tight. They seemed OK on arrival at my overnight stop so I forgot about them and planned to set off at 4am.

In the morning I'd only got to the outskirts of the city and as I was negotiating a magic roundabout, (those which are painted on the road), one of the little buggers slipped off, rolled down the road, flipped its lid off and white liquid flowed everywhere. I have no idea how, but the police were there within minutes.

'Good morning driver. What's occurred here then?'

'Hello Officer. Yes, well I saw a blue bin on the road and as it's similar to the ones I've got on, I thought I'd stop and pick it up.'

'Right driver, would you like to start again before I get my note book out?'

'OK. There were five bins on my lorry and then one fell off.'

'That sounds much more like what happened. Now then, the Fire Brigade will be here any minute.'

'The Fire Brigade? What for?'

'Do you know what the contents of the drums are?'

'I was told it's a coolant liquid for paper making machines.'

'We need you to be more specific than that. We can't let it run into the drains unless we know precisely what it is, and that it's not harmful or toxic in any way.'

'I'll get the tickets and see if it's on them.'

I climbed into the cab and came back with the notes. I gave them to the policeman. He passed them to the fire officer who was now in attendance.

'There's no technical advice on these. Where are they going? Do you have a phone number for them?'

'Yes. I'll get it.'

He took it and went to make the call. It turned out they had to get the general manager out of bed and also speak to my office, all of whom were sleeping soundly. Finally it was discovered it was not a dangerous substance. They flushed it down the drains, cleared up and said their good-byes. Only the police officers and I remained.

'Now then driver, that's all cleared up apart from you. You understand this constitutes an insecure load?'

'Yes Officer.'

'Look, we're coming to the end of our shift and we're not really looking forward to doing a lot of paperwork. So I suggest you secure your load, properly this time, keep your trap shut and clear off. How's that sound?'

'Excellent Officer. I can do all of that. Thank you for all your help.'

It wasn't quite so simple back at base. There were a lot of sleepy, bad tempered managers to confront. I kept quiet for all of it as there was no way I'd gain the upper hand. I knew I'd just have to accept the outcome. In fact the outcome was to spend a week in the dock to help Harold shunt trailers back and forth. It could have been worse. I didn't want to lose my job as I'd prefer to leave on my own terms. All in all I was lucky. It was my own fault and I'd upset a lot of people in the middle of the night. I remained silent and got on with it.

Paper Pushing

At the weekend I spotted an advertisement by a small engineering company in the local paper. Transport manager required. I rang them up and he asked me to go round on Saturday morning. The interview was probably the briefest I'd ever attended. In the country everyone knows everything about everyone else. Tongues wag all day long.

'Hello Hugh. My name's Nigel. I'm the general manager here. I've actually heard a bit about you over the years so we can make this fairly brief.'

'Good morning, Nigel. I had no idea I was so well known.'

Still I could have guessed, having had 49 jobs, of which nearly all were in the same area.

'Well, I don't know if you are but I used to meet Mr. Rodes at various gatherings and he's spoken of you.'

'That's good news. Despite what he may have said, I have no managerial experience whatsoever, but I could do with a change.'

'There's no way of saying this diplomatically. There's an extreme lack of experienced transport managers out here in the sticks, and so the next best thing is an experienced and recommended driver. It's not very difficult work and we only have eight lorries. As you know, none of them are 32 tonners. I can explain what's required within an hour or so, if you'd like to take the position.'

'Yes. I know basically what's required of me. I'd have to check drivers' hours, plan loads going out, and presumably back. Liaise with customers and sales, plan vehicle maintenance. Deal with breakdowns and also with the drivers as and when.'

'That's it in a nutshell, but we don't do return loads because we only have an own account operating licence.'

'They always come back empty?'

'Yes, unless there are any sales returns.'

'It all sounds pretty straightforward. I'm sure I can handle it. What will you pay me though?'

'After the money I imagine you earn at Rodes it might be a bit disappointing, but it is all there is available. The wage is £150 per week gross.'

Jesus! It was going to be a bit of a climb down, but on the other hand it was the change I wanted. It would be less hours and it would give me a different experience.

'Yes you're right. It's not a lot. I expect your drivers earn more.'

'Sadly it's all I can offer you. I've had my own instructions from head office.'

'OK Nigel, I'll give it a go. I accept the job is new to me and also you don't know how I'll get on so it's a testing ground for us both. I have to give a weeks' notice to Rodes. I could start on Monday week.'

'That's excellent news Hugh. I hope you'll be happy here.'

I returned to the yard and announced my departure amicably.

Job No50

I arrived on the first day of my new job with a mixture of anxiety and excitement. I wanted to be good at it but realised I knew very little about the management of lorries. It turned out my instruction lasted no more than half an hour. The introductions to the rest of the team took most of the morning. There was the office team including accounts and sales, which was really no more than the telephone receptionist and the office go-for. We moved on to the factory. I was shown what they made and introduced to the production and workshop manager and then the 'procurement' manager, or store man. The drivers were all out delivering so I'd catch up with them later.

As it turned out my duties were particularly limited. I tried to settle in and make a few friends, but apart from the office team who were very friendly, it was the hardest part of the job. The factory managers, and as I learned later the drivers needed a transport manager about as much as they needed a terminal disease. The whole operation was tiny from the point of view of transport. They did fabricate an amazing amount of stuff but it was all to order. There was little or no stock held apart from fast moving items. Eight small capacity lorries were not very difficult to organise, despite there being a lot of multi-drop loads.

On day one I checked all the drivers' hours' log books, which hadn't been done for weeks. I talked with the sales woman about what had definitely been ordered and what the delivery addresses were. I went through any customer complaints which were current and what returns were due for collection. After that was completed it was lunchtime. Afterwards I talked with the production manager to see how many of the orders had already been made and what the time scale was for the rest. I planned the next loads for when the lorries returned. It was then I discovered a peculiar working practice in the drivers' pay agreement.

Each load had to be given a sensible time limit to complete the deliveries and return to base. For example, if the transport manager deemed a particular load capable of being delivered within three days, the driver was required to do it within the period stated. If he did it in less time he took the period saved as time in lieu. The records showed nearly all the drivers were only doing a four day week, and a few of them only three days. It meant if the factory was busy there'd be two or three drivers sitting at home enjoying themselves. Shorly Shum Mishtake. I took it up with Nigel who told me firstly, it was the best pay agreement they could get, meaning most inexpensive I supposed. And secondly, the factory was never very busy, and thirdly if it ever was they'd just pass the extra work to the factory in Bridgwater.

By the end of day three I was beginning to think there really was no need for a transport manager. The work could easily have been shared between the other managers. I stuck at it for about two months in all. There were times when I thought it more boring than hoeing cabbages in a forgotten field, which was job No 8 some years before. There were very few amusing moments which were memorable. I suppose it was mostly because just about everyone was underworked. It must have been a tax loss operation.

Mable was the accounts department, and she had the loudest voice I'd ever worked with. Several people remarked on it but she took it in her stride and never fought back. She was a cheery soul with a ready sense of humour. On one occasion she mentioned even she was bored with her job and perhaps she should look for something else. I left it a few days and then one lunch time I told the whole office, and Mable, I'd heard of a job which might suit her. If she liked the idea I could put in a good word for her.

'Oh thank you Hugh. That's very kind. Where is it? I don't want to travel far.'

'It's in Watchet.'

'Yes, that's good. It'll only be a couple of miles for me. What's it doing?'

'It's on the dock Mable, working for the Harbour Master. He's looking for someone experienced to be a fog horn for the dock as the mechanical one is beyond repair.'

'Oh Hugh,' She shouted, 'You're taking the mickey! You're very naughty. I'll get my own back you know.'

Yes. I knew that.

One day I had to go into the factory to check on production of some orders for a load I'd arranged. With the information I'd then have to phone the customers to confirm a delivery date which was mutually acceptable. I returned to my office and was about to start re-planning when Julie, (front-of-shop sales department), said,

'Hugh, urgent call to return. There's a man called Rawlings who's just rung about the immediate supply of several tombstones.' Tombstones were a line or rail of inverted steel loops, joined together. They were used for cattle to put their heads through to feed. They were wide enough for their heads but narrow enough to stop them moving their neck far enough to steal their neighbours food. 'I've put his number on your desk. Do you see it?'

'Yes thanks. I'll call him as soon as I've sorted this load.'

I completed my plan and lifted the receiver.

'Rawlings. How can I be of service?'

'Hello Mr Rawlings, My name is Hugh from Country Engineering. I understand you've just made an enquiry about the immediate delivery of some Tombstones, cattle handling equipment, so what can I do for you?'

"Ah, I think you may be the butt of some joke, Hugh. This is Rawlings Funeral Service and we already have a suitable supply of tombstones.'

'I see Mr Rawlings. I apologise. I'll try and get to the bottom of it. Many thanks for your help.'

I put the phone down.

'Mable. Was that your joke?'

'Yes Hugh. Did you like it?'

'Yes Mable, very amusing. Have you thanked Julie for her input?'

It was funny actually, and more so than the fog horn. I'd have to improve.

Two of the drivers were very difficult to get on with and were always whining about the work I gave them. Yet they always seemed to get their days in lieu. It was a bit like the situation between Gerry and I at Rodes. I was starting to understand the other side of the coin. Additionally the lack of things to do was making me depressed, so I found a way to amuse myself by giving those two drivers more deliveries than normal and shorter times to get them done. It was just to see really. It never gave me any satisfaction and they always succeeded. One Thursday evening I put a load together for one of them which totalled 97 deliveries. It started in Cheshire and did a loop all the way through central Wales to the south. The last one was near Bristol.

'Mr Transport Manager, you are taking the piss! It's Thursday night and obviously tomorrow is Friday. We're always home on Friday.'

'They're all urgent, behind schedule and they've got to go this week. You're the quickest driver we've got and I know you can do it if you go tonight. It's not as if you've done anything today so you've got plenty of time left.'

'Well fuck! I'm going to complain about this on Saturday.'

'That's your privilege, my man.'

'Damn right it is.'

He had two days to do the trip and all the deliveries were to farms so he could get everything off at any time of day or night. If there was no one there he could leave it and put a note through the door. The only times he would need the customer present were if he needed help lifting something. He didn't have any heavy items on his special load.

I went home with a clear conscience. On the Friday morning I arrived later than usual, which I'd cleared with the general manger beforehand. I spent a couple of hours at home phoning the local haulage firms to see if I could get a driving job. But as happens from time to time the next job, number 51, was elusive.

On Friday evening I called Gerry and he said to go and see him on Saturday morning. Better to go back to Rodes than die of boredom. On the way home on Friday night I spotted the 97 drop lorry standing empty outside the drivers' house. He won't have much of an argument when he makes his complaint, I thought. Life is all about priorities and his life was no different. He just had to answer his own question. 'How much do I want to be home on Friday night?'

I still had a clear conscience. When I thought about all the full weekends I'd worked in the past, I knew he was getting upset about nothing.

'Hello Hugh. How are things? Are you looking for another change?' "Gerry, the truth is I'm bored to tears. There's not enough to do. I've learned a bit about management, but right now it's not for me. I have asked at other hauliers but there's nothing available, so unless you take me back I'll go out of my head.'

'I wouldn't want that to happen. I'll be happy to take you back, but on my terms. You're a good worker and an experienced driver but I can't handle your previous attitude. If you keep your mouth shut, do the work as before and behave in general we'll get on fine. What do you say?'

'I can handle it. I understand a little more about what you do, so I'll just do what's required. How's that?'

'Excellent. I'm happy to have you back. You can have your old lorry. It's been looked after and all your expensive extras are still in it. Start in a week?'

'Done. Thanks Gerry.'

Job 51 secured. The Guinness Book of Records must have been cheering for me by then.

Having told Nigel the news, I could not wait for the last week to pass. It takes more than two months to get over an addiction to lorry driving.

Job No 51. Everyone deserves a 2nd Chance

My old lorry was in a surprisingly clean and tidy condition. The night heater and the air horns still worked and the sun visor was undamaged. I took the storage cabinet out and used it for firewood. I'd made a new start and my intention was to try and keep it all as clean as the last driver had done. I was impressed. Even the CB radio was still there, but it wouldn't have mattered if it wasn't.

The first job on my return was to help clear out a board mill in Bristol which had closed down. A bunch of us had to move the paper stock from the mill to a store in the country. It was going to take most of the week. The approach to the mill was quite complicated because we had to go past Temple Meads railway station and do lots of lefts and rights down narrow lanes until we got to the river.

The concrete apron was wide and spacious and had a downwards ramp to the loading bays. Recently the laws on maximum weights had changed to 38 tonnes and the trailers had to have an extra axle making them Tri-axle, (or three axles as opposed to tandem axle, or two axles). It increased the weight we could carry to 24 tonnes or a bit more depending upon your tare, or unladen weight. The major difference for the driver is that tri-axles behave differently when cornering and especially reversing. Normally when reversing the movement pivots on the trailing, (most rearward), axle but tri-axles tend to pivot on the centre axle. It took a bit of getting used to, most especially when using ramps. I'd give you a class in geometry, but it's all a bit long-winded and I know it'd bore you to death. Similar to calculating hill inclines.

I was on my own for the first day at the mill. I checked in with the loader and he said he'd watch me in to the loading bay. I started my reversing trajectory towards what I perceived as the point where I was required to arrive. The loading foreman was in position beckoning me back and then suddenly started doing the windmill dance procedure. It was pretty obvious where I needed to be but his dance got more agitated and aggressive. He started shouting. I couldn't hear a word but I could see he was getting very angry, so I stopped, turned off the engine and got out.

'Why don't you do what I'm telling you driver?'

'Because I can't hear a word your shouting and your signals have so far failed to make any sense at all.'

'They make sense to me.'

'Yes, I'm sure. But you clearly can't drive one of these and they don't make sense to me. Look, let's do this the easy way. You tell me precisely where you want me to put the trailer. Then you go and have a nice cup of tea and when you come back we'll be ready to start loading. How's that sound?'

'It sounds like a good idea driver but I'm sure you won't be able to do it without my directions.'

'Well, the benefits for you are you get a nice cup of tea, and if we're no further forward when you come back we will only have lost five minutes.'

'Alright,' he said very reluctantly. 'I want it precisely here.' He indicated.

'Excellent. I'll put it there then.'

He rolled his eyes and set off for the kettle.

Of course it wasn't as difficult as he'd made out. What he'd failed to make clear was that he wanted the trailer between the marked out loading spaces. He would then be able to pick up the paper on the loading bays from ground level. I completed the task and waited for him to finish his tea.

'You made a good job of that driver, I am impressed. Right professional, I never thought you could do it on your own. I was watching you from behind a roll of paper. OK, let's get on with it.'

The forklift driver had spied on me to see if I could reverse a lorry. Some people are very proud of their responsibilities. He went to get his forklift. We were relatively good friends by the end of the week.

It's been said a lorry driver's life is lonely, but loneliness is a state of mind. If you crave constant companionship, working friendships and the to and fro of chats during your working day then it's probably not for you. A driver can always find someone to exchange a few words with during rest periods, whilst loading or unloading, or at an overnight stop. Furthermore, modern life has brought the mobile phone, so if you use it responsibly you could chat all day. Before mobiles there were CB radios. It's true human beings are for the most part gregarious, but it doesn't mean they need constant communication with others.

Most long distance professional lorry drivers enjoy the solitary life, which is quite different from loneliness. It often involves long periods of working alone, and the majority of drivers are happy with their own company. Most of them don't like to talk when they're driving. They just like the peace. Inside modern lorries it is very peaceful. They're all very quiet and insulated. Nothing like it was in Harold's day. There's a lot to look at and they're all very high up, so you can see for miles. You can listen to the radio or play your own music, or you can dream. I miss that part of the job. I miss the hours and hours of continuous driving without someone breathing down my neck and telling me to get a move on.

However there are those who get a serious dose of verbal diarrhoea in the instant they stop at a café.

I was returning from a tiring day after waiting in the long queue to unload at Bolton. There weren't enough hours left to return to base so I stopped in Sandbach services for the night. There were several of Rodes' lorries already there. We were all returning empty as there was a ship load of timber for delivery to the north. I found the quietest spot I could and went inside to wash. I returned, changed and headed in for supper. There were half a dozen drivers eating together so I joined them. We greeted each other.

'All of you lot going back empty?' I asked.

'Yup.' was the group reply.

'I think there's a boat load in so we'll probably be up again tomorrow.'

'I hope not,' said Bob, 'I want to be home tomorrow.'

'You might be lucky.'

We talked about the usual things for half an hour, like deliveries, journeys, loads, and lots about lorries. At last I said,

'Can we talk about something else lads? I've been driving one all day and I don't want to talk about it all night.'

'What do you want to talk about Hughy?'

'I don't know. Has anything happened at home that I don't know about?'

We chatted on about this and that, and after a pause Dave mentioned,

'I bought a new car the other week, well new to me. Actually it's a bit old.'

'Oh yeah? What is it?'

'It's a Humber Snipe.'

'A bit old? It's a museum piece.'

'Oh but it's soooo comfy.'

'Sure, and I expect it does a massive 8 miles to the gallon.'

'Yeah, it's not great on fuel but it's in really good nick.'

Bob spoke up,

'They were fantastic cars in their day. Yeah, they were really pres…prest…presi…can't think of the word.'

'Presumptuous?'

'No that's not it"

"Pentecostal?'

'No, of course not!'

'Pricey?'

'They were, but it's not the word.'

'Presidential?'

'No, that's not it either.'

We suggested a few more without success.

'Come on Hughy, you're an educated man. What's his word?'

'I've no idea. He hasn't told us what it means yet.'

'What's it mean Rob?'

'You'll know when I think of it.'

'That makes sense, unless we don't.'

'I hate it when I can't remember something. I'll go and have shit. It'll come to me then.' He set off for the loos.

'If he has to have a shit every time he forgets something his cab would be a real mess.'

'It's not very pretty when he's got total recall.'

'Coo, he's got a stride on him and he bounces up and down while he's walking. Look!'

'That's why he was christened Bob see. Cos he bobs along!'

'That don't make any sense, Micky.'

We chatted on for a bit and then Bob came back.

'It's no good, I can't think of it but it will come to me.'

'Don't worry yourself Bobby. It's not important and Dave's got a comfy car. That'll do.'

'Right boys.' I said. "I'm going to turn in so I can make an early start. Around 3.30am.'

'Yeah. Sparrow-fart. Excellent time to go. Three o'clock cup of charley?'

'Nice one. See you tomorrow.'

I slept soundly through the night until there was a knock on the door. I glanced at the clock. 2am.

'What?' I shouted without leaving the bunk.

'Hughy, It's Bob. I've thought of that word.'

'Good. Fuck off!'

'But I might forget it again.'

'Brilliant Bob. It's 2am now go away. Piss. Off!'

'You miserable bastard.'

I managed another hour of uninterrupted sleep and then the alarm went off. I got up, went to wash and then got a cup of tea with the others. 'You don't look too good Hughy. Anything happened?'

'I'm not talking about it.'

Bob came in and I gave him a nasty look.

'I've forgotten it again.'

'Try another shit.' Someone ventured and we all roared with laughter.

We drove back in convoy, stopping at the Smokey Hut for an early breakfast, and got into the yard together at about 8.30am. We dropped our empty trailers and formed an orderly queue to re-fuel. While I was waiting, I said,

'Give me your delivery notes and I'll get our new ones.'

Bob came bouncing down the line just then.

'I've got it, I've got it, I've remembered the word. It's presteeeejuus,' which translated into normal language is prestigious.

'Nice word Rob,' said Alan. 'What's it mean?'

'Come on, give me your notes you lot and we'll call him Steeejuus from now on. Sounds better than "Bob".'

I did the paper exchange in the office and returned with the new wad.

'Hey Steeejuus, do you know what this is?'

'Yeah, It's a delivery note.'

'Exactly, but do you know what it means?'

'No. What does it mean?'

'It means, my man, you are going to have another night out. We're all going to Bolton again. ♪ Oh, the joy of the open road ♪'

'Shit. I wanted to be home.'

'There's nothing else. No locals, only Bolton. ♪ Oh, the joy of the open ♪'

'Steeejuus, get your lorry off the pump. There's a queue waiting.'

'Gentlemen,' I shouted. 'We've all got Bolton. Again. All of you have tractors back from Coventry, but I have the special load of beer from somewhere near Preston, worst luck.'

'Is it from Samlesbury Hughy?'

'Yes.'

'That's a fantastic load Hughy. You'll be amazed. It's all automated loading. You never seen ort like it. Make sure you're there half an hour before your loading time, and they'll load the full load in less than a minute. It's fantastic.'

'That's good. I can't wait.' I wasn't all that impressed, because tractors were dead simple. They were easy to secure and a fairly light load. Still, I supposed someone had to do the beer.

'I'll tell you how to get there in a minute Hughy. It's in the country, not far off the motorway.'

'Thanks Mike.'

We set off for the north at intervals as and when we'd found our respective trailers and secured them. Bolton was becoming a sort of home from home after going there every day for a week, but it was a pleasant journey with plenty to see from on high in the cab. We met up at the delivery point to park for the night on the concrete apron outside. It was too late to unload because they closed at 4.30.

The last stretch of road before arriving was wide and pretty much traffic free, despite it being on the edge of the city. However, it had double yellow lines preventing parking on both sides. It also had a very good pastry shop which sold scrumptious pasties, pies, cakes, bread, sweets and the like. I always used to stop there to pick up something to munch while I was waiting in the queue.

I stopped there again in the late afternoon. I got my provisions and as I came out there was a traffic warden writing out a ticket in front of my lorry. I started to say something apologetic, but I saw that look on her face which says, 'I've started, so I have to finish.' I hurriedly climbed behind the wheel, started up and pulled onto the road. In the instant I did so, she was just about to put the ticket under my windscreen wiper, but she was fractionally too late. I waved of course, and gave her a big smile, but I'd got away with it. There were no or very few sticky tickets then and they had to be attached to the vehicle by hand to secure a fine.

I learned later, traffic wardens can't give you a ticket if you park your vehicle on the zigzag approach or exit from a zebra crossing. Neither can they fine you if you park on the crossing itself because it's considered a traffic offence which can only be prosecuted by the police. Interesting isn't it? I also learned if you park in a public pay car park and put a full cover over your vehicle, you can't get a ticket from a warden. The reason is the cover has to be removed to put the ticket on it and they might damage your vehicle in the process. With reference to my introduction pages, I believe that to be a bureaucratic nonsense, despite wanting to avoid parking fines. What's your view?

Space age automation

We had a rowdy night together in a nearby pub. We didn't have to go anywhere early in the morning. It was one of the few mornings for a lie in.

'I was thinking,' Mike said before we left the pub, 'Hughy ought to tip first as he's got the furthest to go.'

'It's a nice thought Mike, but I'm last in the queue again.'

'Yeah,' said Bern, 'why are you always last?'

'It's because I'm a lazy bastard.'

'OK, you go first and we'll have a lie in.'

'Thanks, it's a deal. See you back at the yard.'

'Just make sure you get up on time. They start at 7.30.'

I was on time in the morning, unloaded first as previously agreed, shouted my cheerios and set off for Samlesbury. I followed Mike's directions and found my destination with ease.

Imagine yourself in the early 1980s as we were, hydraulic machinery had only recently been adopted as the norm for loading purposes. Even so, hydraulics had been around in a basic form since the 1930s or before. I was used to having to do a lot of my work by hand, but was by then getting accustomed to there being a forklift available to do the heavy work. Nevertheless Samlesbury came as a shock.

I drove up to the entry barrier where the gate man took my details and then directed me inside the compound.

'Drive into the compound and park up facing the factory, driver. At the top of the building you'll see a screen with a number on it. Your number is 54. When you see your number illuminated, drive into the warehouse from the right hand side and follow the traffic light instructions. Understand?'

'Completely. Thank you.'

'You shouldn't have to wait more than ten minutes if all goes to plan.'

I parked up facing the building, spotted the screen and waited. It was only about five minutes before number 54 appeared. I followed my instructions and as I entered the warehouse there were traffic lights with arrows on them, which suggested where I was to put the lorry. On the right was a platform like a railway station which I had to drive as close to as I could. I stopped when the lights turned to red. A voice from nowhere said,

'Ensure the handbrake is engaged. Turn off the engine. Remove any equipment from the trailer. Wait in the cab until the lights turn green.'

I did all as instructed. Within a minute a giant forklift came out of the darkness of the warehouse bearing twenty pallets of beer. In one go it placed the whole lot on exactly the centre of my trailer. Then it vanished back into the darkness. How did it know?

The disembodied voice returned.

'Put your equipment back on the trailer. Continue to the next stage when the lights turn green.'

Oh, yes please. I went on and stopped at an office which was at my level. A lad gave me my delivery notes.

'This is bloody superb.' I said to him.

'State of the art, driver. Dorchester is where you're going, yeah?'

'Yes, Indeed. Thanks. Oh, whose is the voice from within? It's very commanding.'

'Mine. Drive into the next building and park between the platforms. Hopefully you'll be able to sheet down there without falling off your trailer, and if you do it won't be very far.'

I took it as a joke, but in fact the height of the platforms came to half way up the height of the load. It would make it only a two foot fall if I did slip. The lorry cab poked out of the end of the platforms allowing me to open the door. I covered the load, pulled forward a little to get the ropes over it and was ready to go. The light was still red with an arrow pointing down to something like a parking ticket machine. I pulled up alongside, pushed the 'finished' button and a numbered ticket popped out. I assumed it was my exit pass although no one spoke to me from the bowels of the factory.

Mike was right. I'd been there a total of 40 minutes and most of the time had been my own in securing the load. It was a bloody fantastic experience. It never happened to me again. Not even once more in the coming twenty eight years.

I arrived at the yard just as the others started rolling in with their tractors on board. Perfect timing for us all to get a pint at The Star and talk about lorries for the whole evening. Bliss. They had other loads to find for delivery on Monday but I kept mine on for the trip to Dorchester. It was the end of another full 65 hour week. It was nothing to complain about, and it was perfectly usual.

Highlands and islands

I was in Dorchester on Monday morning and unloaded by 9am. After a call to the office I returned to the yard and checked in.

'You like nights out Hugh, don't you?'

'Oh yes, Gerry. I can't get enough of them.'

'Good, because I've got a little trip here which most of the others will moan about.'

'Mmmm? OK.'

'Do you know where Wick is?'

'Yes. Of course, I'm good at geography. You're not going to send me all the way up there are you?'

'You are exactly the right man for the job. Two drops Wick. Twelve crates containing stuff.'

'Stuff?'

'Machine parts might be the better description.'

'Yeah, it's certainly more descriptive than stuff. Are they a secret or something? Because there's an army or navy base up there, isn't there?'

'There might be but you will not be carrying military material. It's for onward delivery to various islands.'

'I could take them all the way to the islands.'

'No you can't, and it won't be necessary.'

'OK. Pity. Have you found anything to come back with?'

'Not yet but I thought you might have more luck than me.'

'I could ask around, sure. Are these crates to be sheeted?'

'Oh yes. Must be kept dry, it says here. Here are the delivery notes. Enjoy yourself. See you in a couple of months.' He laughed.

'Great, thanks and see you soon. I'll be in touch if I can't find a return load.'

Yippeee! Northern Scotland, I thought, my favourite. I'd be away all week. Wonderful and it was late spring so there shouldn't be a snow problem. I'd never been so far north. I looked forward to a new experience.

'Before you go north Hugh, you could do a quick one to Chard. There's plenty of time. It'll take you more than a day to get all the way up there.'

'Yes. OK. I can do that.' It was another quick earner for me before being banished to the northernmost regions.

As it turned out, there was a delay in Chard. On my return and having swapped trailers and secured the crates of stuff, I only had about three and a half hours left in my day. I wanted a quiet night, so instead of stopping at Hollies I chose the other side of the motorway where I knew there was a lay-by with a pub close by which served food. Fortunately the lay-by was empty and I had a noise free night to myself.

There was no rush in the morning because even from there I knew I couldn't get to Wick in a day. On closer inspection of the delivery notes I discovered I wasn't going to Wick. In fact I was bound for Thurso, or more accurately Scrabster and Gills Bay ferry port. Nowadays Thurso is seven hundred miles from Watchet, but in those days the UK wasn't littered with motorways like it is now. It would have been closer to eight hundred miles then. Even with the speed limit of 60mph, which was quite often broken, the average speed on motorway work was approximately just less than 50mph. It meant the entire journey would be a minimum of sixteen hours. Even though I'd done around three hours to get to my lay-by it was still going to be more than a day to reach my destination. Superb. It was to be a whole day to myself with practically no agenda. There would be no one to call and no rushing about for the next load. Complete freedom. I had a lie in and set off at 7am.

You would think there'd be nothing as boring as driving a slow moving vehicle for nine full hours, predominantly on a motorway. Of course it wasn't slow all the time. In fact downhill could be quite rapid but going up the other side generally reduced velocity to a snail's pace. Despite the slow progression the time passed quickly. I used to listen to the radio in the mornings and particularly enjoyed the stories on Radio 4. Sometimes I'd even listen to the Archers!

Compared to a car or van a lorry is very comfortable. Modern ones more so than a luxury limo although in the early 80s it probably wasn't entirely true. They were all high and have exceptional vision, complete with large mirrors to keep track of where you'd been. Some even had electric windows, but mine didn't. As a rule, a long journey at those sorts of speeds takes less time to accomplish than in a car. It's a tortoise and hare story. From the West Country to Glasgow I would often be passed by the same car half a dozen times. Four hours or more driving a lorry is much easier than the same time in a car because you are in a more comfortable position. Therefore in a car you would require more rest periods. It's curious, but the best way to calculate any journey time, especially a long trip, is to take 50mph as your intended average speed. It's not important that your vehicle may be capable of speeds in excess of 100mph. You still won't arrive much quicker than a fully freighted lorry. Try it and see.

Many years later I met a motorcyclist on the ferry to Spain and I asked where he was going.

'I'm off to Delores mate, near Valencia.'

'Nice.' I said. 'Where are you going to stop the night?'

'Oh I'm not stopping. We'll be off the boat by 2pm and I'll be there in time for tea, at 6pm.'

'No, you won't.'

'Course I will. Google gives it as only 600 miles and I can get a steady 120mph out of this baby.'

'OK, I'll have a gentleman's bet with you. I calculate you won't arrive in Dolores before 2am. I'll give you my email address and you send me a mail when you get in. Agreed?'

'No, you're wrong mate. I'd put money on it, but you won't be able to pay me. But yes, give me your email and I'll send you one at six o'clock when I'm on the beach.'

We parted to go our separate ways. He sent me an email at 1.45am.

'You were right, son, I'd never have believed it. I'm really glad I didn't put money on it.'

So returning to long journeys by lorry, there are lots of things to do to for amusement. I used to look out of the windows at the passing landscape. Sometimes I'd play the game of whether I could see through almost 360° without seeing a single man made dwelling. I discovered in thirty five years there is nowhere from the roads I travelled in the UK where that is possible. It is possible in Spain where they have more space. I had the opportunity to make a cup of tea on the move, roll incessant cigarettes, look for better cassettes to play, dance in my seat and have long conversations with myself. I still talk to myself now, but only in the confines of our kitchen. My wife has considered having me sectioned whenever she catches me at it!

Recently I've read several news articles about people who have seen lorries veering from lane to lane on motorways. One person said he was absolutely certain the driver was too tired to do his job. I dispute his certainty. Lorries do tend to drift. Right hand drive heavies tend to drift left and left hand drive ones tend to drift to the right. It is almost a natural phenomenon. As a general rule lorries do not veer radically from left to right or the opposite, unless they are involved in an emergency. The perceived movements of a heavy vehicle are mostly gradual when travelling at speed. Drift often occurs naturally or as I said could be induced by, rolling a fag, looking for something in the cab, reaching for a cup of tea, dancing or anything else which comes to mind. It does not necessarily signify fatigue.

When you do a particular type of work day in day out it becomes almost automated. Driving continuously and professionally is very similar to doing a monotonous and repetitive job in a factory. You could almost do it in your sleep.

Your eyes see the road and your brain perceives the hazards without having to concentrate. When a hazard becomes potentially dangerous your brain wakes you up and you take appropriate action, unless you really are asleep, (joking). It was also suggested in some articles the possible new law of allowing drivers to do an extra hour twice a week would lead to many more accidents on the road. See my opinions on drivers' hours rules. It would not lead to fatigue. Professional drivers know when to stop and rest. It's not controlled by the law, the office or the mother-in-law. I appreciate sensational news stories sell newspapers, but I do think some absolute nonsense has been published recently with regard to lorry driving. That, and the continual implementation of laws which govern the profession.

There, you see? Doesn't time fly when you're enjoying yourself? I'd passed Glasgow already and was heading up towards the Cairngorns. From about Preston going north the views were spectacular and become more awe inspiring as you pass through the real mountains. There are castles and tiny crofts, rolling grazing lands and open moors. The colours change from grey and green to pale yellows and purple heather. There are dry stone walls and hastily erected ancient fences, and later the open moorland. The architecture changes from flatter roofs in the south to steep sided ones in the north, built to cope with severe weather. It's all very fascinating.

I had planned on stopping for the night at Inverness, but things had gone so well I thought I might make it a little bit further. Possibly even Dornoch. I had already stopped for a large and tasty lunch just north of Carlisle. There used to be a small and popular transport café there, but Google Maps show it as disappeared now. Whenever I'd stopped there before it had been frequented regularly by a transport company from Devon. They did a lot of work into Scotland. At one time the drivers were paid on mileage. It wasn't unusual to see some of their lorries with the drive axles jacked up and left in gear while the drivers had a meal!

Dornoch is a pretty little town which would have been classed as a village forty years ago. It was small but perfectly formed with a large market square. It was useful as there weren't any tiny roads to negotiate. I managed to park adjacent to the Castle hotel, which I notice now has a sign to instruct NO OVERNIGHT PARKING. It hadn't been erected back then when I arrived, so I did. As hiking is not one of my pastimes, I was also pleased to note it was only ten long strides to the hotel bar. I filled out my tachograph and put a new one in for the following day, drew the curtains and marched to the bar.

I went to reception first.

'Good evening.' I said. 'I'm a lorry driver and I've stopped for the night. I was wondering if you might have a room I could use to shower and change. Afterwards, I'd like to have a basic dinner with a glass of wine. Could you help, please?'

She was an attractive woman, in her late forties I guessed.

'Well now,' she said in fluent Scottish. 'It's not normally something we offer but as it turns out we're not very busy. I think there's a room I could offer you, but it won't be free of charge.' That was the fluent Scottish bit.

'Of course. You don't get very much for nothing. How much will you charge me?'

'Well now,' she repeated, 'a room for an hour to wash and change, a three course dinner with a glass of wine and coffee to follow. I can do for, let me see, £15. The bar bill would be extra. Would that be alright Sir?'

'How about £12?' I said hopefully.

'No Sir. £15 is the best I can do.'

I thought it was a bit steep for rural Scotland, but on the other hand it was a matter of priorities.

'I'll go for the £15 then. Thank you.'

'In advance Sir, if it's not an inconvenience.' She hadn't trusted the lorry driver part of my introduction, but I was used to it.

It wasn't inconvenienced and I rummaged around for the amount.

'Thank you. I'll just go and get my wash kit and a change of clothes.'

'Very good Sir, ring this bell when you come back and I'll show you where to go.'

Our overnight allowance was £9, so by the end of the evening I would have spent more than double that. I'd be on a starvation diet the next day.

The room was five stars by lorry driver standards, complete with a four poster bed and an excellent bathroom with a powerful shower. I could have gone wild and got the bed for the night for £30, but then I'd be getting into Bingo winners spending. I spent a good long time in the shower. I climbed into my glad-rags and took my work clothes back to my private wheeled hotel. I returned to the warm and welcoming bar and announced myself.

'Hello. I'm the driver who's booked a table for dinner, but I'd like a glass of beer to start the evening off.'

'Of course Sir, and your name is?'

'Hugh.'

'Ah yes, I have it here. It's a good Scottish name if you spell it without a W. Where are you from?'

'I live in south west England at the moment. Yes it's with a GH, but where I come from my work mates pronounce it with a Y on the front because they can't say H. In fact my antecedents come from Aberdeen and our clan emblem is an oak tree.'

'Och, the Sassenachs. Dreadful race but there's got to be one or we'd have nothing to moan about. So you must be an Anderson then. Those who saw off the cattle thieves with their archers, killed the lot and doubled their herds, if I'm not mistaken.'

'You're very well read. I'm not sure my family were part of the archers, but the story is correct as far as I know.'

'It's one of my hobbies. Scottish clan warfare. It's really interesting.'

'It looks like I've established myself as friend not foe, so moving forward, what's on the beer front?'

'They're all marked on the front of the pumps, but if you don't recognise any I recommend Gunfire. It's very smooth and powerful.'

'I'm always game for something new. I'll go for the smooth and powerful.'

'Good choice Hugh. Let me know when you're ready to eat and I'll inform the waiter.'

'There aren't many people in here tonight.'

'No. It's a quiet period, but the locals will be in after supper time for a wee dram or two.'

Transport cafes, bars, cheaper restaurants and especially motorway services never offered particularly good food for travellers or drivers. Though I can safely say they were ten times better then, than what appeared on your plate from the turn of this new century. I nearly always chose to eat at least one good meal each week when I was away from home. My personal feeling is motorway service station food nowadays ought to carry a government health warning. I imagine there would be many people who would vehemently disagree with me but I enjoy my food and food-for-fuel is not how I like it. Perhaps I'm fussy, but I doubt anyone would take their family out for a meal at a motorway service station. If the food were any good perhaps they would. Airports are another case in point. I recently saw a Facebook post on a friend's page showing a reasonable breakfast but unbelievably small with two tickets alongside. One was the breakfast receipt for £35, and the other, his airline flight ticket to Ireland for £33. Get your head round that.

I told the barman I was ready to eat and sauntered into the dining room. There was no choice but I hadn't wanted one. The first course was a really warming and tasty fish soup. It was followed by home-made steak and kidney pie with fluffy pastry and accompanied by new potatoes. You can get very bored with chips. There were also fresh peas present and all served with plenty of gravy. It was accompanied by a very palatable red house wine, though I didn't know which it was. I finished off with home-made lemon cheesecake and some strong black coffee. I took an hour eating it and felt it had all been extremely worthwhile. I went back to the bar to see if it had got any busier. It had, but not much.

'Hugh,' the barman greeted me, 'your meal was a pleasant experience?'

'Yes very much so, thank you. I'd come again if wasn't so far.'

'I'm glad. Let me introduce you to Bruce. He was just complaining about a bloody great lorry parked outside the hotel.' He laughed. 'Bruce, meet Hugh. He'll give you more information than I can.'

I smiled as broadly and sincerely as I could.

'What would you like to know Bruce?'

'I can sense the two of you are taking the mickey out of me. Hugh, what do you know about the monstrosity parked outside, and why is Alan laughing?'

'I have no idea why Alan's laughing, but I can tell you I'm the driver of the offending vehicle. I've come a long way and I needed good food, a wash and to relax. So far those wishes have all been accomplished. Are you looking for an apology for making the village look untidy?'

He laughed loudly and said,

'I knew I was the butt of this. No, not at all lad. It's just that you've parked where I always park. We get used to our habits up here in the wilds.'

'I'm sorry Bruce. You should've left a note on the lamp-post. I'm new to Dornoch.'

'Now Bruce, Hugh should've cleared up your problems. Hugh, what can I get you? A wee dram?'

'I'll try a highland malt Alan. Recommend one to me.'

'Very good. Try this one, Sir.'

Bruce piped up again.

'Where have you come from today Hugh, and where are you off to?'

'I was just north of Birmingham last night and I'm bound for Thurso in the morning.'

"That's a long way. You've picked a good spot for the night, though it's a pity you parked in my space.' He laughed again. 'If you want to make a round trip of it tomorrow, I suggest you turn left at Helmsdale and go north to Golval. Then pick up the main road to Thurso. You can come back down on the A9 and the coast road. It's a bit narrow up to Golval but lots of lorries use it. It'll be more scenic if you haven't been up here before and I suppose you've plenty of time. Thurso is not far.'

'Thanks Bruce. I'll give it a go.'

I drank my whisky, ordered another and asked Alan for the bar bill.

'£2 for the beers Hugh. The whisky is on the house. Come back soon. Bruce could do with another shock.'

I thanked him, said my goodbyes, shook Bruce's hand and turned in for the night, but not without thanking the lady on reception for her help and an excellent meal.

As I remember it, the road from Helmsdale to Golval was not without its scenic views, as Bruce had pointed out. Although not mountainous, it was extremely narrow. It was predominantly a single track road with passing places. The land was pretty flat and looked like boggy moorland, but I'm no farmer and it probably had more value than I thought. The land along the coast from Golval to Thurso was more inspiring with rocky inlets and sandy beaches.

Reverting to the previous evening, what I'd learned from several years of driving was you never got offered basic amenities by anyone, with the exception of the cold store in north London. If you didn't have the brass to ask, you'd never know the answer. Most people were kind and helpful but prejudice was always rife. Trust was difficult to obtain, especially if you appeared itinerant.

Religion is another factor. Not only must you fear God but you must also fear strangers. In fact it's much more prevalent in the British Isles. Perhaps it's because of the countless times we've been invaded and conquered. We wouldn't want it to happen again, would we?

Thurso looked like an interesting town to explore, but there wasn't time and I never got the opportunity again. Later I did return to Dornoch. I was on holiday with my beloved of the time. We stayed there for a couple of nights in a four-poster suite. It was excellent.

Scrabster was desolate and windy, but it wasn't difficult to find the address and I was unloaded swiftly. Next up was Gills Bay port with just one crate left on board. They were less enthusiastic, but still I found my trailer empty before lunchtime. I asked around for telephone numbers of transport companies to find a return load, but was greeted with shaking heads. I reckoned the only stuff they exported to my end of the world was either refrigerated or wool, if it was in season. There was nothing for me. So I drove south to the next centre of civilisation, which was Wick, and got the same response. I settled into a lay-by with a phone box and had a ring around to my contacts in Glasgow and Edinburgh. After half an hour of inserting 2p coins I got a response.

'The highlands and islands are a bit out of my reach driver, but quite by chance I have a load for Liverpool from Nairn. Know where it is? Never mind, no-one else does either, but I'm assured it is on the map. It's timber. The net rate to you is £150. Does it take your fancy?'

'The load does mate, but the rate is a bit poor. Can you improve on it?'

'No driver, that's it. Take it or leave it. If you take it I'll buy you a dram when you pass by as I could do with clearing it, but I can't offer any more money. What do you say?'

The Scots were very fluent, I thought.

'It's better than a kick in the teeth. I'll take it. Thanks. And the details are…?'

I scribbled it all down on the back of my hand, thanked him and confirmed with my office,

'OK Hugh, if it's all you can find, it's more than I've got for you and the week is running out. The good news is I know there's a pair or three JCBs for Taunton from Knowsley. If you can get to Liverpool before lunch I'll book them for you.'

'Lunch on which day? If I can load today and night trunk it, I might make it for the following day. I'll call when I'm loaded.'

I headed south along the coast road, which was more exciting than Bruce's scenic route and a bit wider. The A9 was considerably better than in the days of the 17th century when it was first constructed, but it was still narrow by modern trunk road standards. I passed through lots of villages and skirted round Dornoch before getting closer to the sea. There were plenty of bridges in Scotland built to shorten the northern journeys. The important ones crossed various firths or inlets. They were great feats of engineering. In the late 1970s not all which exist now had been built, or even thought about. The Kessock bridge immediately to the north of Inverness was open, as was the Cromarty firth bridge. The Dornoch firth bridge was still a plan which meant I had to take a longer route through Bonar Bridge. It all took a great deal more time than you'd think when looking at a map. Bonar Bridge is worth a visit though. It's a lovely bridge.

As an industry, tourism was only just starting to get a hold within the economy. In those days most people went on holiday to places they knew or wherever had been recommended, or they went abroad. Much later it became more important and lots of places put up big signs on the main roads to promote their towns. Nowadays, you often see signs to say 'What to see and do in…wherever', and it's especially popular in Europe. I only mention this because there's a place near my home called El Tomillar. El Tomillar has absolutely nothing to offer. It's in the middle of the country on a main road. It probably has forty houses of dubious construction and a church. In the blink of an eye you've passed it. I would imagine there's nothing to see or do, and nowhere to get pissed because there's no bar! So why is there a big and expensive sign? But I digress.

It took me almost four hours to reach Nairn from Wick, and of course on arrival, it was very nearly the 'grab coats and hats' time. I found the collection address after a bit of searching and asking around, just in time to be told,

'You're too late to load today driver. They're all going home.'

'OK. What time do you start in the morning? And can I park here for the night?'

'7 o'clock sharp. Yes, you're welcome to park the night. If you want to wash I'll show you where to go. You can park over there next to the fence.'

It's a curious thing and despite its geographical location, the indigenous people who live along the coast from Inverness to Peterhead speak the purest English in the land. I was very surprised by the lack of brogue or other accent from the 'meeter and greeter' at the saw mill. Initially I thought he wasn't a local, but after a foray into town for beer and food I had the same experience. None of the people I spoke with had any accent or dialect. It wasn't monarchical English who speak of their "haises" in the country or putting on a clean pair of "traissers" for dinner. It was just pure English. There's an interesting bit of trivia for you.

They were on time and swift in the morning. I was loaded, sheeted and secured by nine o'clock and then I phoned in.

'I'm loaded and ready to go Gerry.'

'Good, I'll book you in for the JCBs for this afternoon.'

'As you think fit, but I won't unload today.'

'You will if you get a move on and pull your finger out.'

'It's an eight hour journey, Gerry. If I pull my finger out, as you flippantly put it, and don't stop for a break which is against the law, the earliest I could arrive is 5.30 pm. If I do stop to rest and by the time I've found the place, it will probably be 6.30 or 7pm.'

'Yeah but…'

'Gerry. How often do you look at a travel brochure, (map)?'

'From time to time.'

'Well, scrutinise it more intently today. Have you any inkling where Nairn is? I'll be in Knowsley tomorrow around noon. If you can arrange a Saturday morning delivery in Taunton I could be there by 8am. Would that suit you?'

'I could probably arrange it.'

'I'll check with you when I've got the diggers on. Have a nice day.'

I hung up. Traffic managers were a wonderful race, but they weren't very good at map reading or calculating time and distance. I set off with an achievable plan in mind.

In those exciting days drivers were mostly left to their own devices. It was beginning to change a little as transport traffic offices arranged more work than before. But even so the general haulage industry is a very minute by minute business. Things can change rapidly and it's not always possible to plan for many days in advance. The only means of communication with the workforce was by telephone which often required leaving messages. There were no 'phone texts or electronic mails. There were no satellites or remote cameras. A driver was fully aware of what had to be done and after a short while would learn how best to go about it. As in any employment, if they failed to do what was required they'd lose their jobs. None of us wanted to lose our jobs because it was the best thing since sliced bread. We spent our days roaming around the country and the only thing we had to do was keep the lorries loaded. In return we got paid, and for several years we got paid well. Very well in fact, so whenever I felt the need for a whinge I'd have good long think about the period when I was working in the garage. It was less than a decade before.

The advent of mobile communication was a double edged sword for professional drivers. It became much easier to get quicker and better information, but we learned within a short time it was a method for the office to be on our backs hour on hour. I think many of us could remember the time when the office was calling every half an hour to ask, 'Where are you now, driver?'

The speed of business increased, but the speed of the vehicles decreased with the introduction of speed limiters. It was very difficult to be on the winning side with modern road transport. The new inventions became a means of control which up to then had been impossible to the same extent. For many it took away the enjoyment of the job, which allowed us to take any route we pleased and stop to eat or rest whenever and wherever we wanted. The freedom of the job was reduced. Beforehand, drivers had to work on their own initiative. Office control soon took over. Plenty of drivers who were new to the job never discovered the freedoms and abilities which many of the old soldiers had. Personally I thought it was a pity.

The plan went well and I arrived, but too late to unload. There was a pub close to the destination. I parked in front of the gates to be sure of being first in the morning. They were early to start and I was unloaded before eight thirty in the morning. I left and was loaded with two JCBs by eleven o'clock. I enquired about a delivery time and was told I was booked in for Monday morning. I set off for base. There wasn't any point in calling Gerry. He'd find out what was going on by lunchtime. I was back in the yard by five o'clock with another long week notched up. It had been good to be away for so long without having to work to tight deadlines or having to ring in every night.

Wine

Monday brought a special load of china crockery in cardboard boxes for London. Several deliveries of cases of wine for Michael's business associates around the city were added to it. After I'd delivered the JCBs and returned to base, I discovered my load was ready but it wasn't covered. I had to set about doing it in a strong wind.

It all looked a bit rickety. I pulled it gently out of the line of loaded trailers and climbed gingerly to the top. It was windier up there. I wasn't sure if I could get the sheets unfolded and get down again without them being blown away before I'd had time to tie them down. As I was struggling with this problem a large black car drew up. Here come the suits for a laugh, I thought but Michael, the boss, jumped out of the back seat all suited and booted and came over.

'I'll tie the corners for you Hugh.' He shouted over the wind, 'Spread out the front sheet and then come down carefully.'

'Oh right. Thanks. There's another pair of gloves in the cab Michael.'

'No need for them. I can wash up afterwards.'

I got down to ground level and thanked him again.

'You've got the wine on this load, I think. Sorry to give you a run around but someone's got to take it to the money men. There's a bloke called Hillier. You'll see it on the tickets. He should have three cases but he's only got two. Make up some plausible excuse for him could you?'

'Yes of course, and thanks again for your help.'

'I always lend a hand when I can, lad. It's pretty windy today. It makes it a difficult job on your own. I've got to go now. Oh, all the wine is door step delivery only. You are not to go hiking it round people's offices. Understood?'

'Yes, that suits me fine.'

It was a high load but quite light. It probably only weighed about ten or twelve tonnes but it tended to blow around on the open roads and in high winds. I got it to a place just off Wapping High Street without mishap for first thing the following morning. Delivery was to a high rise warehouse in an older part of the city and each box had to go up on an old pulley with a platform. There were a lot of boxes and it took most of the morning. Towards the end, the boss thanked me and said I could take one piece as a tip. I laughed, but thanked him. All the pieces were cheap tourist stuff and I picked out a small garish bowl which I reckoned I could use as an ashtray. It was horrible by aesthetic standards but served me well. I've still got it after forty years. Why do I keep such rubbish?

There were four deliveries of wine, and the addresses were all over the place, although mostly in the south. They were all posh houses in secluded roads. Mr Hillier was the third delivery.

'Mr Hillier? I have two cases of wine for you from Michael Rodes in Somerset.'

'Thank you driver. There should be three.'

'Yes I know, but Customs had one away. They probably had to check the vintage.'

I laughed.

'Confiscated by Customs?'

'Yeah, it's quite common at this time of year. Although to be honest, I've never known them sneak off with a pack of timber for inspection.'

'No, I suppose not. Ah well, two is better than none. Thank Michael for me would you?'

I can't imagine how he bought my line, but he did.

'Driver, do you drink wine?'

'Yes sir I do.'

'Good.' He opened a case. 'Take one of these for your trouble.'

'Very kind sir, thank you.'

Result, I thought.

Last up, was a block of offices in the Strand. I'd never been in the city centre apart from darting through it early in the morning or late at night. I think it was No.1 The Strand, but I'm not absolutely certain. I can remember we were in sight of Trafalgar Square and it was mighty difficult to get on to the right road for a correct exit. I pulled up just before the zebra crossing in front of the door to the offices. A uniformed man rushed up.

'You can't park here mate.'

'Good afternoon.' I said.

'You can't park here.'

'I've got a delivery for you. Four cases of wine. Just sign here.' I flourished the delivery notes.

'I can't sign anything. I'm the door man.'

I carefully put the cases on the pavement in front of him.

'Exactly mate. Sign here.'

'I don't know what I'm signing for.'

I showed him the tickets.

'You are signing for four cases marked WINE. As you can see, all these cases are marked WINE, aren't they?'

'Well, Yes…but who are they for?'

'A Mr Jolly.'

'Yes well, he's on the fifth floor. You'll have to take them up there.'

'No mate. I can't take them inside without your say so and that means you have to sign for them. Look, you're not signing your life away. Just sign!'

'Oh OK then, but you'll have to take them to the fifth floor.'

He signed and printed and I put the time on it.

'Thanks. I'm not going to the fifth floor. This is a door step delivery and you are the door step man. I've delivered. You take them up.'

'I can't take them up. It's not my job.'

'I'm off mate. I haven't got time to discuss your job description. You are now in full charge of four cases marked WINE. Have a Jolly afternoon!' I had been envisaging a much more complicated time involving four trips to the fifth floor and a possible parking ticket, but the door man was quite agreeable in the end. I left swiftly, smiling broadly as I went. I don't think I would ever have made a very good van delivery driver. I probably had the wrong attitude. Commercial deliveries were much simpler.

Trouble afoot

I loaded for the return and delivered. I got back to the yard and dropped my trailer in the line. It was about mid-day and there was a huddle of drivers nearby shouting at each other. I wandered over to see what was going on.

'What's all the fuss about? Someone died?'

'They're telling us we all got to be owner-drivers!'

'You got a piece of paper? Got any reasons or explanations? Any details?'

'Just this. You'll get one in a minute when you check in.'

I was handed a short note and read it.

'Doesn't look very exciting, but it doesn't have a date for it to start. I shouldn't think there's anything to get worried about right away.'

'That's not the point Hughy. Something is going to change and I can't afford to lose my job or buy a fucking lorry.'

'OK. I'll go and see if I can find out some more.'

I wasn't a shop steward and in fact none of us belonged to a union. With hindsight it would probably have been easier if we were, but we weren't and the others seemed to have faith in me because I spoke 'proper'. It's not much of a qualification, and as things developed it turned out to be useless.

'Morning all. There appears to be trouble-at-mill. What's going on?'

'Ah Hugh, yes there's going to be some changes for the future. Here's yours.'

He gave me a piece of paper similar to the others I'd seen.

'Yeah, I've seen it, but what is actually happening, and why?'

'Right, well in brief, costs are going up and profits are going down. The company has got to make some fundamental changes to stay afloat for the future.'

'Costs always go up and generally rates are increased to reflect that. It's been going on for years. So there has to be more to it than that.'

'The shipping company's predictions for the future see a big decline in trade, and in the meantime there's talk, nothing more at the moment, of sending more ships to Mostyn.'

'Why Mostyn?'

'It's cheaper. Watchet dock charges are high by comparison.'

'Is it anything to do with the council wanting to get rid of heavy industry in their picturesque community?'

'Hugh, there may be something in what you say, but I really don't know the answer.'

'Which means, yes it is.'

'I don't know.'

'In short if there are less ships there'll be less work, and if there's less work the docks will probably close putting 50 or 60 people out of work, including us?'

'Look, it's nowhere near that yet. We're just preparing the ground for what may happen.'

'Bearing all you've said in mind, what the company is suggesting is the drivers bear the brunt of the cost, by investing their own money in what will probably be over-priced second hand lorries. And to work under contract for a company which will probably go under in the future, but you don't know when.'

'It's not like that. As owner drivers they'll be able to work wherever they like in the event there's none here.'

'Look mate, if you were offered this exciting deal at this particular time would you invest your life savings in it? I think not. Added to which, hardly any of the blokes have the right paperwork to operate a lorry.'

'It's not so bad a deal and the paperwork can all be taken care of by the company. Out of interest, have you been appointed spokesman or negotiator or something?'

"You know as well as I do the paperwork will be a bodge if they don't have their operators CPC, and no I haven't been appointed by anyone, but you are offering the dodgy deal to me as well as the others. I need to know what I'd be letting myself in for, don't I?'

'It's all I know, Hugh.'

'I don't think it is, but it's all you're going to tell me. What's the next load you have for me anyway?'

'You are going to Duckinfield. Deliver in the morning. Take some time to think about what I've told you, but please don't go spreading panic. Nothing is going to change for several months. I can assure you of that.'

'I can be diplomatic if I choose, but they'll want to know the bare bones. If I don't tell them they'll make their own panic in your office. Those who aren't here today probably will anyway.'

'I'm always here to help.'

I gave him a winning smile and wandered back to the group.

'What do you know Hughy?'

'What you found out?'

'What's going on?'

'What's it all about Mr Clever?'

'Listen lads, I just asked the questions. You lot could have done it. I'm not your representative. Being part of a union might have helped, but listen. I have some information, and in the long term it doesn't sound good, but like I said, right now it's not going to happen for a while.'

'What's a while mean?'

'Look, what he said was things are not going well for the company. Costs are going up and profits are going down. The shipping company says it will divert some of our work to Mostyn because it's cheaper. In the meantime they want us all to think about being owner drivers under the wing of the company. We've got plenty of time to think about it, but for what it's worth my advice is to think hard on it. In any case the main man has assured me nothing will change for several months.'

'How many months are several?'

'Billy, one is one, two is a couple, three is a few and more is several. In this case I'd say several amounts to anywhere between four and twelve. Make it nine as a rough guess. It's fair to all of us. If you want to bail out, you have a sensible amount of time to organise it. If you don't, we have to fight it. But frankly I can't see fighting as being a very good plan. Just think about it, and we'll have another regroup in a week or so with the whole fleet. Perhaps down the Star on a Friday night? You lot alright with that? It's all I have to offer.'

'It don't sound at all good Hughy, but at least we have more news. Thanks for finding out. You're right, we'll think on it and have a meet in the pub over a beer or two.'

'Right then, I'm off to find my load and think. What say we organise a meet for later on at the weekend?'

I took a good long time to go north and I spent a lot of time thinking about my/our predicament. Mine mostly, if I was honest. I had always been master of my own destiny, although always reliant on others for employment. The deal on offer could give me complete independence, except I'd be tied to a contract with a company which didn't appear to be going anywhere. It didn't seem to make sense to me.

If I intended to start my own haulage business it had to be on my own terms with my own work and my own documents, which I had already acquired. What was the point in staying with a sinking ship? There were things we could do to try and solve the problem. For instance, asking for help from our MP. I doubted he'd do anything to prevent the loss of only 50 odd jobs. But who knew?

Searching for job No.52 seemed the best answer, while I still had plenty of time. I resolved to go to the meeting and keep my mouth shut. I would listen to other points of view before putting my thoughts forward. The others had more local contacts than me and got on better with the dockers. Perhaps there might be more points of view, more information and a possible solution. What about a co-operative? Surely it was a possibility.

Rodes had been a good employer. I'd learned a lot and Michael had helped me from the very beginning. It would be a great shame if it all caved in. Even so in business these things happened, and much more frequently than before. Owner driving was for a much more distant future, although there was no harm in finding out the details.

The work continued much as before but there was more disagreement amongst the drivers and panic was afoot. We'd arranged a meeting for all the employed drivers for the following Friday evening. Some owner drivers would be present as well. The more the merrier I thought. We met and I got a pint, sat and listened. Jonny was the self-appointed chairman, and after we all had some beer to be getting on with, he called us to order.

'Right lads,' he began, 'we all know why we're here. Has anyone found out any more details so we can get a better idea of what we're dealing with?'

'It's true about more of the ships going to Mostyn.' Someone offered, 'Shop steward down the dock told me. He thinks there'll be some lay-offs, but he didn't know for sure. It just points that way.'

'Well, it definitely means less work for us, but in the past when there hasn't been a boat in we've found other work by tramping.'

'Yeah, but there's not so much now and we know the rates are crap. You owner drivers won't put up with it for long will you?'

'OK, but none of this is news. We need to find out is why the dock charges have gone up because that's what's forcing the shipping company to go elsewhere. Anybody know anything about it? Can anyone find out?'

'The docks are controlled by the council, which means politics. It also means the costs truly have risen higher than Mostyn or someone is getting back handers, don't it?'

It felt like my turn,

'We could find out about the costs without too much trouble. If something dodgy is going on we'll get stamped on when we try to get to the truth. It will just bear out what we're all thinking.'

'What are we all thinking Hughy?'

'Well, I'm thinking for several years, since the influx of rich people buying holiday homes to live in for three months of the year, there has been a lot of ear bending with the council to try and stop lorries operating in the town. To a certain extent it has been successful because our yard is now out in the country. If I'm right, this is the next step to make it impossible for the shipper to come to Watchet.'

'How will we find out about the costs?'

'I should think the harbour master is a good starting point and possibly customs? I'm only guessing. The next port of call, so to speak, is to go and see our MP when he's next down in Watchet. Whether we have proof of wrongdoing or not he's probably going to run a mile, but it's worth a shot in my view.'

'OK,' said Jonny. 'We're getting nearer to a plan. Has anyone else got anything to offer?'

Ray, one of the owner drivers, stuck his hand up.

'This isn't really my concern as I'm self-employed, but at the moment none of you know what you're being offered. If you found out anything about the council what would you do with it? If you see the MP what are you going to complain about? No one has fired you yet and no one has told you to be owner drivers. Before you go any further and get stuck into upsetting a lot of people, I would suggest you find out a lot more about the company plans. What sort of contract they'll offer you, what the lorries cost, what the terms of the contract are. Stuff like that, because without it any MP is just going to laugh you out of his office. At the moment you've nothing to moan about. They're only guesses, and they might be wrong. It's certainly true that costs are rising and the rates aren't. It's also true the most expensive part of any business is labour. You lot need to have all the facts before you worry yourselves to death.'

Silence descended around the table. Everything he'd said was true. We knew nothing.

'Yeah.' I said. 'It's all true. So Jonny, perhaps we should find out enough so we can have a proper argument with someone.'

'Who's going to find out then?'

'I could do it but it would probably be better if we get the office to tell us altogether rather than individually.'

'You'll ask Gerry then?'

'Yes, I'll do it tomorrow. I'll come down here afterwards and leave a message or see you here, say twelve o'clock?'

Nods of agreement all round. We had several more beers and left but it was clear some blokes were not happy.

The following morning I went to the office and asked the question. I was told the company would print a document outlining the terms of the deal within a couple of weeks. Which lorries would be available, approximate costs, what company support there'd be, etc. But there would not be a group meeting with the drivers. Everyone would receive the proposal and those who wanted to progress further could do so on an individual basis.

I reported back to driver HQ, (The Star), and they all decided to get drunk. Everything was normal so far.

When it arrived, in my view the proposal was far from exciting. The most important advantages were no one would have to spend any money initially, and all costs would come out of earnings on a monthly basis. I thought it would probably attract a few drivers because in practice it would almost be the same as before. The difference would be that weekly pay would change to monthly. I decided to find out a few more details from the office.

'Gerry, this bit of paper suggests to me it's not so much a proposal as a statement of intent. Is that the case?'

'In effect, yes. We will change to an owner driver operation at the end of the year.'

'Which means if no one takes it up we'll all be out of a job?'

'Well yes, but it won't happen suddenly. As drivers leave, retire, or God forbid die, we'll replace them with owner drivers.'

'The proposal says we'd be bound by the contract to only work through Rodes office.'

'Correct.'

'Which vehicles will be available at what price?'

'The vehicle you drive regularly would be priced at £15000.'

'£15K! You must be joking. It's not worth more than 5K.'

'Remember, you're not putting any money up front and you'd pay it off in three years or less. There's no interest on the payments.'

'And the rates will be the same as they are now? Meaning they're not likely to increase while fuel costs will?'

'The rates will be the same, yes. And no, an increase is unlikely in the near future.'

'Well boss, if you get anyone to go with this you'll be on to a winner, but I can't see it happening myself. I could be wrong.'

'It's up to you Hugh. No one's forcing you, but after a while there won't be jobs here for employed drivers.'

'OK. Thanks for the info, see you next week.'

At HQ there was a big crowd of drivers, most of whom had seen the proposals.

'Did you get a price for your lorry Hughy?'

'Yes. £15K.'

'Our prices are about the same. It's a lot of money to buy our jobs.'

'We also have to wonder how long the work will last.'

'Why don't we go and see our MP? Maybe he will help.'

'I shouldn't think so but anything's worth a try.'

'Will you go? You'm more edjucated.'

'I don't think it's about education, but if you want me to I'll try it.'

I arranged a visit for when there was another MP surgery, and went to see the big man on a Saturday morning. He wasn't very helpful but I reported back to the crew.

'What did he say Hughy?'

'It didn't go very well. I outlined our problem and situation and he told me what we already know. We still have jobs. We haven't been threatened with dismissal and it's just a business change of direction. I told him about the rip-off prices of the lorries, and he said it wasn't his job to get us cheap lorries. All of which is true. Then I made the mistake of suggesting he was involved in encouraging the out-of-towners to influence the council in doing away with industry in favour of tourism. Also, despite being our representative in parliament he didn't give a damn about sixty odd of his voters being made unemployed.'

'What did he say to that?'

'He finished the meeting and asked me to leave.'

'Oh Christ Hughy. You lost your diplomacy at the most important time.'

'I did say I probably wasn't the best man for the job.'

'You didn't actually call him a cunt then?' Don chipped in.

'I didn't use that word.'

'I'll go and tell him. Then I'll hit him.'

'I think he's already gone.'

'If he has I'll come back and hit you.'

'Yeah OK Don, but whoever you hit won't solve the problem.'

'Sit down and drink your beer you daft idiot,' said Jonny helpfully.

'What choices are there then?' Someone asked.

'Look, as I see it there're two choices.' I said. 'We can keep working as we are till we get laid off or we can do the deal offered. From my point of view I don't think the deal's a very good one. In our favour we don't have to pay any money out initially, but we can't be sure how long the work will last. Lastly, we can look for other jobs, which is what I'm going to do while I'm still being paid. It's every man for himself.'

I set about it the following week. The hunt for job No.52 was on. The Guinness Book of Records must have been pretty excited.

When you're still employed as a driver you have the advantage of paid transport to search for other work.

I asked in a lot of places.

I went to all the closest and obvious ones like Taunton Valley Transport and another that might have been Bartlands. I went to Wentworths, and as I wasn't concerned about the distance to travel to work I asked in Avonmouth and Bristol. I asked in south Devon and even in Dorset. I looked amongst companies which operated different types of trailers like bulk tippers and tautliners, although I didn't actually have any experience with either. I had no success with any of those enquiries. I visited companies which had own account operations. They were those who only hauled their own goods like Country Cider, which later closed down. In short, after a couple of months I was pleading, but still to no avail. Looking back on it now, I really wonder how there could ever be a shortage of lorry drivers. I'll tell you how I believe it happened towards the end of the story. Meanwhile, I was becoming more than a little desperate.

Quite frequently I used to stop for the night with my brother in Hampshire. He had a groundwork business and various excavating machines. We had a sort of distant relationship which became marginally closer the more frequently I stayed with him. He had bought an old lorry and a low-loader trailer to haul his machines from site to site.

I visited him again.

'So if you have a six month contract, and after you've got all your machines in place what happens to the lorry?'

'It just sits there until we've finished. It's all paid for so there are no outgoings. It doesn't cost me anything. Why?"

I explained the situation at Rodes, and said I was looking for another job. 'There're hundreds of jobs about Huff, (amusing pronunciation of GH in my name). It doesn't matter to you where it is, does it? You're on distance work all the time.'

'I do spend a lot of time living in the lorry it's true, but it's good to go home once in a while.'

'So what have you got in mind?'

'There's a transport company near Taunton which uses a lot of owner drivers and other transport operators. I was thinking you might be interested in putting your lorry with them and giving me the job to drive it. At least it would be earning something instead of sitting here rotting between contracts.'

'I'll think about it. It certainly makes sense but I need to know exactly what they're offering before I commit. I won't be able to pay you very much.'

Oh, here we go, I thought. I knew instinctively I wouldn't earn a lot, but it would keep me on my own patch amongst people I knew. I could just tick over until something better came along. I'd learned over the years that drivers' wages were cyclical. I wasn't really motivated by earning a lot of money. For a short while I just needed something different which paid my rent and put food on the table.

'OK, thanks. I'll pop in and see them when I get back and let you know.'

'Ideal. Now come and see this mammoth excavator I've just bought. It's not new obviously as they cost hundreds of thousands, but it's in good nick and it's only done a few hours.'

I didn't know much about construction machines at the time, but I looked politely and asked what I thought were intelligent questions.

I called in to Taunton Valley Transport on my way home. I spent ages waiting to see the man in charge. Eventually I was able to ask him about the possibilities of what I had in mind. He was interested but thought the lorry might be a bit old. It was. In spite of his reservations, he said if he met the owner and had sight of all the pertinent paperwork like insurances and maintenance sheets, he couldn't see any reason why we couldn't proceed. In the first instance it would be a short term contract of perhaps a year.

I reported back to brother and he said he'd come down when he had a moment. Job No.52 looked like it was in the bag, so long as brother did actually take time out to go to Taunton. I waited but in the meantime I had to keep working. It was fortunate there was plenty to do. It kept everyone else from becoming unhappy as well. It was just like the days before we received the bombshell. Even the office was in good spirits. Some drivers started leaving and sure enough they were replaced with willing owner drivers who all had proud, smiley faces. Was I having second thoughts? No, I thought. Stick to the plan.

Panda

I was in the office one day exchanging signed delivery notes for new ones. 'Hugh.'

'Yes boss.'

'What do you know about Bethnal Green?'

'It's in East London.'

'Anything else?'

'It's near Spitalfields.'

'I know where it is. What happens there at night, for example?'

'Can you get to the point boss?'

'You know we have a lot of stuff going to London at the moment. Recently, a lot of drivers have been signing off their days at Bethnal Green.'

'When we did a lot of work to the north, a lot of drivers used to stop for the night in Sandbach until they closed it off to the rest of the world.'

'Yes, but I think there's more to it than that.'

'Really? Like what?'

'That's what I want to know.'

'It sounds more and more like you want me to spy for you.'

'You have never told me a lie as far as I'm aware.'

'OK, but I could just tell you my registration number when questioned.'

'Look...'

'OK, I'll have a look. Give me an easy one for London, and I mean easy, with a super fine rate, and I might just report back.'

'Thanks. Timber for Purfleet and return with 42 Berth timber.'

'You're spoiling me.'

I found my trailer at the dock trailer park. Red was there roping his load down.

'Hughy. Where are you off to?'

'Purfleet and timber back.'

'Easy one. I've got cork to Joan Street and waste paper back to the mill. Why does he always give me the high loads? He knows I'm shorter than most.'

'Probably thinks it's funny. I've heard there's a new overnighter at Bethnal Green. Do you know where it is and what's so special about it?'

"Yeah. It's brilliant. Easy parking, loads of take-aways, plenty of pubs close by and free to park. I'll show you how to get there when I've finished this. I'll be there tomorrow night if I get finished in time. Are you going now or tomorrow?'

'It's a bit late to go now. I'll have one of those rare nights at home.'

Red got out his A to Z.

'Look mate, it's right here next to the railway arches, between the A10 and A11. Easy one, off the A13. Got it? It's best to get there around six or seven or it starts getting crowded.'

'Thanks Red. I'll catch you there tomorrow.'

I set off in the middle of the night as it was best to get through the city early in the morning. I delivered in Purfleet and stopped for breakfast at the Noakes, which now unfortunately seems to have disappeared. It was really popular with lorry drivers. It had a fuel station next to it as well so it was a useful refuelling point. Many of those old cafes we used to stop at have long vanished, along with the good food. I got loaded at Tilbury and was ready to go by lunchtime, so I went back to the Noakes. I had to waste a bit of time until I could get on to the park at Bethnal Green. We didn't get many easy days which required no waiting around. They mostly happened when we didn't want them. I had plenty of time for a wash and change so I wouldn't have to hunt around for a wash house in central London. It's quite amazing the scarcity of places to wash in the biggest city in the world.

I eventually found the recommended park quite easily. I noticed there were five of Streets lorries already there, but not Red's. He must have got held up, or couldn't find a ladder to get on top of his load of waste paper. By seven thirty there were a total of nine of us and Red had finally arrived. Several other lorries parked there as well. Don was there which meant there'd be some heavy drinking.

The parking was similar to Sandbach in that it was fairly central to the pubs and take away shops. Of course it had the obligatory railway line behind it, which was supported by low arches. We parked facing the pubs, of which there were plenty and some more along the side of the cobbled parking area. I got out for a chat to see who was staying and to find out what all the fuss was about. Usually, one overnight stop is much the same as another apart from the company you had for the evening.

'You found it alright then, Hughy.'

'Yes. Pretty easy Red, even for me.'

'It's a useful stop because it's only half an hour to get out to the country in the morning. It's also a good, rowdy place for the night.'

'Which is the best pub? If I had one in each to find out, I'd never find the lorry after.'

'They're all good but most of us use the one with the bright lights. Hey, come on, let's get some fish and chips unless you fancy the Chinese.'

'I always throw up after beer and Chinese. I don't know why people don't just buy it and chuck it down the toilet to cut out the middle man.'

'Fish and chips it is then. There's no Boddingtons here so we've got to drink the southerner's muck.'

'Southern beer's fine Red. You're just not used to it.'

We all ate something and headed to the bar.

Within half an hour it became clear why Bethnal Green was so popular. The stripper started at eight thirty.

'They got a stripper in every pub here but we reckon they're prettier in this one.' Red shouted above the music.

She danced and stripped for half an hour and then took a break. Another girl came on and repeated. The girls were followed by forty five minutes of loud music while we got drunker and drunker. Yet another stripper started dancing. Don was becoming louder and very drunk. He stood right in front of the girl and was almost touching her. We told him to back off and behave. He took no notice. Then the barman came out and pulled him back to the bar. It didn't go down well, and he started getting punchy while shouting and swearing. The end result was he was physically thrown out by a couple of heavies who probably worked for the pub. It seemed like they often had to deal with bad behaviour. They certainly didn't seem at all concerned about getting rid of Don.

We all thought he'd go back to his lorry and sleep it off, but he kept shouting and knocking on the windows. Some of us went out to calm him down, but without success. In our absence the barman had called the police. A Panda[2] car turned up and two uniformed coppers got out. By now it was fairly clear who the culprit was, so they spoke to Don.

'The barman called us out, young man. Says you're causing a disturbance and won't go home.'

'Ssssnot me ossifer.' Was Don's weak response.

'Well you're clearly very drunk.'

'Arrrdly shtarted yet.'

'We think you've definitely had enough beer for tonight and it's for the best if you come with us.'

'Carrnt go nowaare wizs yoooz. Gotta go 'ome shoon. Mahh lorrrysh jush over zare.'

They made to get hold of him.

'Nah, nah carrrnt go wizg you. Look ossifas, if I tellsh yoooz a good joke will yoose lemme go back to mah lorrrry?'

The coppers looked at each other, and one said,

'If the joke is really good and we haven't heard it before, and we've heard a lot, we will escort you back to your lorry where you will stay. Do you understand?'

'Yessher absholutely!'

'Right go on, let's hear it.'

'Yeah, the joke. Whash the diffrensh tween a pair of knickersh and a Panda?'

They looked at each other and at us. We shrugged, and then they looked back at Don.

'We don't know lad. What is the difference between a pair of knickers and a Panda?'

'Oh itsheaaaasy! You can only get one cunt in a pair of knickersh.'

---

[2] Apart from being a large furry bear affair, a PANDA was a black police car with white panels painted on the side to make it more visible. They later became blue and white. They were phased out in the mid-1980s in favour of the 'Jam Sandwich'.

We really did think the Old Bill would arrest him immediately. They looked at Don with big smiles and then burst out laughing.

'It's not often we hear a good one from a drunk. OK, now just piss off back to your lorry and not another peep out of you. Got it?'

'Yesshh, oh good fankyoose. I'll go now. Whish one issshit?'

Three of us bundled him into his lorry and locked the doors. He was lucky. We apologised to the barman so as to preserve our standing for future visits. He laughed it off and said it happens quite often. 'You carrot crunchers often get over excited about our luscious girls.' Personally I thought his remark was overstated, but so what.

We woke Don up at 5am.

'I'm not very well. I don't want to go.'

'It's understandable, but if you don't go now you'll be blocked in all day by the cars which park here.'

'Yeah...don't want that.'

'We're going in ten minutes.'

'OK. I won't be far behind. Breakfast at Theale?'

'Good idea.'

We sat down to breakfast about an hour later.

'You look like shit, Don.'

'Thanks, but these bangers and beans will spruce me up.'

I delivered in Yeovil and got back to the yard by mid-morning. None of the others were there.

'Morning boss. 007 reporting for de-briefing.'

'Yes. Good morning Hugh. Good night? Now, tell me all about it.'

'Gerry, I can't be heard recounting this. I'll get lynched.'

'OK. Let's take a stroll.'

'Well like I said, Bethnal Green is much the same as Sandbach, but as you know there are a lot of railway lines at the back. They're raised on arches and each arch has a door. Inside there are workshops and small stores from where they distribute their stuff.'

'This is sounding interesting.'

'Yeah, well we didn't go anywhere near the stores under the railway lines. There're a lot of pubs and take-aways close by. We spent the night in one."

'Why one?'

'Because it has the best strippers.'

'Strippers? Is that it?'

'Yes.'

'Do they strip off…well…completely?'

'Oh yes, absolutely completely.'

'Isn't that illegal? I mean in a pub?'

'Probably. Nearly everything else is, but if you're concerned about the amount of flesh shown to your lovely drivers you should take it up with the Home Office.'

'You're taking the piss Hugh. That's it? There's nothing more?'

'No. Nothing more. What did you think was going on?'

'I thought the same sort of thing you all did in Northampton with the toilet rolls.'

'What was that sort of thing Gerry?'

'Christ Hugh, did you think we didn't know?'

'Didn't know what?'

'Oh never mind. Just forget I asked you to do this job will you?'

'I'm really good at forgetting things Gerry. I might even get a degree in it.'

'Yes, good man. Right, there are cork bales for Chingford. Delivery tomorrow and you can do one to Chard now to fill in the time. Then tomorrow there are CKDs from Leighton Buzzard for return to the dock.'

'Great, we have a plan.'

Don rolled in at that particular moment and gingerly got out of his lorry.

'Don doesn't look very well.'

'It might be his age.' I said helpfully.

'He's only twenty-six!'

'Exactly. I best be getting on then.'

Acronyms

Later in the day I picked up my load of cork bales for north London. Although I'd never asked for details, I supposed the bales were constructed by forming a make-shift crate out of small pallet planks. A hessian sack was put inside and then stuffed full of all sorts of small corks. The whole package was stapled together with an industrial stapler. That's what they looked like, anyway. They were all loaded and unloaded by hand. They could get a fair number on a high load which was then sheeted. The cork would eventually go to companies which supplied stoppering for bottles and jars.

We got a lot of cork of all varieties from Portugal. Every different cut and shape had a different use. We used to take the bales to a distribution store in Chingford for the most part, but there were other destinations which were nearly all in London. The drop in Chingford was only just off the North Circular Road so it was easy to find, but you did have to go early in the morning. Consequently, there was always a queue waiting to unload. There was a permanent crew of blokes to help with unloading and to be fair they worked hard and swiftly.

They were all equipped with a 'dockers hook' or 'hay hook', sometimes called a grip. It looked like an upside down clothes hanger, but with most of the arms missing. The short horizontal piece was the grip which was normally wooden. A long hook with a sharp spike protruded from it. It was used to stick into a bale, which made it easier to manhandle and drag to where it had to be put. We didn't have any hooks, but we were required to present each bale by hand to a man who did have one. He'd drag it up onto the heap.

I always remember one of the crew had a permanent nose dribble. It was as if he had a constant cold and had forgotten his handkerchief. It's was really off-putting if you had to work next to him. If it was a cold, he'd had it for more than five years! I don't know why I didn't ask him, but it was a bit personal and he didn't ooze personality. It was probably best ignored.

Finally I was away to Leighton Buzzard where the same crowd of us would form another orderly queue to wait to load CKDs.

Now CKD was another bit of curiosity. What did CKD stand for? You'd think it would be an acronym for a really complicated and intelligent piece of engineering, wouldn't you? It could have signified really long words which no one outside the business could possibly understand. You'd be wrong. It stands for Completely Knocked Down. CKDs were basically car kits. They were a cheaper way of exporting complete cars and they would be assembled by other companies in the country of destination. They could have been called Ks, or kits, but I suppose that'd be too simple. The previous night Don himself could almost have been described as a CKD. I have often wondered who would be offered a job to think up ridiculous names and acronyms for stuff. I should think its good work for someone with loads of imagination.

Much later and in between haulage jobs, I had cause to find out what foodstuffs attracted VAT. The list of things which did or didn't is gobsmackingly long. In fact it was so long I never found out the answer to my enquiry, as I ran out of time. In my search, I did discover Ginger Bread Men did not attract VAT. Ginger Bread Men with two chocolate dots for eyes similarly did not attract VAT, but Ginger Bread Men with two chocolate dots for eyes and one extra chocolate dot for a nose did attract VAT on the whole Ginger Bread Man product. I also discovered cream did not attract VAT, but Baked Alaska did, whether it was warm or not. The list was huge. I kept thinking to myself, why would a government spend soooo much time and money on making a list so extensively long and exact just in order to raise revenue and show a profit. Tax has to show a profit or there'd be no reason to raise it, would there?

While we're on the subject Taxi is another interesting word. Its origin is from the Greek but obviously it's spelt differently and it means tax. Would you believe it?

It's quite interesting to know these things because as a nation we pay more tax than you can shake a fist at. It wasn't always so. In my working life there have been all sorts of exciting new taxes invented. Community tax, airport tax, insurance premium tax, national insurance tax, city congestion tax, fuel tax, VAT, etc. Forgive me if I've missed some out. I know there are hundreds more. Then, of course there is income tax which is a tax for permitting you to work your ass off. I'm really surprised there hasn't been an uprising by now. We Brits do tend to just sit on our hands and encourage governments to dump shit on us. If it were an annual international competition we'd win the gold every year.

Curiosity has always been a major part of my personality and for that reason I always carried a dictionary/thesaurus on my travels. I later bought a book on word origins too. Fascinating stuff.

How time flies. It was finally my turn to load cars in boxes. In honesty, we didn't have to wait long. It wasn't just waiting for the sake of it which so many hauliers have to endure. The lorries were loaded as they arrived and we only had to wait for the queue to diminish. Every driver waited until the last lorry was loaded and we helped each other to secure them. We'd all return together.

Camaraderie was pretty strong in those days, especially amongst same company drivers. If we saw a driver from our region who was broken down, we'd always stop to see if we could help. A useless exercise in my case! The custom decreased as more and more drivers became self-employed or were paid on difficult-to-earn bonuses. Many good human customs changed in our quest to worship our new god, money.

There were bridges to negotiate when leaving Leighton Buzzard and CKDs made quite a high load. We were soon all ready to leave. 'Anyone know how high the bridge is on the Wing road?' Al asked.

'About fourteen foot?'

'About, is not very accurate is it? Either we can get under it or we can't.'

'Depends how high these loads are, dunnit?'

'Not entirely no, but anyway they're not more than fourteen foot cos it's the law, innit?'

'Is it?'

'Who's got a tape measure?'

'Doesn't make any difference how high the loads are if we don't know the bridge height.'

'Good point.'

Al asked one of the loaders.

'Thirteen feet nine I think, mate.'

'You think?'

'Look,' I said. 'I'm going to go the long way round. You lot go whichever way you like and I'll see you for a cuppa in Leigh Delamare.'

'It takes ages that way.'

'It'll take longer your way if you can't get under the bridge. I'm off.'

I stopped at the motorway service station and waited half an hour until a couple of the others showed up.

'Where have you lot been? You said it was quicker under the bridges.'

'It's like this see. Ray went first and he got stuck under the bridge. It is thirteen nine and I reckon his load was thirteen nine and a quarter. Anyway he went under. Really slowly like and it cut all his ropes. He had to stop and retie them all.'

'And you lot?'

'We stopped all the traffic, backed up, and came out the long way. The Old Bill turned up half way through. To assist, they said.'

'What a palaver. Still we know how high it is now. It's probably time to invest in a measuring stick.'

'They're called tape measures now.'

'Thanks Dave. I'll remember that when I go to the measuring stick shop.'

'Ray's not very lucky with bridges is he? You remember when he brought tractors back under the bridges at Combe Florey and bent all the exhaust pipes to right angles?'

'Yeah, I was in the dock when he came in. I liked the modern design.'

More owner drivers had joined the fleet. I thought Job No52 was a long time in the confirmation, so I planned to call in on brother at the earliest opportunity. I had tried ringing him but he was never at home. In the meantime, there were a few loads to go to the north. I was assigned one for Golborne and a return load from a tinned food factory in Wigan. It had a loading time set at 11.30am so it had to be another middle-of-the-night start time. It wasn't actually a return load. It was bound for a supermarket RDC, (regional distribution centre), at Weybridge in Surrey. I was to be given a timed delivery when I loaded.

I accomplished the first part of my mission without mishap. I don't know why but it was an effort to get out of bed in the middle of the night. I checked in at the gatehouse to the food factory, fifteen minutes before my booking time.

'Morning driver, what's your loading time? Do you have load number?'

'Load time is 11.30am and no, I don't have a number.'

'Destination?'

'Weybridge'

'Hang on a minute.' He made a phone call,

'Your load number is 101.'

'Oh goody!'

'Right driver, go over there and wait with the others.'

'I don't have to wait mate, my loading time is only five minutes away.'

'Everyone's gotta wait mate, it's how it is.'

'OK, I'll wait.' I said, not wanting to upset the first line of defence.

I parked behind the rest of the lorries in a queue and waited, and waited, and waited. After about forty minutes I got out of the lorry and wandered over to the others in the queue and asked the question,

'How long have you blokes been waiting?' The immediate reply was,

'I been here since 7.45am. I got an eight o'clock loading time, but it's always the same every time I come here. Loading times don't mean squat.'

'I got an 11.30 booking so I could be here for days.'

'No mate, not days. They have to clear the back log for each day, on the day. But yes, you could be here a very long time.'

'So the delivery time'll be altered to suit?'

'No, they don't give a shit about drivers' hours. They don't give a shit about the other end. They just don't give a shit, period!'

'Wonderful. Is there anywhere to eat?'

'No, nor anywhere to wash up if you're a late loader but there's a really good café round the corner, about a quarter mile away. It's open till midnight. I'll show you if we're still here together at lunch. I'm sure we will be.'

'Lunch? You're kidding, right?'

'No son, just sit and relax like you're waiting for a hospital appointment.'

'I might need one if it's a very long wait.'

'I should call your doctor and book one now, then.'

We did have lunch together with several others. It was excellent, as my companion had said. The queue moved forward very slowly, but if you'd been monitoring the movement you'd probably have given up the will to live. I was finally called in to load at 5.30pm. I'd been sitting on my hands for six hours just waiting to load despite having arrived at my allotted loading time. The loading crew were a happy bunch, as they often are in the north. They explained the booking time farce was put together by an office whose staff had never set foot in the factory. It wasn't their problem and it wasn't their job. They joked about the left hand not knowing what the right hand was doing. Generously, they gave me a 24 pack of baked beans for my trouble. It might prove handy for supper. I finished covering and securing the load at almost 7pm and was given my delivery notes. They stated I'd been allocated a 9.30am delivery. I worked it out quickly. If I were to stick to drivers' hours rules, it would be almost impossible to achieve. I pointed it out.

'It's your delivery time driver. I don't know and I don't care about drivers' hours laws. That's your problem. If you're not there on time they could reject the load. If the load's rejected and it's your fault, you probably won't get paid. Work it out for yourself. Bye.'

I worked it out and knew I'd have to find another ingenious way to bend the law. It also meant less sleep but I slept less when I was driving than I do now. I phoned the office to explain the dilemma.

'I thought you might have phoned me if there was a problem.'

'There's no public phone on site.'

'OK, well find some way to do it and don't tell me about it. So long as your records are more or less in order, it'll be fine.'

'Fuck the records. Call you tomorrow.'

I hung up. I wasn't very impressed with the support I was getting, but it's the lorry drivers' life.

I'd been clever enough to take my tachograph card out before I loaded and I knew I could park up at the café. It would incur only about two hours and one mile without a card in place. I reckoned nobody would notice. It would give me ample time to even get to France, (I wished).

I ate well, had a couple of beers at a nearby pub and slept well. I was on the road heading south at 3.30am, knowing I had plenty of time. There would be no rush. Breakfast at Hollies seemed like a good plan.

Breakfast was tasty and heartening. There was plenty of good company to talk with about interesting stuff like diesel engines, gearboxes, different types of loads and of course, wages. I enjoyed it for once. I was on my way 45 minutes later and I arrived at destination at 09.25.

'You got a 9.30 delivery driver.' The gateman said, sounding like he thought I was late.

'Which means, John, I'm early.' Everyone was called John.

'Only just.'

'There's no just about it. Either I am or I'm not, and I am.'

'Alright driver, there's no need to sound cocky.'

'What's next?'

'Go over there, back into the line of lorries and wait your turn.' He said, almost excitedly.

'You're saying all of them are going to unload before me? You're joking.'

'It's no joke. Join the gang.'

Despite being a surly little git, he wasn't wrong. I waited and waited and…well you know the rest.

Eventually, I was empty at 5.30pm again. It seemed like a popular time in the food industry. I may well have let loose a few 'FUCKS' at the staff, but it didn't do any good, and I didn't get any 'thanks-for-coming' 24 packs of anything. It could be my attitude, but for goodness sake what goes on in that business?

I thought at the time perhaps it was a one-off load and I was just unlucky, but after talking to other drivers, I discovered that it was normal practice. I'd spent nearly a whole duty period waiting to load and unload. In the future, as an employed driver, I was to do no more than about half a dozen supermarket RDC deliveries. They were all the same regarding waiting times. When I became a haulier in my own right I refused several supermarket RDC deliveries, because it was more profitable to return home empty than to waste time waiting for them to do something.

I called brother and told his wife I'd be later than expected but I was on my way. She told me she was going out. The main man would be back soon and it was his birthday. Did I know? I made a mental note on an old fag packet to buy him something on the way. In those early days of mechanical tachographs it was possible to disconnect the speedometer cable, which in effect disabled the spy machine. Whilst it was disabled it registered as 'REST' on the graph. This was true even if you were flying along at 60mph. It was quite handy in times of need, but not to be used too often. If you were spotted, or worse stopped, it would become apparent you weren't doing exactly what Whitehall had instructed. God forbid. Later the disconnection practice became impossible but there were other methods. Necessity is the mother of invention.

I think this is a good time to give you my informed views on the modern problem we're all experiencing with supply. Fast forward to 2021/2 →

Hurry up and wait

The word chain has several meanings in modern English. However, to most of us it represents a piece of engineering used for pulling, lifting or lowering objects. An anchor chain would be a good example. A supply chain is very similar but figuratively used. A chain has several or many links, but all the links have to be joined together in order for the whole to function correctly. In the UK the supply chain is a misnomer. Whilst it has many links they are not joined together. We'll call it a system for now. In fact it's a failed system. Highways authorities refer to roads which are no longer fit for purpose as failed.

The function of a supply system or chain is to deliver goods from their manufacturing origin to the end user. There are various methods including rail, air, sea and road. All of those methods require the use of a lorry because an airport, sea port and rail terminal may not be right next to the manufacturer. It is not yet possible to tele-port goods as they do in sci-fi movies, so at some point in its journey everything has to be moved by lorry. It follows road transport is the single most important link in any supply chain or system.

The UK supply system is a series of disconnected links which have neither interest nor intention of making the whole work together. The UK is not unique. The problems we've experienced recently have been reported throughout Europe, and even in the USA and Canada.

The cause of the UK supply failure has been blamed on the road haulage industry. Haulage associations, the serving government and the media in general were in agreement. They believed the root cause was an unprecedented lack of professionally trained drivers.

There is a shortage of drivers, and there has been for more than twenty-five years. Our new generation are not keen on doing a job which is poorly paid and involves many hours work. Existing drivers are getting older and approaching retirement age. It's all true.

But consider this. Before the government decided on implementing Brexit and before the pandemic, the shortage of drivers was still evident. The problem has been brewing for thirty years but was seldom mentioned. Then suddenly it was. In those days no one felt it necessary to act, because to an extent the supply system functioned.

Those who laid blame very recently agreed on a figure to represent the shortage. It was 100,000.

It's curious to note that everything in our lives, our environment and our society throughout our planet is mathematical. It even includes music. So the 100,000 perceived lack of drivers is an excellent lead-in to my informed opinion.

I'd like you to cast your minds back to the short passages regarding drivers' hours' regulations, and the last story about my journey to Weybridge. Firstly, a professional LGV driver is not permitted by law to work more than 13.5 hours in any daily duty period of 15 hours. Secondly I think we can agree my experience in a RDC could not be taken as an average. I can be reasonable when I feel like it.

We'll assume the average waiting time for a lorry driver before loading and before unloading is two hours. It would therefore total four hours of unproductive time in any one duty period.

Both government and haulage associations have been quoted as saying there are 268,000 LGV vehicles licenced to operate throughout the UK. With regard to the shortage of drivers neither government nor haulage associations have been specific. It wasn't said whether we lack 100,000 lorries with drivers, or if we already have 100,000 lorries standing idle because there's no one to drive them. If it were the former it would mean we need to increase the total UK operating fleet to 368,000 vehicles. I don't think that's the case. The latter might be true but I believe the figure is closer to 50,000 because several vehicles are operated for 24 hours with two drivers. My estimate would reduce the lorries actually operating in the UK to 218,000.

218,000 lorry drivers who are unproductive for four hours in each daily duty period equals a total of 872,000 lost man hours every single day. If we were to take the lost man hours and divide them by 15 hours which is the total daily duty period allowed to LGV drivers, the answer is 58,133.

If the existing workforce did not have to spend its time waiting, 58,133 drivers would be back on our roads immediately, working their asses off.

Our apparent lack of highly qualified driving personnel is because supermarket warehouses, container ports, (to name two of the very worst culprits), factories in general and archaic British working practices are wasting our time. I find it laughable the man government has recently chosen to investigate the crisis is an ex CEO of a global supermarket company. Even if he managed to uncover the truth, he is very unlikely to stick his hand up and say, 'I have to take 50% of the blame for creating the failure of the supply system,' is he? Government incompetence is awe inspiring.

Very recently, a newspaper called Trans Info reported both the Portuguese and Spanish governments had issued a directive. It stated all vehicles delivering or collecting at supermarket RDCs have to be loaded or unloaded within one hour of arrival at their premises. When one hour has passed, hauliers are entitled to charge for waiting times. Unfortunately the directive was not applied to container terminals. There were several caveats applied to the directive and a period to phase it in. I would guess at least a third of their driver shortage problems will disappear.

When Trans Info got in touch with the UK for a comment on the Spanish directive, a government official said the major problem was different in the UK. They always do, don't they? It was solely down to staff shortages. I can assure you the reply was wholly incorrect because there were no staff shortages in the last part of the last century. I can remember people clambering over themselves to get a job in a RDC. The problem is exactly the same now as it was then. The failure is because of a complete absence of effective management. If it were true staff shortages were hampering unloading times, why doesn't management alter the work load to compensate?

The incumbent British government of 2021/2 was not content with a domestic supply system failure which had been brewing for over 30 years. So it decided to invent its very own international supply system failure with the implementation of Brexit customs rules. It appears to be working admirably!

According to reports the new customs system is not fit for purpose. There are media reports that drivers have had to wait eight hours in each port. That's sixteen unproductive man hours. I don't know the number of lorries which used to pass through the ports on a daily basis. When you have the information, you can do the same mathematics as I did.

As a note, my analysis of the supply failure has been borne out by recently published reports in the Wall Street Journal, which confirm the same story in the USA. Hauliers sometimes have to wait 15 hours or more before loading or unloading.

Birthday dinner

I didn't forget brother's birthday and called in at an off license. I bought a bottle of whisky in a presentation tin. It was decorated with pictures of Scottish soldiers in bearskins playing bagpipes. It resembled a box of tea biscuits. I hastened over to his gaff, fixed the tachograph intervention and went in to see him carrying my overnight kit. I was looking forward to sleeping in a real bed for the night.

'Hi Bruv, how goes it my man?'

'Huff. Excellent. I've just got in and found the note with your name on it. Wife's fucked off for the night so we'll have to entertain ourselves. Probably take you to dinner. Fancy that?'

'It sounds good. Happy Birthday! I was warned but I only had time to get you a small present. There're not many places to stop in the lorry, so I was only able to get you a tin of shortbread. Sorry.'

'Oh thanks, yes, It's kind of you. No problem, I like shortbread. Occasionally.'

He shook my hand, took the gift, gave it a quick glance and a shake, (it was well packed inside), and he put it on the top shelf of the kitchen dresser. We talked about this and that. I had a wash and change and then we headed out for a couple of drinks before dinner.

Over drinks Bruv told me a few funny stories about his business. Groundwork, as the name suggests, is about the first stage of construction. The land needs to be cleared before the building work can begin. It's not always the case but on top of most virgin land is topsoil. Topsoil is a saleable commodity because in most areas you need it to grow things. Beneath is subsoil which is normally less productive. I'll tell you more when we cover my experience in construction transport. Most ground workers know the value of topsoil and everything they dig is considered salvage. Topsoil is generally saved for sale at a later date. Bruv did a lot of soil removal, and on quite a large scale. On any job he would scrape off the topsoil and haul it to a store before commencing on the initial dig for building. Of course there were many others who knew the value of topsoil. He employed various owner operator tipper drivers and they'd all talk amongst themselves in the pub. Quite often those who weren't contracted on a job would join the queue to load, and then sell what they loaded. It was theft to all intents and purposes. To stop it happening, Bruv told me he'd invented a system of passwords. The driver had to give the correct password to the digger driver before he'd be loaded. On his birthday night he'd rung the digger driver for the following days' work and given him the password.

'And what is it for tomorrow?' I asked.

'Bosoms.' He said. 'No one's going to think of it first time unless the digger driver is tricking me. Clearly it's not fool proof but it's worked for a few weeks. What do you think?'

'Excellent password!'

'I thought so. Come on. Let's have dinner, I'm starving.'

Dinner was good and in some local swanky restaurant. I thought it a bit overpriced but I wasn't paying. When we reached the coffee course I brought up the true purpose of my visit.

'Look,' he said. 'I've got a big job starting the week after next, so next week I'll be moving all the machinery over there. When it's done the machines shouldn't move for about ten months to a year. It depends how it goes. Before I start the move, I could go down to sleepy Somerset and meet your man. If he tells me what I want to know I could start a contract with them on the first Monday of next month. You set up a meeting for the Saturday morning coming, let me know and I'll go down. How's that?'

'OK. It should work. I'll do that then.'

'Good man. Do you want a Cognac?'

'Yes, thanks. Don't forget the paperwork he wants or it'll be a wasted trip.'

'Two Cognacs please,' he shouted and then to me he said, 'Surprisingly I've got the paperwork ready to go.'

I called the office in the morning.

'Where've you been Hugh? I had a load ready for you at two o'clock yesterday afternoon.'

'I was waiting in the queue. There are no phones, no café, no wash houses, no nothing. I got out at 6pm, but I'm not far away. I'm near Byfleet.'

'Oh OK. Another day, another adventure. There was a load of tiles near Theale to go to Penzance and return with clay for export. I'll check if it's still there. If you don't hear from me in 15 minutes just do that. Collect from…'

'I know where it is.'

'Yes Redlands, excellent. If you don't hear from me soon I'll see you tomorrow.'

What a stroke of luck, I'd be able to pass by Taunton Valley on the return from Penzance. I'd be home on Friday night ready for a meet with Bruv on Saturday morning. I love it when a plan comes together.

I didn't have to wait in Redlands. I was in, loaded and out before ten o'clock, with plenty of time to deliver in Penzance. The clay collection place worked 24 hours so there were no worries there. I would probably be returning to base on

Friday morning with plenty of time to call in at Taunton Valley and arrange a meeting.

I even had time for a filling Devonshire lunch at Whiddon Down. I managed to load directly after discharging the tiles and I called into Taunton Valley just before lunch the following day. The manager was in a good mood and we arranged a meeting with brother for Saturday morning at eleven o'clock. I had an early finish back at base and returned home. I called him to confirm the meet. All fixed.

I arrived on the dot, but my brother didn't. We waited and then we waited some more. At 12.30 the manager said he was going to finish up soon for the weekend. Brother still hadn't arrived. I called him and his wife said he'd left home at 6am so 'he shouldn't be long.' Finally, at quarter to one he turned up.

'Where the fuck have you been?' I said.

'Yeah, sorry, I had a lot to do for next weeks' move but anyway I'm here now. I have all the papers. Where is he?'

I showed him in and did the introductions. They were only in there for about ten minutes and then brother emerged.

'OK, it's all set up. Start Monday after next just in case I have problems with the machine move. You do exactly what Dave tells you and I'll pay you. What could be easier? They pay by self-billing at the end of each month. You alright with that?'

'What are you going to pay me?'

'What do you get now?'

"Depends, but on average £350 per week plus expenses.'

'I can't pay you that much. Make it £300 including expenses.'

I knew it wasn't going to be a lot but I also knew my time was limited at Rodes. This would have to be a stop-gap.

'Well, OK, but it will be every week, yeah?'

'Of course, I'll send a cheque made out to cash. Understand? You will effectively be self-employed, got it?'

This wasn't going to be very good, I was thinking.

'Got it.'

'Jolly good. Pick the lorry up two weeks from now. You can get a lift up I suppose?'

'I'll think of something.'

'Great, well that's it. I have to go. See you soon. Ring me before you come up. Bye Huff.'

And he was gone. Job No52 was confirmed, but I was a bit anxious. In hindsight it was a good thing, as life got considerably better in the future. I had to break out of the rut I was in at Rodes which was not going to last long. It was time to bite the bullet. I bit, and never looked back.

I gave my notice the following Monday. Gerry said he was sad to see me go despite our turbulent history, but remarked, if I had no intention in being an owner-driver it was probably in my best interest. He wished me luck and I reciprocated.

When I left I received my 'week in hand' which was only the £150 less tax I'd earned as basic money the last time I'd re-joined. It was better than nothing.

I managed to get a lift up to Hampshire to collect the new lorry with a friend who was going to the airport.

Job No52. The Flying Dune

My brother's lorry was a Seddon Atkinson of dubious and indeterminate age. It had spent a good deal of its life in Saudi Arabia so the registration plates were for imported vehicles. It had a full sleeper cab. It was equipped with basic comforts and surprisingly, it was very clean. It even had a working radio. I think it was powered by a 320 Cummins diesel and it smoked a lot. Apparently the smoke was caused by the air cleaner having been removed more times than it had been fitted. They said the sand and dust of the desert kept clogging it up. Mechanics would correct me I expect, but it's what I was told. It didn't seem a very good idea but anyway it worked fine. The Seddon was also amazingly powerful compared to what felt like a lifetime with Magirus Deutz.

The gearbox on the Deutz took a lot of getting used to, but Bruv's Seddon had what I think was called a Fuller H box. On the trip home I was getting very confused when shifting gears. First gear was where it usually was, but second was where third normally was and third was where second should have been. Then it had a range change to give it an extra layer of gears and you could split each one. I'm not going to bore you with lorry gearbox configurations but you drivers out there will know what I'm talking about, won't you?

The paintwork was somewhat faded and it had no markings or signwriting, so I was incognito.

Dave started me off with shunting trailers from the South Molton chipboard factory to the yard at Taunton. The Seddon certainly did fly up and down those steep hills. It gave me a good opportunity to get to know the vehicle which was to be my home for a while. It wasn't to be a very long because working for family is not always a good solution. In the end, I did manage about six months.

There weren't many memorable occasions but there were a few.

I found the start off period seemed to go on forever and eventually had a moan in the office about the lorry not earning very much. I was only doing two local trips a day. In the end brother came down and had a shouting match in the office, and I was given long distance work at last. Their fleet drivers were nearly all owner-operators. Some were happy and doing well but at least half were always moaning about the money. It appeared if you had friends in the office everything went swimmingly. If not, well, life was hard. At the time I felt it wasn't really my concern so I just did what I was told with a smile and kept quiet. The earnings did go up a bit but it was clear brother wasn't going to make a million. However, it made a small profit and it was better than standing idle waiting for the next machine move.

At the time I was living in the country with my girlfriend. You didn't think I had any of those did you? It was convenient because the village headman said I could park the lorry in the square when I was home. It saved me the commuting time.

The Flying Dune was very reliable despite its age and outward appearances. I was surprised. I got back into the routine of long days and very early morning starts. I quite enjoyed it but I missed the camaraderie of Rodes transport, and to an extent the friends I'd made there over the years. Most of the new work I was doing was confined to southern and south-east England. It was all controlled by the office, so there was no chance of wandering the world again.

One day I did a delivery to somewhere in Suffolk and was told to go to Harwich dock to reload chipboard for Devon. One of our owner-drivers was already there. We had a chat while we were waiting. I sat in his cab and he offered me a cup of tea which he'd just brewed.

'This is a great lorry.' I ventured.

'Oh yeah, the bees-knees mate. It's brand spanking new. This is its maiden trip. Pulls like a train. It's a 290.'

'I expect it's better on fuel than mine too. Not that it's my concern really.'

'Well, it's not so hot. They're all about the same, but I would hope it'll return about 7 or 8mpg.'

'You've got all the kit haven't you? It's like a camper.'

'It's got every extra there is.'

'Ah look, seems you're next. I'll give you a hand to sheet it later.'

'Thanks, I'll look out for you.'

Some drivers can be very proud of the lorries they drive and obviously if you've bought one, you'd be even prouder. I always liked to personalise mine but I only added things which made life more comfortable. As I've said, cleaning wasn't something I ever got to grips with, so on the whole I didn't do it.

We helped each other to secure both loads, and when we'd finished my new acquaintance said,

'You know your way out don't you? Yeah, well there's a good café once we get over the big long hill. Why don't we meet up there and get a bite to eat?'

'Sounds like a plan,' I replied. 'Yep, I know my way out. Catch you at the café.'

He climbed into his cab and looked as proud as punch.

'I'll wait for you there because I expect I'll get up the hill long before you've started,' he laughed.

'You're probably right. See you later.'

He started off quite well and his lorry did seem to have a lot of power. He was about 150 yards ahead of me at the bottom of the hill and going well. I gave The Dune as much 'welly' as I could muster. Great clouds of black smoke blew out of the exhaust stacks as I raced up the hill behind him. Within only about a minute I was right behind. I knew I was going to break the law of etiquette but you can't just slow a lorry up on a hill to be polite. I pulled out to overtake. I could see smoke like an old steam engine in the mirrors and the engine noise was like an inferno. The cab was shaking and I was starting to go up through the gears. Unheard of! Very soon I was alongside his cab so I waved as I shot past. He looked straight ahead and made no acknowledgement at all. He was a speck of dust in the mirror glass when I pulled into the café. I parked up and waited. After what seemed an age he drove past without stopping. Oh dear, I thought.

I've blotted my copybook. Some people have no sense of humour. I thought it was quite funny but he never spoke to me again.

Getting paid though was no laughing matter. For the first two or three weeks the cheques arrived on time but then there were gaps. Sometimes the gaps were a fortnight but later on it became a month or more. I continued to work, but in the end we had a row by phone. He promised to pay me on time in the future but nothing changed. Job No53 was looming large. I'd worked through the autumn and winter for my brother and had rarely been paid, so as spring began to appear I spotted an advert.

HGV Class 1 Driver required for exhibition work.

It sounded different so I rang them up. I met the man one Sunday morning. We liked each other and he was happy with my references. I omitted the brother experience. He explained what the work was all about and told me it was seasonal. Which is to say it was only from April to September, but on-going each year. The wage wasn't jaw dropping but I felt sure it would be regularly paid. We agreed, and I was to start in early April which was only three weeks away.

I worked for a time without receiving any wages from my brother. Then I phoned him up at a time I knew he was always at home. 3 o'clock in the morning!

'I've had enough of this.' I started. 'I go to work every day at two o'clock in the morning. The lorry earns you money and they pay you, but I haven't had any money from you in six weeks.'

'Huff, I know you're angry. I've had a hard time here and I've just forgotten. There's so many things to do and…'

'That's bollocks! I've got another job and I start tomorrow. I've told the office. I'm going to park your lorry somewhere safe and when you pay me what you owe me I'll tell you where it is.'

'That's theft.'

'You'll find it's a moot point in a court of law. I'd call it Goods to the Value of. Anyway, be that as it may, it's what's going to happen.'

'I need the lorry in a month or so for another machine move.'

'Now you know how to get it. Stay in touch Bruv.'

I hung up and my girlfriend and I had a party in the evening to celebrate.

Job No 53. The itinerant barman

Even though I'd worked at so many jobs, exhibition work was not something I'd ever done before. I was looking forward to it. To be completely honest it was nothing to do with mounting an exhibition. What I had was a forty foot step frame box trailer, which meant the floor was much lower for the last three quarters of it than at the front. It was converted into a very basic hospitality unit. The main entrance area was in the middle and above the fifth wheel was an office with a door for more intimate business dealings. At the back was a minute kitchen affair which served as a bar. It was a hospitality unit on permanent hire to Pixy Oil, who eventually went bust, or got bought out or something. They sold lubricants and fuel to all sorts of businesses including farmers. I only saw the agricultural ones. It turned out I was nothing more than a bar steward with a lorry license. It was quite a fun and rewarding job and I liked it.

I had to take the lorry and trailer to all sorts of major agricultural shows and events like ploughing matches. I had to find the pitch to set it up and transform it into the meeting and greeting unit and serve hard liquor and tea/coffee to all the punters. The local sales reps for Pixy always met me on site and organised all the business. It really couldn't have been easier. I had plenty of free time. It was very simple to find each site because they were all signposted from miles away. Setting up the unit was the only part which required any amount of intelligence. Even so, it was only required to be level 1.

Unfortunately, I was never supplied with a level and I never acquired one. In order to get the whole outfit sitting more or less correctly I used a glass of water with a line on it. It could have been a glass of beer, but sometimes it can be a bit frothy which would obscure the line. It didn't have to be perfect. It was only to be almost sure the wine wouldn't tip out of the glasses when they were set down on a table. The only bit of DIY, which I've always loathed, was assembling the aluminium approach steps and railings. Then I had to hide the lorry bit round the back and roll out a built-in awning. Job done. Except of course, for putting out the cheap garden chairs and tables for the few occasions we had a little warmth and no rain.

The lorry was a short cab which meant it had no bunk, but I had a whole bedroom to sleep in at the front of the trailer. Obviously there was a bar so I could take a night cap before sleeping.

My first assignment was the Ayr Agricultural show in southern Scotland.

Scotland was a long way and it felt even further with my mobile bar because I was equipped with a very old Saviem. A Saviem was a sort of early type

Renault and less powerful than my first Volvo at Rodes. It only had to pull a practically empty trailer but it was still very slow and quite cumbersome. It blew about in the wind because it was so light. Although the vehicle was a set-back for me, it was relatively comfortable and driving was an enjoyable job. It took me more than a day to arrive at Ayr. There was almost no paperwork to gain entry as the trailer more or less said it all. I was guided to my pitch and left to set it up. The show started the following day. As it was my first time out with it, it took me nearly four hours to get it looking presentable. I later learned hardly anyone cared so long as it was almost level, the bar was open and I was wearing a tie. It was a dry but cloudy day with a brisk north wind making it quite chilly.

Just after I'd finished the Pixy rep showed up sporting a pair of tailored shorts. It was only then I realised I was actually in Scotland.

'Hello there, you must be Hugh? A good Scottish name laddie! I've been told you're new to this sort of work so they've asked me to come along a bit earlier and see if you've got everything you need. My name's Alistair, by the way.'

'Good afternoon, Alistair. I think everything is in order. You're the boss. Is there anything amiss? Do you want anything added or removed?'

'It all looks just perfect Hugh. Well done, good job. You could just add a glass of whisky to my hand, if the bar's open.'

'The bar is open Alistair. It's always open unless I'm driving.'

'I'm beginning to like you already, Hugh.'

Of course, it was just a 'jolly' for the reps. They had to do a certain amount of work, but fuel and lubricants are a necessity rather than a choice. It was simply a matter of keeping existing customers on side. Some of them were for life, provided the price was right. Not many changed suppliers because we were all creatures of habit. As mechanics often say, never repair something which is working.

'Here you are, Alistair. It's not the best but there is a lot of it.'

'Thanks. No, probably not, but after a couple no one cares. Especially if it's for free. Do you like whisky?'

'Oh yes, I'm a big fan.'

'Good, but don't drink it all before tomorrow.'

'If I drank all I've brought you'd find a corpse on the floor in the morning.'

'That's very heartening, Hugh. I'm sure my customers will love you.'

'I'm just the barman Alistair.'

'Yes of course, but there's nothing worse than a grumpy sober barman.'

'I'll try my best to roll around the trailer with a smile on my face.'

'Brilliant. Thanks for the drink, I needed it. I've had a hard day. I'll get here about nine thirtyish. The others will be a bit later. Can you rustle up bacon sandwiches for breakfast?'

'Anything, if it's not cordon bleu.'

'Great. See you tomorrow.' And he was off.

I went out to see what else the showground had to offer.

It was a county show and not just agricultural. There was something for everyone. There were all the local businesses and the national ones as well. There were fun fairs and tens of bars and restaurants, if they could be called restaurants, mostly set up under marquees. Of course there were plenty of moos and woollies with various demonstrations for people from the cities to understand that milk doesn't in fact, come from a supermarket. The old ones are the best.

I learned fairly soon there were plenty of people who travelled around like me. They went to all the different shows, either for themselves or for big companies. All the major lorry companies made an appearance, including DAF, Volvo, MAN, ERF, Ford/Iveco. I had a wander around all of those while taking in a few beers on the way. Most car manufacturers were there, at least those which had a local distributor. Even supermarkets had a presence. There were artisan/craft shops and thousands of handicrafts and local food stalls. Initially it was quite interesting. I'd never really had the time or opportunity to go to my own local shows so I was quite taken with it all.

At the Ayr show I met a bloke called Terry who flew a balloon for Michelin. It was a big oval yellow one. It was all he did. Obviously he had to get it there, tether it to the ground, inflate it, fly it and then just keep an eye on it. Each day he had to take it down and repeat the process the following day, but it didn't seem too taxing.

'To be frank mate, I spend most of my days in the bar, and I'm getting paid for it.'

'I run a bar Terry, so I can't get out of it if I wanted.'

'Great. I'll come over and visit you.'

'Remember to say you want to buy mega-quantities of lubricants.'

'Oh yeah Hugh, I'm well practised at scrounging.'

Most of the shows ran for one or two days and then it was time to pack up and move on. Some of the bigger ones like The Bath & West ran for about a week, which could get a bit dull after the first tour of the ground. There's hardly a job in the world which is so exciting every day you can't wait to get breakfast over with and get on with it. In fact I think it's safe to say there isn't one. After all I was quite experienced with jobs even in those early days. The Ayr show was open for three days, so if I missed anything on day one there were always two other days for further investigation.

After opening everything up each morning there were a few things I had to do to start the day off. The first of those was to get fresh bread, bacon, sausages and eggs. I was supplied with most other snacks and there was a fridge to keep it all from going off. Tom, the boss, gave me a money float for those extras, and when I first started doing the job I bought newspapers because I thought it was a nice touch. Later I discovered many of those who came to the stand were illiterate, so I gave up on that. They were very pleasant people but they just couldn't read. Alistair was punctual and I made him a bacon sandwich before his team arrived. 'Oh yes, great sarnie Hugh. Where did you learn to cook?'

'Back there, in what we laughingly call the kitchen. I picked up a smattering of cooking skills this morning before you got here.'

'You're obviously a quick learner. My colleagues will arrive soon. Only the best performers get free tickets to the show so the slackers probably won't make it. That'll make about five of us in all. Hopefully there'll be a lot of punters though. It's a really good opportunity to do some serious business.'

'OK, I'll get more coffee on the go and boil the kettle.'

'When they've all had their fill and if it looks a bit quiet, you can just sneak off for a bit. In a while you'll be able to tell when it might be busy and when fuck-all happens won't you?'

'OK, fine.'

Right then seemed like an opportune moment to sneak off and get myself a professional bacon sandwich. So I did while Alistair shuffled his paperwork. I wasn't going to trust my cooking to my own stomach.

It was quite a busy day although I had no idea at that stage what was busy and what was quiet. There was an almost continuous flow of existing and potential customers. Terry didn't make it so I wandered over to his plot. He wasn't there and there was no balloon in the sky. I figured he must have had to rush off to another show. I had a few beers around lunchtime when there were less punters pushing in for a free whisky. Then I nipped down to the toilets before returning.

Makeshift toilets are like the end of eternity, as many of you will know. For most of the night it had been a bit drizzly and it was all very mushy under foot. The toilet floor might originally have been concrete, but the day I visited it was like a slurry pit. While we were all there doing our business, a woman rushed in shouting apologies and dived into a cubicle. Nobody said a word apart from one who politely offered consolation. The bloke next to me said,

"If any of us had done the same in the Ladies there would have been cries of rape and anguish before we'd got near the door.'

'Probably, but no one can get near the door for the queue. They only put up half a dozen women's loos compared to the lines and lines which we have.'

'Yeah, I suppose. You working or drinking?'

'Both really, I'm the barman on the Pixy Oil trailer.'

'That's handy. Fancy a pint?'

'I've got to get back mate. Why don't you come along for a freebie and buy some fuel?'

'It sounds good. I could do with some fuel as it happens. What is Pixy Oil?'

'It's a French fuel and lubricant company.'

'I'll go with that. I could do with a change from the English.'

'What do you do then?'

'I've got a farm contracting business. Harvesting, ploughing, drilling and any other stuff my customers want me to do. I've got plenty of big tractors and machines.'

'You'll be very welcome I'm sure. Come along with me.'

We wandered over to the Pixy business centre.'

'Christ Hugh, where have you been? We had a rush on and had to do all your work.'

'Sorry about that. I've found you a prospective customer. He's a farm contractor with a good business. Alistair, meet Calan.'

'Oh thanks. Come aboard Calan. Hugh, could you get a glass of wine for the large lady over there?'

'OK Alistair, which colour?'

'Hugh, you can see there's no one of an ethnic minority here.'

'I spotted that. Which colour wine?'

'Oh, yes of course. White, please.'

I went to work.

The next day I spotted the yellow balloon flying again. After the breakfast rush, I wandered over to see if Terry was back in control.

'Hi Hugh, some fucking kids untied the guy ropes and the flying advert disappeared. We had to chase after it nearly all day and eventually it came down near Edinburgh. Helluva mess!'

'How do you know where it is when you're on the road?'

'It's got a sort of radio tracking device on it, but it's relayed to a central office. They use a radio to show us where to go. It's chaos really, but we were lucky because if it had gone out to sea we'd probably have lost it.'

'Do you have to do it all on your own?'

'No, you couldn't do it on your own. There's a team of us, and we have to inform the show authorities who inform the police. The air traffic control has to know and by the end of the day I reckon the whole fucking world knew.'

'Anyway, all's well that ends well. Fancy a pint?'

'Yeah. Good idea. I just have to get the girls to sit on the guy ropes, and then we'll shoot off for half an hour.'

We wandered around the showground aimlessly, buying one or two beers on the way. There were loads of arty-crafty stalls with mostly Scottish knick-knacks and plenty of local produce including home-made whiskies, biscuits, bread and cheese. Then we had a look around the car and lorry dealerships. There wasn't anything of great interest although I drooled over the new lorries on the DAF stand. I saw the big Eddie there who later ran one of the biggest haulage companies in the UK. I never realised who he was at the time because he hadn't really got started in those days. However, looking back it was my only claim to fame at the Ayr county show.

Except on a few occasions the shows were never back to back for me, which was lucky as I always had to return to base to restock with booze and other provisions. It was mostly alcohol I needed because they got through an amazing amount in just a few days. The only one day events I went to were ploughing matches, which were great fun. There were one or two racing events which were always noisy but never raised any enthusiasm in me. Most weeks it meant I'd have about three days or sometimes less between each job. I got paid by the day. I can't remember how much, but it was a less on the days I wasn't at a show. It was all planned a year in advance and then divided out, so I got the same each week. I know it wasn't much, and certainly nowhere near what I could have earned on general haulage, but it was a job and quite an easy one. I knew I'd have to start searching for **Job No54** before the season ended. When October came round I'd be out of work until the following year. I soon realised nearly every show was the same and the novelty wore off quickly. Even so I had to remember they were all the annual highlight of one local community or another. Fixed smiles were a necessity. Only a few were memorable for one reason or another and the others have become a bit of a blur.

The Lincoln show was one I enjoyed. It must have been summer because I recall the sun was out and it was warm. Most of the men were in shorts. In general Brits have a knee-jerk reaction to mild temperature increases. Most will drop the roof on their convertibles. Some would leap into a pair of shorts whenever there's less than 50% cloud cover, even if there was ice on the road. It's a British peculiarity. Anyway it was warmish. The whole showground was almost completely flat, which made it so much easier to set up the trailer.

As usual the leading Pixy rep came round to watch me prepare and get the first beer out of the bar. They were always very pleasant and some even jovial. I can't remember any one of them being difficult or fastidious. After all it was an opportunity for a free jolly, paid for by head office. Who would moan about that? I can't remember the main mans' name, but I do remember Dave, his second in command who always arrived at the crack of dawn each day. Sometimes it was even before I'd managed to crawl out of bed. It was 7.30am at the beginning of the first show day when I met him.

'Hello Hugh. How's it going? Did you have a good trip up? Found the place alright? Met the head man, I hear. Got any coffee on the go yet? I hear you're a wizard with breakfasts. Oh, I'm Dave, I didn't say, did I? I do work for Pixy. I'm not just scrounging. Well I am, but officially.'

'Morning, Dave. Yes is the answer to most of your questions. You're too early for breakfast but I can put some coffee on when I get back from the wash house. Can you stand guard while I'm gone so I don't have to lock it all up?'

'Yes of course, but you're not going to be long are you?'

'Probably about the same amount of time as you spend in the bathroom, plus the time to walk there and back.'

'OK fine. I'll stand guard then.'

The show didn't officially open to the public until 9 o'clock but those with trade passes could get in from six.

'The office bit is out of bounds till I get back because my bed's still set up in there, OK?'

'Gotcher.'

Despite the state of the loos in Ayr most showground wash houses had separate ones for trades people, and some even had showers. On the first day at least, most of them were clean. I was lucky at Lincoln. They even had hot running water which was a wonderful step forward into the twentieth century. Consequently, I was a bit longer than Dave normally spent in the bathroom.

Dave turned out to be a really nice bloke, although he did always arrive far too early in the morning to be absolutely normal, even for a hard working salesman. On my return he wasn't very interested in coffee.

'Is everything alright Dave? Nothing untoward occurred? I see you found the bar OK.'

'Yes. It wasn't very well hidden so I sort of helped myself. Is that alright, or have I usurped your position?'

'It's absolutely fine Dave. It's Pixy's bar, I just drive it here. What have you got? Do you still fancy a coffee?'

'It's a Martini. I hope you've got plenty because it's pretty rare on show grounds. No, I'll skip the coffee course but I could manage a bit of breakfast when you're ready.'

'There's half a case of Martini as you've already spotted, but if you get through all it there's no more. I'm not allowed to top up from anywhere except base. I can get you a bite in half an hour after I've moved the bedroom back to the lorry. That suit?'

'Half a case will do just fine. Just keep it a secret will you? Yes, no rush for brekka. Whenever you're ready, mate.'

It looked like we'd moved on from first name terms to bosom buddies during my swift trip to the wash room, or in Dave's case the bar. Christ, it wasn't even nine o'clock in the morning, but time and alcohol don't have much in common. Who was I to tell him what hour he could drink liquor?

The Lincoln show was one of the happiest I attended. Everyone was in good spirits every day, especially Dave, and there were no harsh words from anyone. Several customers invited me to go to their own stands and talk about their businesses and lorry driving, which for some reason everyone finds fascinating although nobody actually wants to do it. Dave was coming back to the bar every ten minutes to get another Martini.

'Haven't I just poured you one, Dave?'

'Oh probably, but I've mislaid it.'

I realised Dave had brought his own cheap coasters and a selection were in Hi-Viz yellow. On each one stood a glass of Martini. He couldn't possibly mislay one in his rush to sell more lubricants.

'Do you drive home each day Dave?'

"No, I get a lift here each day with a farm worker on his way to work. That's why I'm always a bit early for you. In the evenings one of the others runs me home.'

'You got it all worked out then.'

'Oh yes, it's a very ordered life. Can you pour me another please? I'm parched.'

In mid-July while I was on my way home from one of the northern shows, I stopped for a snack and a cuppa in a motorway service station. A lorry pulled in at the same time and its door was sign written with the name Reynolds and Somerset. I wandered over to see if the driver was chatty.

'Morning driver, you're from my neck of the woods I reckon. I work out of Taunton.'

'Yes mate. Our yard's about twenty minutes away from the big town.'

I told him about my job and that it was only seasonal. I asked him if his boss ever took on part-time drivers in the winter.

'Yes mate. Winter is our busiest time. We take sugar beet to the sugar factories where they produce a waste product for cattle feed. We deliver all of it to hundreds of different farms and mills. If you go and see him soon you'll definitely get a job fixed up for the winter. The Campaign as it's called runs from about October to February or March. It should suit you well.'

I thanked him and he gave me his boss's name. We had a cup of tea together. It seemed like I could be in luck to secure Job No54 in good time. It wasn't as if I hadn't heard of Reynolds. I remembered they used to load out of Watchet docks when Rodes were very busy. I was told they were a bunch of cowboys who never stuck to the rules and worked all the hours God sent. That wasn't something which really bothered me. I just wanted to keep the money rolling in. I was still suffering from the irregular payments from my brother. I never got paid all my wages from him but I did get a string of excuses and several ugly phone calls about the whereabouts of his lorry. I never found out if he ever discovered where it was or not. I supposed he must have.

On my return I re-stocked the trailer with more alcohol for the following show, and then took a day off at home. The first job was to call Reynolds. The transport manager sounded hopeful. He said I could call in anytime I was passing during normal office hours, but to confirm beforehand. It sounded fairly positive and put me in a good frame of mind. I aimed to see him after the next show which was somewhere south of London. In fact it was just off the Brighton road. It was quite hard to find because there were hundreds of different signs for different entrances. Of course I picked the wrong one. The official was quite pleasant and directed me through the trees to a big open space which was the real showground. At the entrance there was a map with the site numbers marked. It was a simple matter to follow the paths to my allotted site, which was on the peripheries of the main arena. Nothing new occurred during my stay there. I met up with several of the nomadic people who went from show to show and a few days later I was back home for a four day break.

I rang Reynolds again and confirmed a meeting for the following morning. The transport manager asked me for my references prior to arriving including my present employers', which I gave him. Tom had OK'd it because he knew I'd need work in the winter but was hopeful I'd return for the following season. Of course I would. A different job for winter and summer was quite a good idea, so I'd have continual employment through the year. Furthermore, The Guinness Book of Records was bound to be interested in my ability to keep the number of jobs increasing with such alacrity!

I arrived at Reynolds' yard on time. I noticed the final 100yds of the approach to the yard would be very difficult with a forty foot trailer. There was a small bridge immediately before the turn, but I supposed it was manageable because otherwise the yard wouldn't be where it was. The office was clearly marked OFFICE, so even I couldn't make a mistake.

'Good morning, I'm Hugh and I'm looking for Roger.'

'Good morning Hugh. You've found him. Drag up a pew and sit down.'

'Thanks. This is my licence. Do you need anything else?'

'That's good, it's clean I see. Have you ever had any run-ins with the police?'

'No, none.'

'Good. I've checked your references. Rodes gave you a good report. They say you're a hard worker and experienced. Though I don't know him, your present employer said you were probably better suited to general haulage, but he didn't want to lose you for the next summer. There won't be a problem there because the sugar beet Campaign finishes around March. Sometimes it's a bit later, but it won't be a necessity for you to see it out to the end should your season start early for any reason. From those points of view you seem pretty well suited. Anything you want to add?'

'No, although Tom is probably right. Exhibition work is fine, but there are lots of periods of inactivity and I'm not a born part-time barman. I enjoy driving and being occupied. As far as Rodes is concerned, I loved my time there, although I preferred it when Michael was in charge. Gerry and I had a love-hate relationship, but in hindsight I was probably a bit outspoken. I had a six month break during the six years I was there. It must have done us both good, but in the end I worked out it wasn't going anywhere from my point of view, so I moved on.'

'Where to? Directly to Tom?'

He obviously knew the answer.

'No. I worked at Taunton Valley with my brothers' lorry but it wasn't a great success.'

'I heard.'

Rural communities are more in touch than any other.

'So here I am.'

'OK, well the work is hard. There's a lot of work by hand. Are you up to it?'

At that point the owner walked in.

'Has he come for a job, Rog? He'll never hack it. I've seen more meat on a butcher's pencil!'

Rick rolled his eyes and left.

'He was our esteemed leader, in case you were wondering.' said Roger. 'He's right, it is hard work. Are you up to it? Through the winter it's continuous. There's no let-up.'

'Yes, certainly I am. I've done my share of handball. We did plenty of fertilizer bags out of Avonmouth and Spilldry out of Watchet. Just about everything was by hand when I started. It's not a problem.'

'Right then, I'll give you a go and see how it pans out. If you're no good you'll be out. Your drivers' hours' records must be in order when they reach my desk. If there are any infringements I am required to inform you. If they continue you'll be out. It's the law. You know as well as the others how the law can be bent, but I don't want to know or see evidence of it. Is that clear?'

'Yes, perfectly clear.'

'Part-timers, of which you will be one, are required by the company to be self-employed. Which means you'll be paid the gross amount and you do your own tax returns. You will be paid the standard expenses as per an employed driver, but you will not be entitled to paid holidays, sick pay or the odd paid day off. You will not be entitled to the fall-back pay, which means if the lorry is off the road for repairs you won't earn anything. You'll be paid in cash each week with a week in hand. All payments will be self-billed and you will be given a statement at the end of each month. The pay will be 25% of the lorry earnings. You'll have to trust us with the rates because we are not going to quote you before each job. You can expect to earn between £400 and £500 per week before expenses. Obviously, the more you do the more you earn. Does that suit you?'

'It couldn't be better.'

'You may come to regret your certainty. Anyway, call me when your season with Tom ends and we'll fit you in. There is no exact date for the start of the Campaign. It's different each year as is the finish date, so don't worry about missing out on anything. Do you have any questions Hugh?'

'No Roger, none at all. I'm happy. I'll call you when the bar tendering ends.'

'Good. Thanks for dropping by, see you sometime in September.'

Job No54 was in the bag. I'm an honest man and I'm not going to cheat the Guinness Book of Records by saying, the following year Job No53 miraculously turned into Job No55 and 54 changed to 56 because it would be unfair. They were two jobs which ran concurrently as they did for a couple of years. I am going to treat each period of self-employment as a separate job number, because despite working for myself I was doing a different job. Each time I changed direction I was doing something different. You can put forward objections if you like, but it's how it's going to be.

I'd become accustomed to being self-employed when I'd worked for my brother. It wasn't an inconvenience. I later learned transport companies not only shared work with other hauliers when they were busy, but also drew on a pool of part time drivers to help out.

Many part timers were already self-employed because they ran their own businesses. Often those businesses were quiet at certain times of year like for instance small farms. It was also true of those who had seasonal businesses in the tourist trade. Some of those had HGV licenses which they then used to work for transport companies. Under normal circumstances the tax for which they were liable was calculated from the total revenue received by their business in any one year.

At the beginning of the declared supply 'chain' crisis in the UK, everybody in authority had agreed we had an unprecedented shortage of HGV drivers. Many former drivers were invited to return to work to lend a hand even it was only part time. I received a letter myself, even though they must have known I was approaching 103 years of age.

At almost exactly the same time the Government introduced the IR35 tax law. Broadly speaking it required transport companies to tax their part time drivers at source. It meant some people would be paying tax twice. It didn't take a genius to work out the part time driver pool would shrink to practically nothing overnight.

It does seem government hasn't managed to get a single thing right in twelve years of being in office. It appears everything is ill conceived, ill planned and wildly executed. Is there no joined up thinking?

I told Tom my plan and thanked him for the reference. He was glad I'd found something for the winter which fitted so snugly with his season. If I hadn't found anything to do, I was sure he was planning to offer me something really dull like cleaning and maintaining the equipment. All in all, I think we were both glad it wasn't going to happen.

'Right Hugh, I'm glad you've got yourself organised. The next job is the Royal Show at Stoneleigh. It's a big one, lasts a week and we'll all be there. If you need any top-ups just come and find me and I'll organise it.'

Of all the agricultural shows I attended the Royal Show really was different. I suppose the Queen did turn up, but probably not every year. I definitely never saw her while I was there. It was a pity really, as she might have knighted me for my services to road transport and the gin bottle. Probably not, but it was a pleasant thought. I had actually gained the nick-name of Sir Hugo while I was at Rodes, due my lack of dialect and my educated intellect. I'm not sure about the latter.

There were all the usual attractions including moos and woollies, but also alpacas which were rare in those days, and other furry beasts. There was a small daily circus and in the evenings there were discos for the young and agile. There were hundreds of bars, and near the centre was a jousting ring which was good fun to watch. The colourful knights charged each other on horseback. They used papier-mâché lances in case someone got killed. Around the ring there were big advertisements for various things. One day there was a procession of lorries with a loud speaker. It announced they were looking for drivers to go to the Sudan to work for a charity. Grain needed to be delivered to the interior where people were starving because of the war. I was taken with the idea and decided to investigate further. It sounded exciting.

I found their marquee and introduced myself. They sounded interested and asked about my experience. No, I'd never driven heavy vehicles abroad but I was keen for a new experience. They explained the dangers in as much as I'd be working in a war zone. For some reason it didn't put me off. They explained about the heat and the dust, although I didn't fully take it on board. Then suddenly I was signed up and told to get various vaccinations, including yellow fever and two others. When that was accomplished I was to give them a ring and 'we'd take it from there.' The job would probably start in six weeks or a couple of months.

'Call us when you've had the jabs.' They told me. It all sounded pretty good and I was looking forward to it. It transpired they were a limited company providing transport for the charity, whose name escapes me. I did everything they'd asked and gave them a call. Fortunately I didn't cancel the first plan. In the end, after making several unanswered calls I discovered they had gone into liquidation and the job was cancelled. Looking back now I think I should be truly grateful they ceased trading while I was still in the UK, because otherwise I'd still probably have been in the Sudan to this day, or dead!

The show time finally came to an end, and although I'd enjoyed the season, I was really looking forward to doing some proper work at Reynolds Transport.

Job No54 Driving with the wild bunch

I arranged to go over to Reynolds yard the next Saturday morning, which was only three days away.

I got there about mid-morning and found Roger.

'Hi Hugh. Good time to get here. I'll get the keys to your lorry and show you what's where.'

Within a few minutes he'd returned with some keys.

'OK, come with me. WHA, (vehicle reg.), is yours for the campaign. It's probably the oldest on the fleet but it doesn't give much trouble. Here we are. Have you ever driven a Volvo?'

'Only an F86 when I first started at Rodes.'

'Fine. Well the gearbox is almost the same except you can split each gear so you've got 16 in all. Do you understand?'

'Yes, I've used a splitter.'

'Good. Right, it's got a separate locker which you can access from the outside to store ratchet straps, rope, tools and stuff. Here.'

He showed me the locker which was at eye level just behind and below the drivers' seat.

'You should have 12 straps and you'll need a coil of rope which you can get from the workshop foreman. If you have a puncture you're required to change the wheel yourself. The spare is on its carrier behind the unit, (lorry/ prime mover). It's pretty self-explanatory how it works and you need to bring the old one back with you. Are you clear?'

'Yes Roger, but I've never changed a lorry wheel.'

'It's exactly the same principle as a car but bigger and heavier. You've done one of those before I suppose?'

'Yes, several times.'

'Good. Don't worry Hugh, you'll manage. We all do when we have to. Now, can you splice a rope to make your own lengths?'

'Oh yes, I can do that. Old Harold down the dock taught me.'

'I'm impressed. Most of our lot tie knots in them and they look so untidy. Harold? He's the dock shunter isn't he? He's been driving since they invented the wheel. You've been well taught.'

'Yep, that's him.'

'OK, the lorry has been washed this week and cleaned out. You are required to wash it every week and keep the inside as clean as you can. Got it?'

'Understood.'

'Do you know where the concrete works is?'

'Yes, on the Ilminster road.'

'Exactly. The loaded trailers are left just inside the gate. I expect you've seen them. The delivery notes are put under the electric clip. Always take an empty trailer with you when you go down to collect a load. You will be given a trailer number to pick up and a destination by me or someone in the office. Are you taking all this in?'

'Yes Roger. They say I have amazing recall.'

'I hope they're right because I don't want to keep repeating myself.'

'I'll let you know if I fall behind somewhere but I'm fine so far.'

'Each lorry is supplied with two sheets. One is fifty feet by twenty feet and it's mighty heavy, so build your muscles up. The other is a fly sheet of the normal size. Keep them both behind the cab if you can. It just makes it easier if you don't have to move them from one trailer to another. Do you have any questions?'

'It sounds pretty straight forward so far.'

'Good. We have a canteen over there, next to the workshop. Each lorry has a clip on the notice board where we will leave delivery notes if it's after hours and you can leave the spent ones. There's a kettle and toaster and stuff. The mechanics have a kitty which you can add to. Toilets are in the same building and there's a shower of sorts. That's it. Check your equipment is in order and get some rope. The trailer number plate is in the locker. Pick up an empty trailer and park it neatly in line. When you're ready come and see me and I'll give you a box of tachograph cards. I'll also tell you what you'll be doing on Monday. I really hope you're good at early starts because they're a necessity.'

'I love early starts Roger!'

He gave me one of those 'I bet' looks, but I really did in those days. Nowadays I have difficulty getting out of bed before ten o'clock in the morning.

'I imagine you've brought your bedding and overnight kit with you. It'll save time if you load it up now instead of in the middle of the night on Monday.'

'Yes, I'd thought of that.'

'I understand you live quite a long way from here, so if you want to spend any nights in the yard, you're welcome to.'

'Thank you Roger. Right, I'll get organised and see you in the office in a while.'

'OK. I go home at one o'clock.'

Good grief. A transport yard with a canteen and a shower! What a step into the sunlight. I checked the number of straps and sauntered over to the workshop.

'Morning all,' I hollered.

A head looked out from under a trailer which was over the pit.

'Yeah, what d'yer want?'

'I'm Hugh. I'm a new part-time driver and…'

'Oh yeah, Rog said you'd be over for some rope. Hang on, I'll come up.'

'Are you the foreman? What's your name?'

'Yes, I'm Jon, or Jonny if you like. The rope coil is in my office, follow me.'

'I'm short of three straps as well.'

'Yeah, OK. Here's the rope and oh, a bundle of five straps. Take them all if you want and there's two chains and dogs[3] going spare, if you want to take them on.'

'Thanks Jonny. That's great, I'll take the lot. Do you want me to sign for them?'

'Nah, we don't have nothing as modern as that, but if you want more straps you need to bring the broken ones back, right?'

"Got it. Thanks. How much do the drivers put in the canteen kitty normally?"

---

[3] Dogs are chain tensioners. They have a hook on a short chain at either end of the tensioner which is a bar or lever. The hooks are connected to each end of the securing chain on the load. The lever is then pulled down through 180° until it snaps shut thereby making the main chain as tight as possible on the load. Sometimes an extra bar is required for more leverage. Nowadays chains are usually tensioned with a ratchet mechanism, but we was meant to be 'tuff' in they days!

'Normally? Fuck-all! But if you're going to be honest, a couple of quid a week is fine.'

'I'll do it now.'

As the chains were heavy it took three trips to get the stuff to the lorry, and another to get my bedroom installed. I made up my ropes, stored them, picked up an empty trailer and parked it ready for the off on Monday. It took just over an hour, and then I reported back to Roger.

'All done Hugh? Good. Right, Monday morning go to the concrete works and drop the empty. Pick up trailer 86 and deliver to Hatfield at 8am. Call me when you're empty. Work hard and enjoy. Oh and here is your box of tachographs. Use them wisely. This is a fuel card for when you're away and this is the fuel card for use in the yard.'

'Thanks Roger. Speak Monday and thanks again for the job.'

'No problem. Let's see how it goes.'

Hatfield wasn't far away. Probably no more than three and half hours, but I wanted to be sure I was on time on my first day. I remembered my first day at Rodes and didn't want a repeat. I left home at 1am. It's better to be early than late. As Roger had pointed out, the yard was a long way away from home and it took me over an hour to get to the lorry. Then I discovered I hadn't checked the fuel on Saturday, which was on empty. Despite my idiocy over cards and anything automated, it wasn't rocket science to make the fuel pump work and I was soon on my way.

My load to Hatfield was large culverts which were box sections of pre-stressed concrete normally put under roads to carry water. Mostly all of the concrete deliveries went to building sites, so unless it was a big site the deliveries were short lived and then there was a new one. It was good from the drivers' point of view. It prevented us having to do endless deliveries to the same place, as I was used to at Rodes.

I arrived early at 7 o'clock, so I'd probably got up too early. The site was easy to find as it was on the outskirts of the town. Most building sites have vast signs outside with the contractor's name on it.

'You're an early bird driver. We're just waiting for the crane driver. Just go up there and park under the crane. He'll have you empty as soon as he arrives.'

'Thanks mate. Is there a café close by?'

'Yeah, just down the road about half a mile but don't fuck off till you're empty please.'

'Lovely, thanks.'

'They open at 7.30.'

I parked under the crane. The driver arrived at 7.30, and it wasn't until he blew his horn I realised I had to assist in unloading although I wasn't sure how. I climbed on top of the culverts and found two metal lifters. They had a ring at one end with a spring loaded nipple on the inside and a fixed loop at the other. I struggled to get it to fit on the protruding metal shaft which was topped with a circular cap. The crane driver shouted out of his cab,

'Oi, Mac! Give the driver a hand will yer? 'ee don't know what 'ees doing.'

Mac came over and climbed up to meet me on top of the trailer.

'Are you new to the job, son? Never mind, I'll show you. Watch, the ring goes over the top like this. Twist it round till the nipple catches in the 'ole, then hook the chain into the loop. Do the same with the other. Then get the fuck off the culvert, or he'll lift you up with it. Yeah?'

'Yes I understand. You're right it is simple, but it looked like the Krypton Factor to me.'

'You'll get used to it. Sometimes the work crew do it, but we ain't got enough blokes here for that.'

'Thanks.'

'I'll watch you do the next one. Then you're on your own.'

'Thanks for your help.'

'Think nothing of it, mate. Nothing's easy in life, believe me.'

On that site they were putting the concrete on the ground to use later, but in the future some loads would often be fitted straight into the construction. It takes longer to unload because the fitting has to be exactly precise. I was unloaded before eight o'clock. The crane driver signed the ticket and I was sitting down to breakfast before 8.15am. I called Roger before eating.

'Morning Roger, it's Hugh, I'm empty in Hatfield and I'm just getting something to eat.'

'Good morning. Yes, well done. No rush, enjoy your food. Afterwards, go up to the sugar factory at Bury St Edmunds. Find Gary who works for us and he'll give you a load of pellets. No need to ring again because he'll tell us where you've gone. It's still early in the Campaign so you may have to wait till it's loaded.'

'OK, thanks. I'll ring you when I'm empty again. Bye.'

I'd only met a few of Reynolds' drivers when they'd been loading at Watchet, but not many. There had been some of the others milling around on Saturday morning but they'd paid me no attention. I'd left the Hatfield site before the second load had arrived and I'd seen no-one in the early morning because I'd left far too early. Perhaps there'd be some more at the sugar factory. I was never the social type but I was curious about who my new work mates were. From those I hadn't met I was expecting the same attitude as when I'd first started at Rodes and I wanted to overcome it as quickly as possible.

Gary was difficult to find because the sugar factory was very big, but eventually I came across the pellet store. Gary had a wooden office just inside the gate and it was a hive of activity. He looked up from his papers when I presented myself.

'Yeah?'

'I'm the new boy. Come for a load of pellets.'

'There're loads of new boys and loads of pellets. Got a name? Where are you going?'

'I'm Hugh, Gary. Roger said to go wherever you send me.'

"Well mate, that's easy at least. You better have the next one, well the first one off in fact. That is going to…where d'you want to go?'

'I'm not fussed.'

'You're easy to please. Have this one then. Sherborne. I'll call the customer with an ETA before you go. The shunter'll bring it out of the shed within an hour. He was late getting started this morning.'

'OK. Are any others coming up?'

'I fucking hope so because I got twelve at least to get shot of today. Go and get a cup of tea and I'll give you a shout when it's ready. Drop your trailer off over there somewhere near the loading shed, will you?'

Straw

While I was waiting for my load a couple of my new workmates did show up. They seemed very friendly and relaxed.

'You're a new face. How did you get here so early? Keen to show Roger a willing pair of hands?'

'Er, no. I had the 8am Hatfield.'

'I'll let you off then. I think I've seen you before. Are you Hugh? Used to work at Rodes?'

'That's me.'

'You just here for the Campaign or thinking about a life sentence?'

'This year it's just the Campaign because I've got a summer job with an exhibition trailer and I promised to go back in the spring.'

'Oh yeah? That splits your year up nicely. We heard a bit about you from the Rodes mob.'

'All good, I hope.'

'Well I don't know how to say this, but most of it was OK. Don't worry about attitude from us blokes. We been around a bit. We ain't carrot-crunchers from out west. There's all sorts come to drive for Reynolds during the Campaign. So long as you're not a looney and got some idea of what you're doing we all muck in together. Know what I mean? I'm Len.'

'Good to meet you Len. No, I'm almost completely sane.'

'The almost bit is what gets you membership. Gary's hollering for you. Where are you going?'

'Sherborne.'

'I got Shaftesbury. We'll probably meet up for straw from Cranborne after. Hang on and I'll give you a hand. Mark'll help too when he gets back from the canteen.'

'I didn't know there was a canteen.'

'Oh yeah, you'll find it when you've got to wait more than two or three hours for your load.'

I settled into my new way of life very easily. Most of my workmates were friendly and helpful. The next three years were amongst the happiest times of my career. There were some memorable moments which I'll recount at the same time as separating them from stories of the show grounds. At Reynolds we mostly hauled farm goods to farms and mills and concrete sections to building sites. I learned that builders and farmers were much more relaxed in their approach to life than nearly all other commercial enterprises. Both employed many part time and foreign workers, which gave a balanced outlook. Reynolds office also gave the impression of being very laid back. It made the work so much easier for those of us who had to sweat for a living.

Farm and mill deliveries with sugar beet pellets were indeed very hard work. The pellets were all packed in 50kg/1cwt bags and they were not on pallets. There were 480 bags to a load. Later the maximum weight was reduced to 25kg per bag. It made each bag lighter but clearly doubled the number of bags per load. When the pellets were bagged they were quite often warm, and because they were derived from making sugar they were sticky. That meant when they cooled they stuck together which made each bag a solid mass. The last one to off-load was always the heaviest. It was back breaking work, but we only had to hand them off the lorry. We were not required to hike them around the farms to their final resting place.

Concrete deliveries to building sites were all off loaded by a crane or forklift, so it wasn't all heaving and panting.

On the other hand, straw was. We had to load and unload that single-handedly. No respite in the straw season.

For all the hardship, long hours and the likelihood of seldom being at home, I adored it. I was young of course, and much stronger than before. Quickly I gained considerably more meat on my body than you'd find on a butcher's pencil! Despite the extra meat, I still retained my remarkable good looks. I still have them, according to my wife.

The following day was exceptionally hard work. After I'd unloaded 480 bags of pellets by hand at a farm near Sherborne, I was instructed to meet up with Len near Shaftesbury. He showed me the way to a straw field in the middle of nowhere which I don't think I would have found on my own. Fields don't have post codes or addresses so you just have to know which one it is. It was also lucky Len was with me because we helped each other to load. I can't remember exactly how many bales you can get on a trailer, but it was a lot. Perhaps it was 500 or 600? Anyway it was hot and sweaty work, even with a helping hand. We didn't have to unload them the same day. We dropped the trailers in the yard for someone else to do. It was a fine introduction for what was to come in the following months. The straw season was actually coming to an end.

I remember one year when a group of us loaded straw from Cambridgeshire. The bales were what were referred to as Hesston bales, which means they were probably the largest bales available and had to be loaded by a machine. That was the good news. Haulage of straw was paid by weight and we were paid on a percentage of the lorry earnings. The more you could put on, the better the price or rate you'd get paid. Hesston bales are very big by volume, so we had to be careful of the load height. I think it was usual to load them three high but some drivers were greedy. It had been a long day for most of us so we decided to park for the night at a place near St Albans.

We'd got ourselves neatly parked up in a line and were chatting while we waited for the late comers to arrive. Afterwards we'd go and get a snack and some beer. Within half an hour one of them showed up. The load looked a bit messy and windswept and had ropes trailing behind. The driver stopped and Al got out of his cab.

'Al, it looks a bit messy. What happened to you?'

'Well it's like this see? I decided to put another layer on top, but to be on the safe side I strapped all the bottom ones and then roped the last layer.'

'So?'

'Did you know, in the entire British motorway network there are only three bridges which are sub-standard height? And I couldn't for the life of me remember where the third one was. Now I know. It's at the bottom of the A1M.'

'So you lost a whole layer of straw.'

"Well not lost exactly, but it did come as a bit of a shock when I hit the bridge at 75mph. It swept the whole top layer off in one go.'

'Didn't you stop?'

'First of all there didn't seem much point as I couldn't pick them up. Secondly, the road behind was empty, and lastly I've done twenty three hours already this shift and wasn't going to explain that to the Bill. So here I am. Give me a hand to tidy things up will you?'

'Sure, but they're bound to come looking.'

'And I'll be hiding in plain sight, or the lorry will be and we'll all be down the pub none the wiser, won't we?'

Yes, I thought we would. I expected some farmer would be very pleased to pick up a dozen Hesston straw bales for free. He'd probably get paid for it as well.

'You'll lose a bit on the rate, Al.'

'Win some, lose some. There'll be another day and another adventure.'

For me the defining factor which made Reynolds such a happy place was the constant work. There were seldom moments of hanging around waiting for a load to be assigned. It was a well-managed company, and the office-staff was relaxed and appeared content. Everyone was at ease so long as the drivers achieved the work load they were given. There were very few harsh words, although the minimal company rules were rigorously enforced. Lying was a cardinal sin and most of those who did lie were found out and generally expelled.

On the whole the drivers were tolerant of each other and of new-comers. Moral was high. The pay was good and the conditions were above average for a transport yard of the era although they were the same for everyone on the road and away from home. The workshop-staff was helpful and did most repairs instantly and without complaint. All those things made for a profitable company and a loyal workforce. Perhaps I'm looking through rose-tinted glasses at a period I enjoyed. Maybe there were others who see it differently.

In the first couple of years at least, my advantage was I had two jobs in the year. I didn't have the opportunity to get bogged down in a rut or get bored. The company didn't advocate many accessories for the lorries and shied away from fitting things like night heaters. I'd sold mine about a year before starting there. We regularly went to some mighty cold places and I missed it on many nights. The only way to keep warm was to leave the engine running with the heater on all night. You could never over-heat because there were several holes in the older cabs, of which I had one.

It was during one of those first two Campaigns I found a lay-by not far from Newmarket to park for the night. My pull-in was just outside a small village and the sign announcing its name was directly in front of the windscreen. There was a very chilly wind blowing and as I'd already washed and eaten at the sugar factory, it was simply a matter of bedding down for the night. It was snug in the cab and I was listening to the radio. It was probably early January or maybe late December. As usual, I left the engine running and the heater blowing warm air. The weather forecast came on.

'Not five minutes ago the weather office informed us the coldest place in the UK at this time is…' And they told us all it was almost precisely where I'd parked. 'And the registered temperature is -12° centigrade.'

Oh joy, I thought. I vowed not to pop out for a pee during the night. Despite the outside temperatures it was relatively cosy inside my old windblown cab.

One year I turned the lorry engine on in late September or early October and it ran day and night for the whole winter. I never shut it down until the end of the Campaign in early March. I even left it running while I was refuelling, muttering excuses about having a flat battery. It always kept my work station warm and inviting.

Our deliveries and collections were predominantly confined to the south of England. More accurately, below the latitude which would include Birmingham. But we also went to a lot of places in South Wales. There were several sugar factories of course, but Reynolds' contract was with the one at Bury St Edmunds. From time to time we were asked to make collections from other factories.

Peculiar Highland sports

One day I found myself a little further north than usual and was told to collect pellets from another sugar factory for delivery to Polla in Sutherland. For those of you who live up there, you'd know it's a particularly picturesque part of the very north western tip of Scotland. For the rest of us it's just a speck on the map of northern Scotland if you've got good eyesight. Amusingly, in Spanish it translates as hard-on, prick, chick or bet. All of which except chick are slang. Additionally, it was going to take a very long time to get there and back, so I hoped the rate for the job was sensible. I did love going to Scotland so I was happy to go. Actually I had no choice in the matter, but I also knew I was earning very good money while I was only doing middle distance journeys. Off I went to the land of Bonnie Prince Charlie. Lorry driving can be so romantic.

Polla was approximately seven hundred miles from my starting point on the western fringes of East Anglia. Whilst the first part was very easy going, the last part north of Inverness was slow with many of the roads being single track. It took me two whole days to get there. It was a joy to arrive, not just to have achieved the journey but also for the beauty of the place. It was a wild landscape with rocky mountain outcrops falling almost vertically to within half a mile of the sea. There were lots of little inlets from the ocean and on the evening I arrived it was tranquil. I imagined it was normally a fairly windy region.

Over the sea to Skye came to mind although it was nowhere near Skye. I'd been given clear instructions and a local map to find the farm, which was lucky because I saw not a soul to ask directions. It was winter and there weren't many hours of daylight. It was almost completely dark when I eventually came across the place.

'I'm glad you found it alright driver.' Mr McBride greeted me in the half-light.

'Yes. It wasn't easy but I was given this map and directions.'

'We've only just started doing that. Years ago it took drivers days to find us. Some never did and returned home or perhaps they're still up here searching.' He laughed.

'It's a beautiful place to get lost.'

'Aye, it is. Look, it's the end of a long day for us and probably for you too. So we'll unload you in the morning when everyone's bright and rested. How's that sound?'

'It sounds good to me. Whatever you think is best.'

'Come in with us and share our supper. We can offer you a shower and a bed in the bunk house. Of course you may prefer to sleep in your cab. I know most of you boys do.'

'Thanks. I'll accept the offer of supper and a shower, but you're right I prefer the cab for the night.'

'Well, that's good. Back it into the shed. It'll be out of the wind and weather which will be warmer, and it'll protect the load as well.'

After my shower I was introduced to his large family and a beer was thrust into my hand. Along with several of the farm hands we sat down to fine Scottish fare fit for a king. Everyone had a lot to say and we talked of Scotland, lorry driving, the weather, farming by the sea and past tempests. We ate well and later relaxed with our glasses of whisky and cups of coffee. I was impressed and thanked them profusely before retiring to the cab to sleep and prepare for an early morning start. Some of the farm hands slept in the bunk house but those who lived closer went home.

In the morning at six thirty there was a larger group of men than there had been at supper. All 480 bags were unloaded and stored within an hour. It was good news, but I had to kill some time before my office opened so I was offered breakfast. The food was so good I felt I could've spent a week up there. Mr McBride let me use his phone. The office instructed me to collect a load of seed potatoes from a farm in north Sterlingshire. Mr. McBride told me it was quite a long journey from Sutherland. I reckoned I could get there but it would probably take all day because the roads were so narrow. I thanked McBride again for his hospitality and was on my way.

When I got to the designated farm it was blowing a gale and lashing with rain. At the entrance there was a tiny wooden home-made sign announcing

'Mckays'. I thought it must be it. I'd searched for some time so I gave it a go. The track leading in was rough with several pot-holes and fairly long but did eventually lead to a farm with a low roofed bungalow and several taller barns. The wind was howling and it was dark again. Only Norway could have less hours of daylight in the winter. Or Iceland, but I hadn't been there. I spotted a body standing in the lee of a barn.

'Is this McKay's farm?' I shouted over the wind.

'Of course it fucking is! You must've seen the sign. Where the fuck have you been? Don't you know what time it is?'

'Oh well, that's good. I've been searching for it for a while. Yes, it's seven o'clock and I've been travelling all day just to see you. Good evening.'

'Leave off the crap. This load's got to be in the south for latest on Saturday morning and I've got a meeting tonight at nine o'clock.'

'Excellent, that'll give us a couple of hours to load it then. Where is it?' Christ, I thought, he's a fucking miserable bastard.

'It's in this shed. Back it in from the other side.'

I did, and after dismounting from the cab I discovered the load was on pallets. Wasn't I the lucky driver?

McKay stamped over to his massive and ancient forklift. It didn't sound like it was going to start, but eventually it roared into life amid clouds of smoky diesel exhaust. He loaded it expertly to my surprise despite his dark mood. When he'd finished I started to climb on top to get the sheet over it.

'You can take it outside to cover it driver.'

'No mate, I'm not sheeting it outside in this weather. First off, the bags will get wet, (they were paper bags), and second I'll never get the sheet over it in this weather. So I'll be covering it inside.'

'You fucking lightweight Sassenach.'

I was just getting wound up by then but I bit my tongue.

'You won't be late for your meeting. There's over an hour till nine o'clock. What is it? Darts, or is it something more important like cards?"

'Never you mind what it is. Just get a fucking move on.'

I was all done within thirty minutes and I was ready to go, but filthy dirty.

'Where are the delivery notes?' I asked.

'Oh fuck, they're in the house. I'll get them. Get that lorry out of my shed.'

'OK. I imagine it would be too much to ask if I could use your shower?'

'Are you out of your fucking head? I'm not letting a fucking stinking lorry driver inside my house, let alone my fucking bathroom.'

'You're going the right way for a smack in the gob mate. Just get the fucking notes.'

'No driver talks that way to me. I'll make sure you're fired.'

'Yeah, sure McKay. Notes?'

He stomped into the house, stomped back with the paperwork and thrust it through my drivers' window. He looked like he was about to shout more abuse, but I took the notes and fired up the engine. My parting words to him before revving it up and dropping the clutch were,

'By Christ, McKay, you are the most miserable fucking prick in the whole of Britain.'

As I made my departure the lorry covered him in loose gravel and exhaust fumes.

I was off to a store in Frome but washing and eating came first. There hadn't been any signs of habitation on my approach to the charismatic McKay residence so I turned left out of the drive. Within a mile I came across a small village. On the right was a pub. Mostly they're called hotels up there although many aren't. It was on the right and had a convenient lay-by opposite. It would do nicely I thought. It was still pouring with rain so I grabbed my wash kit and launched myself across the road.

I burst into the bar through a heavy oak and glass door, dripping with water and clutching my meagre belongings. It was a large, old fashioned and cosy bar with a log fire burning in the fireplace close to the door. There were heavy oak beams in the ceiling and a collection of ancient but comfortable armchairs were arranged around the fire. A man in his mid-fifties was relaxing in one and smoking a cigar. He looked at me with amused interest.

'Good God, you look like you could do with some beer quite quickly.' He smiled.

'Thanks. Yes, that would be a good starter.'

'I'll pour it for you.' He got up and went behind the bar. 'I'm not the owner, but Doris is cooking her supper and I don't want to interrupt.'

'OK, it's a bit windy and wet out there.'

'Oh yes, it's blowing a hoolie. Welcome to Scotland. Have you come from the south?'

'A few days ago, yes, but I've just loaded spuds from McKay's.'

'Robbie McKay to his friends, but no one calls him Robbie because he hasn't got any friends. What did you think of him?'

'He's a miserable, ignorant…'

'Prick?'

'Close enough.'

I recounted my experience.

'Come and sit by the fire and dry out.' He gave me the beer. 'Doris banned him because in her words he's so coarse. What she actually did was take down the dart board, and after a lot of shouting and complaining he never came back.'

'There can't be many places round here to go for a beer.'

'Oh there are quite a few, but he's not welcome in many. We call him Tosser McKay and not entirely for the obvious reason. Do you know what a caber is?'

'It's a telegraph pole sort of thing isn't it?'

'Well yes, but it's not so refined. It's a young tree trunk of about twenty feet in length with the bark stripped off. They throw them in competitions and the blokes who throw them are called 'tossers'. McKay is quite good at it so in these parts he is in fact a Champion Tosser.'

'And does he know his nick name?'

'Oh yes, that's the funny part. He encourages people to call him a tosser.' He laughed loudly.

'Ah, here's Doris, and I'm Andy.'

'Good to meet you both.'

Andy told Doris the story of my recent encounter with the Champion Tosser.

'Yeah, McKay. As well as being a total wanker he's got a chip on his shoulder about the Sassenachs and the Jocks. You must have seen his Scottish flags flying over every building he's got.'

'It's a bit windy for flags.'

'Yeah well anyway, there're a lot of sassenachs in this village. Most of my customers are, and so am I. Andy's not, and there are lots of other Scots who visit us quite often. I'm from Sussex myself. I came up here to get away from it all. And you?'

'I'm from the West Country. You've certainly excelled in getting away from it all.'

'Golly, you're a long way from home. Are you on holiday?'

'No, I'm a lorry driver. That's my transport outside. Is it alright there for the night?'

'Best place for it. We won't be getting many people in tonight. My goodness you look filthy dirty. Do you want to get a wash?'

'I do, yes.'

'Well look, I don't let rooms at this time of year and everything is under dust covers till the spring, but if you'd like to use my bathroom you're welcome, and there's a shower too.'

'If you're sure, I'd like to very much.'

'You haven't eaten either I expect. Food is the same as the rooms, but if you'd like to share my supper I'd be happy give you some. There's plenty but it's not fine dining.'

'Thank you very much, Doris. That's very kind. I accept.'

'Get your wash things and I'll show you where it is.'

I came out of the bathroom relaxed and smelling of roses and sat down to a hearty meal of beef stew. It was followed by a strawberry flavoured sponge which was delicious. No one else had ventured out for a drink on such a wild night, so Doris, Andy and I spent the rest of the evening chatting and drinking whisky by the fire. What a difference from the shouting match with Champion Tosser McKay. Who in turn was also an astounding difference from the McBride family in the far reaches of Sutherland. I've always liked the Scots. Well, most of them.

I knew I wasn't going to be able to reach Frome in one shift, so I started at 6am which was relatively late for me. When I unloaded on Saturday morning the first thing the warehouse owner said to me was,

'Morning driver. How did you get on with Champion Tosser McKay?'

I laughed, but I wondered how such an ignorant git could be so well known throughout the length of the UK. I told him and of his threat.

'Don't worry about that. I've already warned your boss he might get a call from Scotland. McKay's a cunt. He's threatened every driver who's been there, but he produces champion spuds so we have to keep sending the unsuspecting to meet the twat.'

The notice board

As my mother used to put it, bad language was an inherent part of the haulage industry. Even amongst the office staff unless they were speaking with a customer. I expect it was the same in all industries where the work force was predominantly male. It was well-known in transport the workforce found it more difficult than most to string together a complete sentence of three or more words without using the words 'fuck', 'cunt', 'twat', 'shit' or anything similar. I'd settled in pretty quickly at Reynolds and most of the blokes had got the measure of me within a couple of months, despite us not seeing each other very often. Word gets around on the jungle telegraph. From my earliest beginnings as a driver I'd got used to the use of slang interjections as a way of getting one's meaning across. It saved using a complicated lexicon like 'very' or 'highly'. After a short period I also found I was earning fucking good money. It was much fucking better than ever before. I didn't spend much of it because I didn't have the opportunity. I was working a phenomenal amount of hours.

With all this in mind, one evening I was taking a legally required rest period in the company canteen. Everyone had gone home for the day and there were no drivers in the yard. I made a cup of tea and relaxed in one of the armchairs. Yes, armchairs! They obviously weren't new, and although they were dirty and scruffy they were mighty comfortable. Sometimes they were even fought over if there were a lot of folk present. I devised a plan, more of a joke really, and went back to the cab for a pen and paper. I wrote out my note in capital letters and I attached it prominently and securely to the notice board. It announced:

I WILL PAY £10 TO ANYONE WHO CAN SPEND AN ENTIRE REST PERIOD OF NOT LESS THAN 30 MINUTES IN THIS CANTEEN WITH AT LEAST 1 OTHER PERSON AND MYSELF WITHOUT USING A SINGLE SWEAR WORD. THOSE WORDS INCLUDE BUT ARE NOT CONFINED TO: FUCK, CUNT, SHIT, TWAT, BLOODY. Signed: Hugh

If any of you have comments put them below and sign your name.

I had a little snigger to myself and went back to work. I was thinking in the morning someone would rip it down and bin it. It was only two days later I returned and there was a full house ensconced for lunch, including the boss. I had a quick glance at the notice board and saw my note was still amazingly in place. There was a comment at the bottom which read, 'FUCK OFF YOU CUNT' and signed by Jamie.

'Hi Jamie,' I greeted him. 'I see you've been educated well enough to write.'

'Tosser!'

'You must be a rich man, or perhaps you don't like freebies.'

The boss piped up then.

'These pricks are all stinking fucking rich, but not clever enough to recognise a quick profit if it were handed to them on a pissing platter. Make me another tea Hughy.'

Someone else started off.

'30 fucking minutes ain't long. I can manage that.'

'I'm sure you can Rick but it'll have to be tomorrow now.'

'Why the fucks that?'

The note stayed up on the board for more than a month and unsurprisingly I never paid a soul. The girls from the office often looked in with messages for the drivers and told me it was really funny as not one of the sods was capable of earning such an easy tenner.

Job 53/2 The wet season

After a really enjoyable first season with Reynolds, I returned to Tom's outfit for a summer in the mobile bar. I had arranged to start again on the sugar beet Campaign sometime in the following September. It was something to look forward to and I had secured a full year of work.

It was early in the exhibition season and my first assignment was to go to a ploughing match in the north. It was very near to a place called Horncastle and it was pissing down. The little lane leading up to the hospitality site took some two hours to negotiate. It needed the use of big tractors to make sure it was possible. Once everyone had been accommodated the approaching lane had become mired. After being pulled into position my particular plot looked quite inviting. It was still grassy but as I was pulled on to it the whole lorry and trailer unit sank into the wet ground. It negated the need to camouflage the wheels for presentation. For the final execution I had to omit one level of approach steps. I realised getting out at the end of the show would very probably create problems for me. But still, there was no need to consider the future yet. I wasn't able to separate the lorry from the trailer because of the wet ground so it had to remain looking exactly as what it was. A lorry.

I had expected the happy and convivial Pixy rep to show up and give me his instructions for the show, but he wasn't able to get there because of the chaos of vehicles on the approach lane. He managed it the following morning and arrived with his suit covered in mud and wearing Wellington boots.

'Morning Hugh. This weather doesn't bode well for doing much business. If it keeps up I don't expect there'll be many people turning up for proceedings.'

'So what's the plan then? Shall I just wait or pack up and go home?'

'Oh no, don't do that. We'll wait and see. It might dry up a bit, and anyway we've paid for the site. Farmers always arrive for a day off whatever the weather but we office boys may not be able to physically drive here, which will be problematic. No matter. I'm sure you know enough to sell lubricants by now, don't you?' He laughed.

'I'll give it a go.' I said unconvincingly.

'Do you want a coffee while you're here. I've got it on the go.'

He settled in and we both waited to see what would transpire. I went to get provisions and rustled up some breakfast for us.

A few farmers showed up during the day, but not many. Not much business was done although enough to justify the trailer being there. None of the other salesmen managed to get to the site and it rained all day. The main man went home early and it continued to rain all night. It was a very boggy place. The wet weather turned out to be the precursor of more or less the whole summer season.

The only show I attended in the year which was dry, warm and sunny was a truck racing event at Silverstone. In those days I suppose I could have been described as a bit of a lorry geek, but I've never been overly fond of racing. In the same way I love motorcycles, but I get bored quickly when I watch them go round and round in circles at high speeds. It was certainly a new experience and the noise of the engines was exciting. In my opinion any machine which has been tuned up for racing bears little or no resemblance to the real working tool.

Being a French company Pixy Oil had a working relationship with Renault, who were also present at the event and had sponsored a part of the hospitality throughout the races. It included the bar/trailer which I took along. They provided hostess girls who were very attractive and a selection of Renault racing cars which were less so. The combination attracted a lot of custom so the local Pixy team were really busy selling lubricants.

What I hadn't been told was a racing celebrity had been invited to the trailer. He was a celebrated F1 driver who had later retired to become a commentator on the car racing sport. Sometime after his visit to the Pixy Oil hospitality trailer he died. In the meantime he stood around trying to look intelligent and to talk interestingly with the punters about engines and his life, which he covered in some detail. I know full well one should never speak ill of the dead. On the other hand, I'd learned long ago it's much simpler in the long run to call a shovel a shovel. I've met very few frighteningly important people at both relevant and irrelevant social gatherings. However, I can say with complete honesty that he was the most arrogant, rude and oversized arsehole I've ever had the pleasure to have been made to shake hands with. I only did so as it was under the terms of my contract. Of the others, one was the MP I tried to negotiate a deal with on behalf of Rodes drivers. He was a government minister for something sensitive at the time. Another was a friend of my father who had suffered an almost fatal air crash and lost both his legs. It's true, they were both overly arrogant and wholly self-serving, but they had considerably more social graces than him with the size fourteen shoes at the Silverstone truck racing event. I've often thought great success either financially or otherwise, will only breed contempt for the minions. I hope I'm wrong. To be fair, it was only for a couple of days I had to put up with him whose body was far too large to fit into a racing car. But within an hour the strain was evident on both our faces. It's very simple to write someone off on a first meeting, but as they say in job interviews first impressions are soooooo important.

Next up was the Norwich Agricultural show which was some time around mid-season. It might have been in late July or early August. It was of normal duration, which is to say about three days. I had some time free afterwards and I'd planned to fly out and see my folks in Minorca for a week or so. As I had expected it rained, with the added excitement of thunderstorms. Luckily it was a mostly flat site and had tarmac roads. In the far reaches of the site they were concrete. My allotted plot was fairly close to what would be the centre of attractions. I was glad because it would provide a better escape route when it was all over. The weather dissuaded many of the sales team from putting in an appearance but the show itself was well attended. The area sales rep was happy with the results.

In my brief periods of respite during the days and in the evenings, I met up again with many of my well-known nomadic companions from different hospitality tents and trailers. I made a few more friends amongst the food and booze sellers, especially those dealing in hot-dogs, burgers and pizzas. One of them was a very entertaining bloke in his late thirties who had an array of stories to tell and some very funny jokes. He mentioned more than once, he'd served in the SAS and was very well trained in the use of a knife. It could be born out he said, by the result of his perfectly cut sandwiches. There were one or two of us who didn't truly believe he'd been in the SAS, but it was confirmed the following day by someone who had also served. Mack the knife was in fact a kitchen porter and completely harmless. I can confirm his sandwiches were cut to precision.

I had planned to fly out and see my parents in the Balearics early on the morning following the end of the show. It meant I'd have to drive the lorry back to the yard in the West Country, go home, pack some summer clothes and drive my car up to Gatwick airport. To be frank, this next story has nothing whatever to do with road transport but it was very amusing, so I've included it.

Comic foreign travel

The weather in Norwich didn't let up throughout the show so at the end we were all waterlogged and very mushy. I had been in a great rush to get out and on the road home. I packed up in double quick time, found a tractor to pull me off the plot, and raced to the exit. I got on to the main road at about eight in the evening and put my foot down. I'd had to bribe the tractor driver because obviously there were loads of others who felt they were in front of me. My lorry wasn't capable of even sixty miles an hour despite pulling an empty trailer, and I thought I'd never get back to the yard. I managed it. I got in my old car and went home. By the time I'd packed a case and collected my documents it was about 4am. At eight thirty in the morning I was sitting in the departure lounge cuddling a coffee and waiting for my flight to be called.

I hadn't taken a flight for years so I studied the other passengers to discover what the form was. There was a bloke reading a newspaper sitting a little way from me and close to the departure gate. A flight number was called but not mine. Various people lined up at a gate. A few minutes passed and the number was called again, and then again. A name was called for the flight and again, and then again. Finally it was announced if Mr Whoever didn't go to the gate the aircraft would leave without him. Very slowly, the guy with the newspaper got up and sauntered over to check in. I wasn't sure if it was cool or not, but he certainly avoided the crush in the queue. His aeroplane was immediately outside the windows where we were sitting. I reckoned my flight would be one of the other planes which I could see from my seat.

My number was called and I waited for the crowd to disperse. It was called three times before I bottled out and hurried over to check in. It was lucky I did as the flight I was on was not parked right in my line of vision at all. We all went down in a lift and boarded a rickety bus. It did a complete tour of the airport while the driver searched for our aeroplane. At last we were all seated and we took off.

I hadn't managed to get a direct flight to Minorca. I was on my way to Barcelona where I was assured I could get an internal flight to the islands. That was incorrect. All flights were booked up for days so the remaining option was a nine-hour ferry journey. If that failed I'd have to spend my holiday on the mainland.

At the port there was a queue for tickets and I waited in it. Then they shut the office for lunch. In the afternoon I queued and waited. Then it shut for the day. The next day I repeated the process which later pushed into the second afternoon. The Guardia Civil who was guarding us, (he probably thought we'd do a runner), had clearly taken a shine to me. It was adding to my anxieties. I knew he was in the Guardia because he was wearing the funny hat called the Tricornio. I don't suppose it was any funnier than the British 'Bobby' helmet, but it is very odd with no particular design purpose. He was holding a menacing machine gun affair. It seemed he was looking forward to an opportunity to use it although it was not apparent when he looked at me. On those frequent occasions he gave me one of those 'I fancy you, boy' sloppy grins. There was an old lady in front of me and the queue had diminished a lot. I was the penultimate. Oh, I was so close.

The ticket man looked up and spoke to Guardia. I didn't speak Spanish in those days but actions speak volumes. He obviously said, 'I'll deal with this lady and then that's it.' Guardia indicated me and replied, 'NO! After this lady the nice young boy, and only then you go home.' There followed a lot of shouting with both men verbally holding their ground. With a much louder voice Guardia said, 'Do what I say or I'll blow your brains out,' at the same time as thrusting his gun right through the glass which divides ticket issuer from purchaser. The seller gave in and agreed.

Well, anyone would wouldn't they, if they were armed with only a ballpoint?

Guardia beckoned me over, gave me another huge sloppy grin and stroked my arm. I gave him the international 'Thanks mate' smile and bought my ticket, which I noticed had a lot of shaky handwriting on it. I raced up the stairs to the ship without looking back.

It was only when I was searching for my cabin I discovered there were two ships in port for different destinations. I was on the wrong one. So I had to return down the stairs and climb up the opposite ones. Guardia and I exchanged smiles during my ship exchange, but thankfully it was the last I saw of him. Oh, the excitement of foreign travel. You can't beat it.

I returned from my couple of weeks' holiday in the sun on a direct flight. I resumed my toil as the part time mobile barman until the season ended for the second time. I'd made up my mind I wasn't going to do it for a third year, but decided not to tell Tom until I'd secured full time employment. I returned to Reynolds for the sugar beet campaign and made enquiries about staying on permanently. It was greeted with 'we'll see' which I thought sounded promising. I determined to ask again after a couple of months.

54/2 Eddy and the force

A new addition had been added to the office staff in the form of a traffic manager. He was responsible for all the day to day organising of loads and work schedules for the drivers. I always liked Eddy but there were many in the crew who didn't take to him. They thought he asked too much of them. It was true, but to Eddy it was a game to give us too much work and see if we could actually achieve it. He obviously knew we'd always be a day or two behind. He never gave anyone a bollocking for underachievement, because it wasn't his job. He could neither hire nor fire. He was really no threat at all to the drivers, but he was in the first line of management if we had complaints or requests. I was introduced to him on my first Saturday of the campaign.

'Good to meet you Hugh. Welcome to the force.'

I wasn't sure if I'd joined the police or not.

'We've got a lot of concrete on at the moment and fertilizer, before the beet season gets fully under way. You can do one to Chichester on Monday, and then almost certainly there'll be a few big bags of fertilizer from Eastleigh to go to Salisbury, but call me anyway when you're empty.'

"I'll do that then. Thanks.'

'Take the one for the 8am delivery, please.' Chichester wasn't more than two and a half hours away, but I went to find the trailer straight away to save me time on Monday. Otherwise I'd have to get up in the middle of the night. I asked one of the other drivers for directions to the building site and also I remarked,

'The new bloke Eddy seems OK, but what's all this about joining The Force?'

'Pass mate. No idea. Maybe he's a Star Wars or Trek fan, but it won't make any of us travel at the speed of light.'

My first Monday back at Reynolds put his reply in some doubt as I raced to achieve everything Eddy gave me to do. I didn't know him well so I was trying to please. It was especially because I wanted to continue working there when the beet campaign finished.

I arrived in Chichester just before the appointed delivery time. Once I was unloaded I found a café for breakfast and rang base.

'OK Hugh, good good. Go to…' and he gave the address in Eastleigh, 'and load fertilizer in big bags for the following farm near Salisbury.'

I wrote it all down.

"It's a big farm. There are forty loads to go there and they're working round the clock to unload. Call again when you're empty, but I expect you could keep doing it all day unless something urgent crops up.'

Over the years I had learned nothing very urgent crops up in a transport fleet. Urgencies usually only occur if there's a breakdown or someone in the office makes a mistake. There is a lot of forward planning and several contingency plans because we all know anything which can go wrong will go wrong. We have to be prepared. In any case, urgencies in haulage are reserved for pizza deliveries! It looked like a nice easy day doing short trips.

I delivered the first load of fertilizer to Salisbury and called in. Then I did another four loads to the same farm and called base again just before 5 o' clock.

'Yeah OK Hugh, can you do another two loads to Salisbury. Then load another, bring it back to the yard, take off your ropes and sheets, drop it off, pick up an empty, take it to the concrete works, drop it, pick up one for Colchester and be there at 8am. Are you alright with that?'

It didn't sound like a direct order.

'Oh yeah, fine.'

Well I thought, he's having a giraffe.

I can't remember how I managed to keep my records looking straight but I must've managed. No one mentioned anything to me until we all went to court a couple of years later.

I completed all the jobs I'd been tasked with by 2am the following morning which was Tuesday. I was absolutely shot. I remember feeling I couldn't keep my eyes open a moment longer. I stopped for what remained of the night at Leigh Delamere services. I flaked out on the bunk with the door open and within a few minutes there was a face in the opening saying,

'Hello Mr Reynolds. I never saw you arrive.'

'Oh really?'

'Christ, you look fucked. I'll leave you be.'

'Goody.'

It was a very long day which is probably why I remember it, but it wasn't a one off. In the beet season the work was continuous. I'd got out of bed the previous morning at four o'clock and worked all day and into the night. It was very nearly a 24 hour shift. It had begun to be difficult once I was back in the yard at around midnight, knowing I had plenty more to do. After getting started on the last journey of the day I felt better, but fatigue finally got the best of me. I slept profoundly for a full four hours and then resumed the journey. I unloaded in Chelmsford at 10am and called Eddy to report the state of play.

'No, you can't be empty! I never thought you'd get there till this afternoon at the earliest, but probably tomorrow.'

'Would I lie to you Eddy, would I li..iie to youooooo?' I sang.

'Probably not. Well you've caught me on the hop, so it's best you go up to Bury and Gary'll give you an exciting destination in the South West. I'll find out where it is later so call me when you've tipped, (unloaded).'

'On my way.'

There were an enormous amount of regulations, constraints and laws to prevent a professional goods driver doing more work than might be considered safe in a working day. The motivation lies in the desire to earn loads of money which unfortunately has become everyone's god. In order to circumvent the restrictive rules you have to be very inventive. Of course it could be argued we never had to do the amount of hours and miles we did. Even so, competition for a good job was strong and if you weren't among the best you could easily lose your position. At the time the basic pay was about £130 per week less tax and so the bonus, which was 25% of earnings was mighty important. While I was at Reynolds I was self-employed so for me there was no basic pay to fall back on in times of sickness or holiday or idleness. If I didn't work I earned nothing. The long and short of it was I had to work my socks off. I was young then and I loved it. I loved the money. I loved the freedom and I loved bending the rules. For some reason age gives you a different perspective.

'Hey Gary, how goes it my man?'

'Hello lover, you're early. Far too early. Go and have a lie down and I'll call you when I've got something you'll like.'

'OK but will I?'

'Course you will. Have I ever let you down?'

'I can't remember. Make it a distance load if you can. I don't want lots of short trips.'

'I'll do what I can. Drop your empty off near the loading door.'

I parked up and lay down on my bunk. I was asleep almost immediately. I woke up and felt hungry. I discovered it was after two o'clock. I went to the canteen, had a light lunch and returned to the cab to read a little. Afterward, I slept through till nine thirty in the evening. Suddenly there was a heavy knock on the door.

'There's a distance one for you Hugh. Penzance. It's loaded, you just got to cover it and delivery time is 08.00.'

'Penzance? That's a ten hour trip man!'

'Yeah, well probably a bit less. You'll make it in eight to nine I reckon. Go early, as the boss keeps telling everyone.'

'OK, thanks Gary, I'm on it.'

'Good, good. See you in a few days.'

There was no time to lose so I got coupled up to the aforementioned trailer and secured the load as quickly as possible. I've always enjoyed driving at night which was lucky because there was an awful lot of night work. We had to in order to cover the long distances and be sure of delivering at 08.00. Of course it's much easier if you know where you're going and the best routes to take. It was something I'd learned over what was by then quite a few years on the road. Anyway I've always loved geography.

Whilst obviously it would be night, it was in fact the best time of day to travel. There was seldom very much traffic and it was peaceful, well as much as it can be while sitting on top of a roaring diesel engine. Despite the darkness outside there were often good views over distant towns and moonlit countryside. I always drove with the interior light on which was the one in the bunk area. It was behind the driver and therefore creates less reflection in the windscreen. The reason was because it reduced the glare from oncoming headlights and helps to prevent you dozing off. It's normally the period for sleeping rather than working. Many drivers used red or other coloured lights which I discovered are better. I believe it's recently become illegal and I imagine it's a law dreamt up by someone who goes everywhere in taxis or doesn't possess a driving licence.

Years later I discovered everything in England is illegal. If you can manage to get from your bed to the front door without breaking a law you'll be heavily fined or taxed or both. Just for being able to achieve it.

I'd left the sugar beet factory just after eleven o'clock which was handy as it meant I'd been able to log a full eleven hour rest period. I wouldn't have to cleverly alter anything on my records.

It was a very leisurely and relaxing trip down to the far reaches of civilisation. I managed to get a couple of rest periods in motorway services for cups of tea and coffee. Everywhere off the motorway was closed at those hours. I also managed an excellent full breakfast in a Cornish café which opened early in the mornings for drivers. Of course the delivery address was nowhere near Penzance. Instead it was out in the middle of nowhere, because it was a farm.

I rolled on to Bert Granger's farm at 08.05, which I reckoned was a pretty good achievement. In any other circumstances it would have merited a medal of honour. I wound down the window and spoke,

'Good morning. Mr Granger? I have a full load of sugar beet pellets for delivery to you.'

'You're late!'

He said it with a heavy Cornish accent.

'Yes. You're right I am.'

No point in arguing.

'I got blokes standing around waiting for you when they could be doing other things.'

'Yes I can see, but I'd dispute how much they could have got done in five minutes. Look I can take it away and come back again tomorrow morning at precisely 8am. How's that suit?'

'It doesn't suit at all.'

'Mr Granger, do you know where this load has come from?'

'No.'

'It's come from Bury St Edmunds. Do you know where that is?'

'No.'

'Well it's so fucking far away I've almost forgotten myself. I left the factory at eleven o'clock last night to get here for eight o'clock this morning. I'm five minutes over time. My apologies to you sir.'

Long pause.

'Christ boy, you been driving all night? You must be fair pooped. I spec you could do with a nice cup a tea and slice of toast. What do you say?'

'It sounds spot on Mr Granger.'

'I'll get the Mrs to rustle it up for you.'

He turned to his men.

'You lads. give the driver a hand with his ropes and sheets and start unloading it while he has his snack.'

Bert, as he insisted I called him, was very amenable. After we finished unloading, Mrs. Granger ordered me to eat the full breakfast she'd prepared. I used their telephone to call the office.

'Ah, Good morning Hugh. Where are you and what's the state of play?'

'You told me yesterday you'd know as Gary would tell you.'

'He didn't.'

'I'm ahead of you again then. I'm MT in Penzance. Well, nearby in the middle of nowhere but close to Penzance allegedly.'

'I'm impressed. You're not pulling my leg are you?'

'I can't see any reason to do so at the moment.'

'OK great. Well by a stroke of luck there's a fertilizer boat docked in Cattedown Wharf. Get yourself a full load and bring it back to the yard for store. See you for elevenses. The load number is...'

Plymouth. Relatively close then. I notice by checking Google maps again to remind myself of various places there are two specific regions in Plymouth, amongst many others of course. One's called Hoe and another's called Hooe. It's a pity there isn't one called Hee and we could all have a laugh. So anyway HoeHoeHooe, we're all off to Plymouth in sunny Devon.

Cattedown was a labyrinth of tiny lanes with various different wharves, so I obviously got lost. Anyway it's not a very big area and in time I found the right one and got myself loaded. I wasn't back at the yard in time for elevenses but I made it for lunchtime. I dropped my trailer and went to the canteen. There was a sizeable group of other drivers taking a break.

'Hi Hughy. What's new in the world of super trucking?'

I told them my story of the last couple of days.

'Christ man, you want to do less or you won't ever become an old timer.'

'You're probably right. Anyone got other stories?'

'Yes,' said Dave.

'I can tell you about the toff in a Roller.'

'Let's hear it.'

'Well, last week I had a load of tractors and machinery for a farm in Dorset. I was going down this single track lane with deep ditches on both sides and this Rolls Royce was coming towards me. So I stopped and waited to see what would happen. The Roller stopped right in front of me and we all waited. He blew his horn and waved his hands about, so I turned the engine off and put my feet on the dashboard. After a while the noise stopped, the driver got out and he waved for me to talk to him, so I got out.'

'Driver says, We're in a hurry. You got to get out of the way.'

'No I don't think so', I said, 'best if you back up.'

'I ain't doing that, he said.'

'OK I said, get your boss out of the back seat and I'll have a chat with him.'

'Boss got out and came over.'

'Driver, he said, I'm in a great hurry. You'll have to move and anyway my car is worth £100,000.'

'It's going to be a lot easier and quicker if you back up your very expensive toy. Besides, my vehicle is worth £150,000, the trailer is worth £25,000 and the load I'm carrying is worth £250,000. The intended recipient of the load is also in a great hurry for it and he will probably make a profit of ten times the value of your toy. But I said, to prevent this discussion developing into a value competition argument, I'd point out my vehicle has got 320hp, is much bigger than yours and weighs in at about 35 tonnes today. I could just push you back but it would cause more problems than we've got already.'

'He looked me straight in the eye for quite a while and then he said,'

'You've made some valid points driver.'

'He turned to his man and he said,'

'Harry, wait for me to get in and then back up.'

'Which he did.'

'Yeah, good one Dave. You know some long words, but those numbers weren't very accurate were they?'

'I been taking classes from Hughy and the numbers weren't important as it got the job done, dinnit?'

'Yeah, OK,' said Mikey, 'nuff stories, change of subject. I got a problem.'

'You got 'undreds o problems Mikey.'

'Yeah, but I got a special one at home. It's electrical. Anyone know a good electrician?'

'Yeah I know one and he's called, hang on a minute,'

'He's called Steve.' I said.

'Yeah he is. How do you know that Hughy? Do you know him?'

'Might do but all sparkies are called Steve.'

'No they're not.'

'Yes they are,' said Rick, 'I know five. They're all good and they're all called Steve. Here look, I got them listed in my diary.'

'You're kidding, you keep a diary? What the fuck do you write in it?'

'Names of electricians. What did you think?'

'So how do you know which one you're calling?'

'I put a reference next to each one like Steve Fatty, Steve Grumpy, Steve Piss-artist, Steve with the absolutely fucking gorgeous wife.'

'I know three myself and you're right, they're all called Steve. That's amazing.'

'Not really, all lawyers are called Anthony and all accountants are called Julian.'

'Yeah you could be right and all traffic managers are called Cunt!'

'That's a bit unfair Bob. Just 'cause you've had a few shit loads lately.'

'Moving on lads. Who wants another cuppa, just like Mum made it?'

'That'd be a first. Yes I'll have one, but scrape the scum off the top for me.'

'Fuck your tea. Someone just give me a number of a good sparky called Steve in Taunton.'

'Coming up son. Just hold your horses.'

East to west exchange

I'm pretty certain it was the same season the competition for the company's work contract with the sugar company in Bury St Edmunds came to a head. The result was we lost an amount of work, but it was compensated for by another contract working out of a factory in Kidderminster. The advantage of the work from Bury was the loads we collected were generally bound for the direction of our home base. Kidderminster on the other hand predominantly sent all its loads into Wales. This often resulted in getting stuck in the Midlands or Wales for weeks on end. Of course it depended on the quantity of work there was from the concrete factory in Taunton. They were our main source of work all the year round. The long and short of it was whenever we found ourselves in the London or south eastern area, we were reloaded to the Midlands so we could work out of Kidderminster before returning home. It didn't affect me personally because I was spending practically my entire working life away from home. For those with wives and family it wasn't so good, although the company did its best to accommodate most drivers' different personal situations. There was still some work out of Bury but not as much as before. Never mind eh? Life is an ever-changing adventure. One advantage for us was the company employed a local shunter in Kidderminster to load trailers and cover them. It saved us some of the dirty work.

Several weeks passed and I seemed to be driving every minute of the day. Even I thought I was achieving an enormous amount of work. For me the money was an absolute fortune. I was paid in cash each week and I seldom received less than £800. It was colossal. I seldom took holidays so the annual amount would have been in the region of £40,000. I didn't compare it with other people in those days. If you were to compare it with drivers' wages in the second decade of the 21st Century, I think you'd find it staggering. I didn't really have time to spend it or enjoy my new wealth. I knew if I kept going in the same vein I could probably afford to buy a lorry of my own. I had a plan.

I was in the office one morning looking for my next load. I was also thinking it might be a good time to ask if I'd be able to continue on the fleet at the end of the beet campaign. I knew I'd need more dosh than I'd accumulated to date to execute the plan.

Eddy wasn't there so Roger greeted me,

'Ah Hugh, you do so much we hardly ever see you in here.'

'Yes. Now you mention it, this is the first time I've seen the yard in daylight for some time.'

'Did you know you've reached the dizzying heights of Star Driver on this fleet?'

'No, I wasn't aware. Is there a prize or a pay rise?'

'No, you'll just continue to get a lot of the work which traffic thinks no one else will do without complaint.'

'No, well I didn't really think there would be, but maybe you could give me a sticker to put in the windscreen?'

'No, and anyway it would now be illegal because the windscreen can only tolerate official stickers like the road tax and stuff.'

'OK, another ridiculous law.'

'Every day. You have to keep on your toes. Right, there're some wide loads for Coventry. They're 10 feet 6 inches wide. Whilst they're notifiable they don't have to be escorted. However you will have to put wide load markers on them which you'll get from the workshop. Put two on the front and two on the back of the load. That's two on each side which makes four in all. Use your ingenuity to attach them, but they must be on the load. It's the law. Ever done a wide load?'

'Once at Rodes.'

'Well they're the same as any other load but they're wider.'

'Gotcha.'

I paced about the office for a few minutes without saying anything although I was aware our conversation had finished.

'Is there something on your mind, Hugh?'

'Er, well, yes actually.'

I was embarrassed but didn't know why.

'You know I asked you if I could stay on as full time after this beet season? It was just I wondered if you've had enough time to think about it, especially as I've now got the accolade of Star Driver?'

Roger laughed.

'Yes, of course you can. I'm sorry, I'd forgotten you'd have to let Tom know at some stage. I'm sure there'll be a place for you bearing in mind our reasonably fast turnover of drivers. If there isn't one we'll find one or create another. That is providing you keep up to scratch, I'm sure you will. Consider it a deal, but on the same terms eh? Self-employed on 25% of earnings plus expenses only. Are you happy with that?'

'Perfect. Thanks Roger.'

It certainly was perfect. I really didn't want to go back to being a temporary, travelling part-time barman on £250 a week even it was for only five or six months. I decided to give Tom the news straight away.

I collected my load for Coventry and it certainly did look very wide to me. Once everything was connected up and secured complete with the triangular marker signs, I sat in the cab to see what it looked like. The mirrors on a lorry are especially important, despite remarks made to me by the workshop staff after breaking one.

"There's no need to worry 'bout that son. They only tell you where you've been. Just keep looking to the front.'

So I looked in them and what I saw were two large slabs of concrete. You couldn't adjust the mirrors from inside the cab in those days, so I was stuck with it. I'd just have to guess when going round corners or reversing. Not ideal.

Drivers who carried wide loads all the time like caravans or portakabins, had mirror arms fitted in the right place so you could see below the load, which was clever. It was not the case for me or for any of us on general haulage.

Ten feet six is not as wide as you would imagine when looking in the mirrors. Under normal circumstances the lorry was eight feet three or four inches, but with the mirror width it was more like nine feet. It was no more than nine inches wider each side but it certainly looked like it. I couldn't ever say wide loads turned me on but I did enjoy hauling long ones.

I took the opportunity to call Tom and tell him I wouldn't be going back to bar tendering in the spring. He wasn't surprised but he sounded a bit sad. He'd have to spend time looking for another suitable employee. He wished me well and invited me to call in whenever I was passing, which I did on many occasions.

All set and I was off to Coventry. I'd been told the load was notifiable but I wasn't sure if it was routed or not. There was nothing on the delivery notes to say so and I thought it probably wasn't. In any event, due to the lack of vision to the rear I decided to take the motorway route. It was easier and the delivery site was to the north of Coventry anyway. Normally we turned off near Tewkesbury and went up through Evesham and Stratford-on-Avon. There were parts which were a bit narrow and I wasn't going to chance a problem I could avoid by going the long way. In any case the M40 didn't stretch as far north as it does now, so there probably wasn't much difference in the journey time. It's really quite distressing not being able to see behind when you're used to it. The delivery site was easy to find and only just off the motorway. I was unloaded swiftly and then Eddy redirected me to Kidderminster, which I thought would be the case. I'd probably have to spend the rest of the week working from there to all points Wales.

Wales

I can't remember the name of the chap who did the loading and shunting of trailers in the Kidderminster sugar factor, but I do recall he was easy to get on with. He lived locally so he was at home each night. We'll call him Anwyll for recognition purposes. On my arrival I introduced myself to Anwyll, and as it was his rest period we had a coffee together in the factory canteen.

He told me he used to be a lorry driver on distance work, but when he and his wife had started a family he wanted to spend more time at home. He had a job in the summer driving a delivery van and for the winter he had picked up the shunting job with Reynolds. He was a happy fellow but quiet, which many drivers are. He admitted the work was back-breaking but if you took it at a gentle pace it was bearable. He loaded about six or seven trailers a day.

Bearing in mind each load consisted of 480 fifty kilo bags, it was a considerable amount of weight he carried on his back each day. The bags came off a chute above the trailer and he had to catch each one and walk them to the front of the trailer to load it. When the load was completed he had to cover it, park the trailer and organise the delivery notes. Those were left in the weighbridge. As you can imagine, it was all fairly time consuming. There were never more than three of four drivers working constantly out of the factory. Any extra loads were carried by anyone passing through the area. It was seldom possible to deliver more than one load a day because in Wales there were a lot of hills and mountains on extremely small roads.

On the whole it was a very enjoyable time and there were no harsh timetables to stick to. We never collected return loads from the centre of Wales, mostly because there weren't any. I had the opportunity to see a great deal of rural Wales while I was working there. I can assure you it was absolutely beautiful and hopefully still is.

'Lunch break is over,' said Anwyll. 'There's one ready to go to LLandrindod Wells. You should be able to get it unloaded and get back this evening. It's a farm so they'll take it off whenever, but give them a call before you go. Then for tomorrow, there's a long one for Rhyd-Ddu which is in the north. It'll be an all day trip. It'll give you a taste of the lakes and mountains. That suit you?'

'Sounds fine Anwyll. I'll have to get my rural maps out for a better shufti.'

'You will that, some of those farms are well hidden away. The Welsh never caught on to the motorway idea apart from the M4 which is an extension of the English one. Consequently, all the roads are almost wide enough for a horse and cart. You'll have a lot of fun up here, Hugh.'

'I'm looking forward to it and I shouldn't think there'll be so much rushing about.'

'Oh, there is sometimes, if there's a lot of local journeys. However, we generally give them to the blokes passing through, if there are any.'

'OK Anwyll, I'm on it. Catch up tomorrow maybe.'

I did my duties without undue problems and was back in the factory by 9pm. I prepared for the following day and was showered, fed, (the canteen was open 24/7), and happily in bed by ten thirty. I was ready for an early start in the morning.

I didn't start really early, but in my opinion any time after 6am was wasting the day. I calculated the journey would take me about four hours on Welsh roads, but in fact it took closer to five. There was no rush as I'd only have time to deliver and return empty. The northern part of the A5, which was the old London to north Wales trunk road was beautiful, but despite its title was quite difficult to negotiate with a large vehicle. The views in the mountains and beyond were stunning.

It was during the period I was there, or perhaps a little before, I'd taken a keen interest in photography. Wales provided some wonderful opportunities for all sorts of different photographic topics.

I had learned how to develop and print my own film, but obviously wasn't able to do it unless I was at home with the darkroom equipment. Consequently, on the very few occasions I was at home I had rolls and rolls of film to process. It was a great hobby and I enjoyed it immensely. While I was learning I was encouraged to take pictures of certain subjects like trees or bridges. It was to help me develop the skill. There were plenty of trees and bridges in Wales and also an abundance of mountains and lakes.

Autumn was turning to winter and the cold weather comes on quicker in the mountains. The ground was hardening more rapidly than in the lowlands. There was a lot of ground frost in the fields and countryside, but also in the rushing rivers and streams. Ice had begun to form and in some places was clinging to smaller plants and leaves. It was magical and I stopped many times to take photos on my journey north.

I'd learned a lot about the darkroom workings and felt sure I could do some amazing transformations with my images. Hopefully it would be before the sugar beet season ended.

I managed to get some breakfast at a café on the outskirts of Oswestry. Afterwards it was only just over an hour before I found the farm. As usual it was hidden in the countryside but relatively close to Rhyd-Ddu. There were lots of blokes hanging around in the yard trying to look busy. The foreman approached me.

'It looks like I've kept you waiting,' I began, 'but it is quite a bit further than I imagined.'

'Good morning driver, not at all. We knew you were coming this morning, but not exactly when and I didn't want the lads getting lost in the fields at the crucial moment. Get your sheets off and we'll have you unloaded within an hour.'

They helped me with the ropes and sheets and then they clambered up on to the load and started handing the bags off to their mates waiting below. When I'd tidied up my stuff and stored it, I climbed up to join them. They laughed a lot and seemed very cheerful, but I couldn't understand a word they said. I reckoned it had to be Welsh. I didn't know people still spoke it. I'd thought it was another dead language like Latin. We were about half way through the job when they stopped for a break. The foreman sauntered over to me while the work crew disappeared into a barn to find their flasks and sandwiches.

'Do you want a cup of tea driver?'

'Yes, thanks.'

'Come with me up to the kitchen. I'll make you one.'

I followed.

'Plenty of drivers who come here, think the boys are taking the piss out of them. They don't like it when they speak Welsh.'

'Ah, it is Welsh, I thought it had to be, or perhaps Gaelic.'

'Oh yeah, it's definitely Welsh. It's not true what the drivers think. These blokes can't speak English, Welsh is their only language. They mean well and they work hard, but they've been brought up in Welsh speaking families and have never left the region. Never! Not even as far as Chester which is only just across the border. I just wanted to reassure you no one's taking the mickey.'

'Don't concern yourself. I don't have a problem with other people's languages. Christ man, there are some English dialects which are incomprehensible. I'm only here to serve, as they say. I certainly do love Wales, it's beautiful.'

'Yeah, most of it is. In the summer it's awash with tourists, and we need them despite the moaning from the locals.'

'Yes, it's the same in the West Country where I live. Do you know the story about the Eskimo touring in Wales?'

'No. Go on, I could do with a good joke.'

"Well, so there was an Eskimo doing a touring holiday in Wales by car, see? And he's driving round some remote and mountainous part of the country when suddenly his car comes to a stop. He knew absolutely nothing about the workings of a car engine, so he gets out and does what everyone does. He looks under the bonnet. Perplexed, he stands upright and looks around. Almost immediately, another car pulls up and the driver gets out.

"Can I help you?" he asks. 'I'm a mechanic on my way home and this is a hell of a place to break down.'

'That's kind of you, thanks.' The Eskimo says.

So Taffy looks under the bonnet and pulls a few wires, tubes and things. Very soon he looks up and says,

'Yes mate, it's OK. I've got some bits in my car and I'm sure I can fix it straight away.'

'Oh, thanks very much.' The Eskimo says. 'What is the problem?'

'It's easy mate. You've blown a seal.'

The Eskimo looked a bit taken aback and retorts,

'So what? You fuck sheep!'

The foreman burst out laughing,

'Oh yeah, I like it. I can't wait to go down the pub tonight and tell my mates.'

The unloading was finished forty minutes later. I said my goodbyes and was on my way. I decided to take the country route as I had all day to get back. I wanted to see the tourist railway train at Ffestiniog, so I headed south from the farm. My route didn't take me close enough to spot the train or even the line, but the countryside and the mountains were awesome. I passed through Bala and saw the lake and then corrected my direction for Welshpool, Ludlow and Kiddermister. I was back by mid-afternoon. As I drove into the factory, I spotted another lorry from the fleet and waved to the driver. I got out to talk to him and recognised him straight away.

'Hi there, Junk. Long time no see. How's it going my little tulip?'

'My name's not Junk. It's Martin.'

'Calm down mate. Everyone calls you Junk. It's because of all the junk you carry around with you.'

'I know why it is, but none of it is junk. It's all really useful.'

'We could debate it if you like. For instance, your curtain pelmet obscuring your view can't be very useful although it's quite pretty. Did your wife make it for you?'

'Just leave it off Toff. I'm not in a very good mood today.'

'I can see. What's troubling you?'

'Well I've been out all bloody week and every time I get somewhere near home, he sends me away again. I've already missed a dentist appointment and I just have to be home by lunchtime tomorrow. My little girl's in her school play.

I just cannot miss it. I keep telling the little wanker in the office, but he don't listen.'

'OK, so where's he sending you now?'

"I don't know. I've got to ask Anwyll, but I bet it'll be into fucking Wales again.'

'Cool it Junk. Let's go and see Mr Shunt and have a nice cuppa tea, yeah?'

'I got stress with a capital S.'

'You have that. You got Junk with a capital J as well. Come on let's go.' We settled down in the canteen with our teas, and shortly afterward Anwyll arrived.

'Hello lads. What's the crack?'

'Well, Junk here's got a problem.'

'It's Martin for fucks sake!'

'OK Martin. Tell me.'

'No, I'll tell you or he'll have a heart attack.'

'Go on then.'

'Junk has been out all week and he absolutely has to be home tomorrow. So what have you got loaded ready to go?'

'Oh is that all? I got a Ludlow, one for Cirencester and one for store at your yard, but none have to be there before tomorrow.'

'Nice. How much time have you got left today, Junk?'

'How many times? It's Martin! I got two hours left today.'

'Fine you take the one for store and arrive at base not before eleven in the morning. I'll do the one for Ludlow now and first thing tomorrow I'll deliver the one for Cirencester. It'll work out perfect for everyone, except me.'

'Would you do that, Toff?'

'It's Hugh but don't get excited Junk. Of course, why not? Ah, but I'll call the office and sort it out cos you'll just get over excited, yeah?'

'OK thanks. I'm S-T-R-E-S-S-E-D OUT!'

'Hi Eddy, it's Hugh. Junk's with me.'

'Hi Toff, it's Martin. He keeps telling me.'

'OK, and it's Hugh. I keep saying so.'

'Moving on?'

I told him the plan and why.

'I want you to do the one to store because he's got time to do the Cirencester and load Avonmouth in the morning.'

I explained the driving time and stress problem and administratively, it couldn't make a blind bit of difference who did what.

'OK Hugh. I'll live with your plan. Tell Junk to get a move on so he can do a quickie to Exeter before lunch.'

'I'll tell him.'

I told him.

'Fuck me Hugh. That's brilliant.'

'What? And die a cripple?'

'What?'

'Never mind. Sleep soundly and make sure you don't have enough time to do the Exeter.'

'It's all settled then,' said Anwyll, and then to Junk 'You need to see a doctor son.'

Stress was not a word which was widely accepted in the English language as a description of a mental health condition until the late 1980s. It was however, beginning to be adopted in the 1970s. Beforehand, it had always been used as an engineering term to address the use and construction of for instance, steel or timber. There was a doctor in the 1930s who described certain symptoms in patients who suffered from mild mental problems as stress. In those days it was not officially accepted by the medical profession. It was only 40 or 50 years later it became a recognised condition.

In my humble opinion everybody will suffer from it at one time or another. Some people have it all the time and some people appear to crave it. Some people can't live without it.

I think it's a generic term for other undiagnosed problems which we already have. In the modern world we just love to put labels on everything. Stress has now become a specific condition which we all understand because it's got a label. Call me old fashioned but I don't think it's anything more than the inability to cope with our problems. It's predominantly temporary as well.

You really shouldn't use it as an excuse to avoid work or school.

To prevent it occurring my advice is,

Don't Worry...Be Happy!

I expect my opinion was really helpful.

The stress which Junk, sorry Martin was suffering from was probably a mixture of inherent worry and not wanting to do any more work in the week.

Another modern phrase we often use now is having a good work life balance. If you choose to work in the 'get-your-hands-dirty' part of the transport industry you cannot expect to have any work life balance. It is most especially true if you do distance or international work. International drivers have been known to spend months away from home. Normally it would not be conducive to having a happy home life. Drivers who are confined to working in the UK can also spend a lot of time away from their partners and children.

There is only one priority in a lorry drivers' life, and it's the job. Even so, in my day I knew many long distance drivers with wives and family. They never appeared to suffer, but it was a long time ago and many things were different.

'Anwyll, can I deliver to Ludlow today? It'll make tomorrow easier.'

'Makes no difference to me but I should give them a call first.' I did so, delivered and was back in the factory for the early evening. I secured the following day's load and hit the sack.

In the morning I arrived in Cirencester at seven o'clock and was away to Avonmouth by nine.

'Your load for Taunton's already gone mate, sorry.'

'Shit. What else is there?'

'All we got left is Telford, but it's not really your direction is it?' I phoned the office.

'Alright Hugh. Have you got time to go to Telford?'

'Yes.'

'OK, do it then and there'll be one for the yard out of Kidderminster. It'll round the week off for you won't it? It's 11.30 already and Junk's still not here. Do you know where he's got to?'

'No idea. Maybe he's had a heart attack. See you tomorrow. Bye.'

They kept me waiting to unload in Telford for hours, and I mean hours. They did promise to unload me on the day, but it didn't happen till gone six thirty. My time was almost up and I knew I wouldn't get back to Kidderminster. I decided on Walsall as a convenient stop. It was in the right direction and had a bit of night life.

Nowadays it probably doesn't look like it did then. Walsall lorry park was a car park by day and was vast. If it were ever full I expect they could have parked more than a thousand lorries on it. Another aspect was it fronted the West Midland Constabulary headquarters. So it had to be safe, didn't it? There were also hundreds of pubs and clubs within easy walking distance. It seemed ideal and I parked. Sadly there was nowhere to wash so I had a strip wash in the cab, which was a bit of a come-down after the luxuries of the sugar factory showers.

I'd also noticed it was alive with girls punting the lorries, but I really didn't fancy it. I had a girl friend at home.

In those years it was widely perceived all transport drivers were boozing whoremongers. It was probably because we were away from home for so long and would crave sexual fulfilment or the need to drown our sorrows. There really weren't many sorrows to drown and as for the former, we weren't very much different from anybody else. Of course there were some who paid prostitutes regularly, but not many in my experience. Not even Jack, even though he seemed obsessed with his tail! As for the beer, well everyone enjoys a good pint after a hard days' work, don't they?

Just as I was about to climb into my glad rags there was a knock on the door. I parted the curtains, wound down the window and put my head out. She was very pretty in a chocolate box kind of way, but not really my first choice.

'Yeah...?' I said cheerfully.

'Want to do some business mate?' She said it in a heavy Brummy accent.

'No thanks love.'

'Why not?'

'I've just had a wank.'

'OK, I'll come back in half an hour then.'

Half an hour, I thought. I wasn't Superman.

I slid into my clothes and headed for the beer sellers.

I was feeling slightly the worse for wear in the morning, but I collected my home-bound load and arrived in the yard in time to avoid having to do any more loads that week.

Not long afterwards I heard Anwyll had handed in his notice. I wasn't surprised. I felt anyone would have to be super human to keep up the amount of physical work he did each week.

Roger called me to the office.

'Hugh, I expect you've heard Anwyll is leaving us.'

'Yes.'

'We're having trouble finding someone to replace him and we need to send a temporary replacement up from here to take his place for a while. Will you do it? It won't be for very long. Maybe for a week or two.'

'What will the money be?'

'How much do you want?'

'Can I work at weekends?'

'Certainly you can. They've only shut at weekends because Anwyll wouldn't work more than five days.'

That didn't surprise me in the least.

'Well just for three weeks then. £100 a day plus normal expenses.'

'Yes, we can run to that. Good and thanks. Take an empty trailer up on Monday, or Sunday if you prefer. You know what's required don't you? And ring me each evening with the days' events.'

'OK.' I wasn't very happy but someone had to do it and it would amount to more than £800 a week.

The first day practically killed me. What I hadn't realised was they were twelve hour days from seven in the morning to seven in the evening. I did get used to it but I wouldn't have wished it on anyone.

It lasted for six weeks, not the one or two. I was only there for five and a bit weeks because I caught a bad dose of flu on week five. I collapsed on the trailer and I was sent to the factory sick bay. It was arranged for me to return to base after I'd recovered a little and I was forwarded to my home. I spent a few days recovering and then went back to work. Fortunately I didn't have to go to Kidderminster.

They started putting the bags on pallets after only a few days of me returning to active duty.

Nutritional warning

Some people attract contrary nicknames. For instance someone who is on the large side might be called 'Slim Jim'. Or if someone else had less meat on them than you'd find on a butchers' pencil, they might be known as 'Big Bob'.

On our crew we had a 'Big Bert', christened Bertram. He weighed in at 24 stone. Allegedly his wife weighed in at 22 stone. Quite a combination when they were out on the town together. There was nothing contrary about his name. He was so heavy he broke the cab suspension in all the vehicles he drove for any length of time. You could always tell which ones he'd driven because they sagged on the drivers' side. He had to chock up the suspension seats because they didn't work when he was sitting on them. I expect he bounced on his buttocks.

Big Bert was altogether charming unless you were foolish enough to rile him. You wouldn't have wanted to be on the receiving end of one his punches. He was also very light on his feet and had excellent hearing. Someone made the mistake of mentioning to a group of drivers,

'You don't want to concern yourself with Big Bert. He's a cunt.'

At the time the big man was on the other side of the yard. He covered the ground like lightning.

'Who's the miserable bastard who called me a cunt then?'

Immediate group dispersal ensued.

When he was quizzed about his size he apparently always replied it was a hormonal problem. It was discovered later his doctor had told him it wasn't. He simply needed to change his eating habits and his diet. He wanted to reduce weight but lacked the will-power to control his food intake. So he accepted a medical process suggested by a surgeon and they wired his jaw up.

He endured the result for several weeks but whenever he stopped for breakfast at a café he'd ask for,

'A full English breakfast please. Could you put it in a whizzer for me? It's just that…'

He was good fun when he was on a night out with other drivers and he had an easy sense of humour.

The only thing he suffered from was vertigo, or so he assured me. We loaded together out of 42 berth in Tilbury one day. I had the easy load. I didn't have to cover it and it was relatively low. On the other hand Big Bert had the high load which he was required to put a sheet over. 'Hughy mate. I can't go up there and spread the sheet because I get vertigo. Can you do it for me?'

'Yeah alright, but you'll owe me a big favour. Agreed?'

He never returned the favour but I suppose he helped someone else with something. It was good enough for me.

I heard another story about him. I cannot guarantee its authenticity and it may be a complete fabrication, but it was very funny. I split my sides whenever I thought about it.

One Saturday afternoon when 'Big Bert' was at home with his wife and all his many kids were away for the day, they decided to take a bath together. The bath was upstairs and it was made of cast iron. They ran the water. They didn't need much so it didn't take very long. They both got into it together and settled down to 46 stone of cuddles. During the settling in period, all the water was displaced and they stuck to the sides of the bath.

Within less than a minute it was clear the bathroom floor was not going to take the strain. The floor collapsed with a great tearing of timber and cracking of tiles. On its downward path it took out the sitting room ceiling. When the loaded bath hit the ground floor it was unstoppable and it descended into the footings.

Now, the thing was they were stuck solid. They couldn't move inside the bath and the bath itself was wedged into the foundations. They hollered and shouted for help and eventually the neighbours found them. Nobody could get them out and no one wanted to break the bath because cast iron splinters and can be dangerous if you're already lying in it.

In the end the emergency services were called and the firemen turned up. After a few attempts to lift them out amid much sniggering in the fire engine, they had to call in a crane. In order for the crane to get access for lifting a hole had to be made in the roof of the house.

They say the incident was reported in the local press, but I never saw it.

Here endeth the first verse. I hope you enjoyed my stories and don't go away. **Job No55** and the others are just round the corner. There's loads more amusing anecdotes in the sequel including super-extra-long cargos, owning my own lorry, working with cranes, office work, building an empire, the police, court cases, part-timing and the best of all, international driving. See you later.